Motorcycle Party Guide to Route 66

Sam Allen

Route 66 MC Publications

Published by Route 66 MC Publications
1200 Smith Street, Suite 1600
Houston, Texas 77002

Manufactured in the United States of America
ISBN: 978-0-9904932-1-1

First Edition

Library of Congress Cataloging-in-Publication Data

Allen, Samuel N., 1955-

Motorcycle and Party Guide to Route 66/Sam Allen

Cover design by Brian Love
Photo of La Bajada Pass courtesy of Kenneth Becker

Many thanks to my brother Dan.
What started as my project became our project.

CONTENTS

FOREWORD

I've been wandering up and down Route 66 for more than 25 years. Most of the time, I had no particular purpose or destination in mind. During the winter I would take a car, and in the warmer months I would ride a motorcycle. Over the course of taking all of those trips, I thought I had been on all of Route 66 at one time or another, but I had never traveled its whole length in a single trip.

At the beginning of 2011, I found myself with a chunk of free time, so I decided to travel Route 66 from Chicago to LA. I thought I might as well take some notes and turn them into a book, a web site or something. I believed it would be a pretty simple project that I could handle during the month I had set aside for the trip. Boy was I wrong.

I figured that there would be a single route with signs all the way from Chicago to Santa Monica. I quickly found that not only were there alternate alignments, but signs were not always available, and where available, they often were inaccurate or out of date. It became apparent that I would have to find a lot of Route 66 on my own.

So, I did what any modern guy would do. I looked for web sites and guide books to help me. Most of the web sites I found focused on selling Route 66 tours or advertising specific Route 66 attractions or merchandise. There were coffee table books that were long on photos and anecdotes but short on detail. There were detailed guide books that were long on information about navigating Route 66 but short on photographs. These books tended to provide so much information that mining the data I wanted was difficult. There also were guides focusing on specific topics, such as lodging and dining. I found only a single guide book focusing on motorcycle trips on Route 66, and as useful as that book was, it was at least a decade out of date.

So far as I could tell, there was no single source providing easy to follow directions, color photographs, information about both traditional Route

66 attractions and off-beat things to look for along the way, and a listing of hotels, bars and restaurants. This book has all of that plus information that motorcycle riders will find useful, such as state motorcycle laws, information about motorcycle rallies, and listings of motorcycle shops and campgrounds.

I also wanted to add some context to the towns through which Route 66 passes. Many of them are small towns today. It's easy to forget that the United States was more rural in the 1920's and during the Great Depression than it is today, and that today's small Route 66 towns also were small back then. Still, they were the leading communities of their day. I wanted to convey something about those towns when Route 66 was established, how Route 66 affected them and what has happened to them since Route 66 was decommissioned.

I wanted to recommend where to have fun. Riding across the country while exploring Route 66 is an adventure, but there is more to it than finding what remains or snapping photos of defunct motels and abandoned roadside attractions. I wanted to direct readers to the vintage Route 66 bars and restaurants, and where the vintage places were gone, guide them to the current hot spots. This is the only book that will tell you where to find all of the traditional Route 66 attractions as well as the best bars, restaurants and other unique places to visit.

So, although this book has a motorcycle tone, it will be fun for anybody who wants to get more out of their trip than just visiting the usual suspects.

This project was more difficult than I imagined. There are Route 66 scholars who have written more definitive guides to Route 66 than this one. I may not have the Route 66 knowledge or experience they have accumulated over a lifetime of traveling a road they love. Still, I'm not a total novice. I have toyed around on Route 66 for years, and I rode it from Chicago to Santa Monica and back over ten times to gather data and take photographs for this book. There are biker bars across the country where I'm now greeted as *The Route 66 Guy*.

So, this book will make its own contribution. I hope you enjoy the book and your Route 66 adventures

Sam Allen
January 19, 2014

A BRIEF HISTORY OF ROUTE 66

The creation of Route 66 began in the early 1920's through the vision and diligence of Cyrus Avery. Avery was born in Pennsylvania in 1871. His family moved to Missouri in 1881. Avery moved to Oklahoma City in 1904 then to Tulsa in 1907. He set up a realty firm and a coal company, and speculated in oil and gas leases. Avery became one of the most prominent citizens of Tulsa.

Avery was an early devotee of establishing a national roadway system. In 1921, he became president of the Associated Highways Association of America. In 1923, he was appointed Commissioner Highways of the State of Oklahoma. In 1924, he was a member of the American Association of State Highway Officials, which at its national meeting in San Francisco, requested that the Secretary of Agriculture underwrite and establish a comprehensive interstate road system. Avery was appointed to act as a consulting highway specialist to the Bureau of Better Roads, which was to create the beginnings of that system.

In 1925, Avery and others began selecting existing roads that would be part of the national highway system. Road clubs around the United States lobbied to have portions of their local roads included. A portion of a transcontinental highway that went from Chicago to St Louis and Kansas, west through Tulsa and Oklahoma City, and over the National Old Trails became the genesis of Route 66.

Before the establishment of the national highway system most roads had local names. The national highway commissioners decided to give roads across state lines shield shaped signs signifying that they were US highways or circular signs for state roads. The most prominent roads were to be designated by two digit numbers ending in zero. Politicians from Missouri and Illinois lobbied for the Chicago to Los Angeles route to be designated Route 60. They lost, and in early 1926 these politicians selected the designation *Route 66* for the national highway from Chicago to Los Angeles.

On November 11, 1926 federal and state highway officials approved the interstate routes for all 48 states, and Route 66 came into existence.

In February 1927, the first meeting of the National US 66 Highway Association was held in Tulsa, and the Association adopted the name *The Main Street of America* for Route 66.

In 1920, the United States had approximately 3,000,000 miles of roadway, but only 36,000 miles had all weather surfaces suitable for automobiles. When Route 66 was commissioned, only about 800 miles of Route 66 were paved. The National US 66 Highway Association, along with corresponding state Route 66 associations, set out to get the entire route paved and promoted as the shortest and most direct route between the Great Lakes and Pacific coast. It took until 1937 to pave the entire route. Advertising campaigns in national and local magazines and newspapers promoted the use of Route 66 and the businesses along the way. These advertising efforts were successful and the towns and businesses along Route 66 prospered.

The stock market crashed and the Great Depression began in 1929, only three years after Route 66 was established. Then, in the 1930's severe droughts in the mid-west and southwest caused the Dust Bowl. Route 66 became the highway that poor dirt farmers hoped would take them to a land of better opportunity. It became romanticized as the road to progress that resulted in the greatest westward migration in the country's history.

Route 66 came on hard times during World War II. Gas and tire rationing made long distance automobile travel impractical. In addition, production of new cars was suspended during World War II, making the purchase of reliable vehicles difficult. Most of the traffic along Route 66 consisted of military convoys and job seekers heading to large manufacturing plants in California.

A second migration along Route 66 occurred immediately after World War II as veterans followed Route 66 eastward from California to their pre-war homes, and families moved westward to California in search of better jobs. Travelers began to use Jack Rittenhouse's 1946 *A Guidebook to Highway 66* to steer them along. 1946 also was the year Nat King Cole released Bobby Troup's tune *Get Your Kicks on Route 66.*

In 1952, the Main Street of America Highway Association (formerly the Highway 66 Association) traveled Route 66 from the Chain of Rocks Bridge, which connected Illinois and Missouri, to Santa Monica, California, and dedicated Route 66 as the *Will Rogers Highway.*

Route 66 was at its peak in the post-World War II boom years of the 1950's. However, in 1954 President Eisenhower established the President's Advisory Committee on a National Highway Program. This Committee designed what became our modern national highway system. Super-highways like I-55, I-44 and I-40 simply bypassed much of Route 66, which no longer could handle the increasing westward traffic. In addition, the 1965 Highway Beautification Act prohibited billboards along these super-highways, making it difficult for businesses in the bypassed towns to advertise. Although some Route 66 towns continued to prosper, the replacement of Route 66 with super-highways and the prohibition of billboard advertising led to an inevitable deterioration of the road that was once The Main Street of America.

Route 66 was decommissioned in 1984. The US Highway 66 Association tried to get the interstate highways over which Route 66 once passed to be designated as Route 66, but it was unsuccessful in those efforts. I-66 now designates a road connecting I-84 in Virginia with Washington DC.

Although a little more of Route 66 disappears every year, there still is much to see. There are lonely strips of concrete that stripe the landscape from Illinois to California. There are small and large towns still displaying the colorful neon signs of the old motels and restaurants where the prosperous would stay during their adventures west, or where weary families would stay in their search of better lives. Travelers today can still feel what it must have been like to travel the Mother Road when it was the gateway to the west.

ABOUT YOUR TRIP

Westward Ho

Route 66 traditionally is traveled from east to west rather than west to east. The rationale is that the US expanded westward, so going west makes sense. So, while I give you turn by turn directions going both ways, my narrative goes from east to west. After all, the Bobby Troup tune tells you *It Winds from Chicago to LA.*

Great Expectations

Finding the signs, advertisements and off-beat attractions that defined Route 66 will be a big part of your adventure. It's satisfying to come across sites like the Gemini Giant or the Blue Whale and find them to be exactly as expected. The problem is that more of these attractions disappear every year. Several have disappeared over the three years that I have been researching and writing this book, and I suspect that some of the places I discuss will be gone before this books is published.

Many of the traditional Route 66 attractions are just plain tired. There are hotels and restaurants that have become "classics" because they survived rather than surviving because they were classics. They catered to folks who needed affordable food and lodging as they traveled across the country. These places are no more luxurious 60 years later, and most don't have the benefit of the year round business they once enjoyed. So, upkeep often has not been good. You should not expect the conveniences that are standard in modern hotels or the up-scale fare offered in trendy restaurants.

Still, there is something romantic about visiting the surviving Route 66 establishments. Many of them are operated by the same families that have been running them for generations. The owners and locals who frequent these places almost always have stories to share about their businesses and of how Route 66 has changed over the decades.

Don't bypass the traditional spots just to save time. Go through the small towns, stay in their hotels and eat in their restaurants. Talk to their residents. If you don't, you will miss one of the richest parts of your trip.

Getting Started

You will find the *Begin Route 66* sign in Chicago on Adams St near the corner of Michigan Ave, but Route 66 originally did not start there. In 1926, it began on Jackson Blvd at Michigan Ave. In 1933, the start and end of Route 66 were moved to Jackson and Lake Shore Drive. In 1955, Jackson was made one way going into town west of Michigan Ave and Adams was made one way going out of town. So today, getting out of Chicago on Route 66 requires you to take Adams.

Finding Your Way

Route 66 was built over several decades beginning in 1926. It originally followed existing roads that were connected to flow from Chicago to Los Angeles. This patchwork approach made for an inefficient and circuitous route west. Much of it was not paved.

The alignment was changed several times to create more direct routes that bypassed town centers and to otherwise make travel easier. As a result, there really is no one Route 66. Instead, there are alternate alignments, some of which still are in use and others of which have been long abandoned.

I have not tried to chronicle all of the permutations of Route 66. Instead, I have provided a primary suggested route from Chicago to Santa Monica designed to give you the most interesting possible Route 66 experience.

When given a choice between a quick route and a comprehensive route, I generally have chosen the comprehensive route that will take you through the greatest number of towns. When given a choice between routing you through or bypassing a town, I generally have routed you through town. Also, when given a choice between a newer and an older alignment, I generally have chosen the older alignment.

In some cases, I have provided alternate suggested routes. A good example is from Santa Rosa, New Mexico to Albuquerque. My suggested route takes the 1926 alignment through Santa Fe. It takes a few more hours than a newer route that follows I-40, but they are well spent hours.

So, I have picked a suggested route I think you will enjoy if you have the time, but I have given you quicker options that you can use if you don't have all the time you would like.

Timing Your Ride

Your ride from Chicago to Santa Monica can be done in 10 days, but that is pushing hard and would leave no time for exploration. Plan on between two and three weeks. If you don't have that much time, pick a portion of Route 66 you want to explore and save the rest for another day.

About 200 miles per day is a realistic goal in the eastern states and 300 miles per day is realistic in the west. You can get more miles in if you do not stop to take many photos, but what's the fun of that. The route sometimes is hard to find and often runs though the centers of rural towns with low speed limits. Some of the sites you will want to see are not directly on the route so some time consuming exploring is required. Plus, the whole point of your ride is to see Route 66. If you rush you will miss things you will regret not having seen. Make sure you see all you can because who knows if you will ever get back.

Travel in the eastern portion of Route 66 often takes longer than in the west. There are more towns in the east, and they generally are better preserved, so there is more to see. Once you get west of Weatherford, OK, an increasing portion of your ride will be on interstate highways and there will be more ghost towns. So, you can make up some time in the west. That's not to say there are no great rides in the west. In fact, the 160 mile ride from outside of Ash Fork, Arizona to Topock, Arizona is my favorite stretch of Route 66.

The ride from San Bernardino to Santa Monica is an exception to being able to make up time in the west. It's only 50 miles, but plan on a full day. Most of the towns have congested local traffic. The last 10 miles down Santa Monica Blvd are brutal. Be prepared for lots of stop and go traffic.

So, budget your time and see all you can see.

HELMET LAWS

Every state has motorcycle laws, but the only ones to which anyone pays attention are the helmet laws. Here they are for all eight Route 66 states.

ILLINOIS: Helmets not required. Helmet speakers allowed only for communications.

MISSOURI: Helmets required.

KANSAS: Helmets not required for riders and passengers over 18.

OKLAHOMA: Helmets not required for riders and passengers over 18.

TEXAS: Helmets not required for riders over 21 if a motorcycle safety course has been passed or if the rider has $10,000 in medical insurance. A state issued sticker is required to evidence compliance with these rules. These are crazy laws that are not enforced. I sent away for the required sticker, but the state never sent me one, and I don't know anyone who has a sticker. For all practical purposes, Texas does not require helmets.

NEW MEXICO: Helmets not required for riders or passengers over 18.

ARIZONA: Helmets not required for riders and passengers over 18.

CALIFORNIA: Helmets required.

TOWNS ALONG THE ROUTE

This Chapter includes information about each town along my suggested route from Chicago to Santa Monica. There is a State Page for each of the eight states through which Route 66 passes, followed by separate narratives for each town in each state in the order you will pass through them going east to west.

In some cases there are alternate routes with a discussion of the pros and cons of each alternative. The alternate routes and related town narratives appear at the end of the suggested routes for each state.

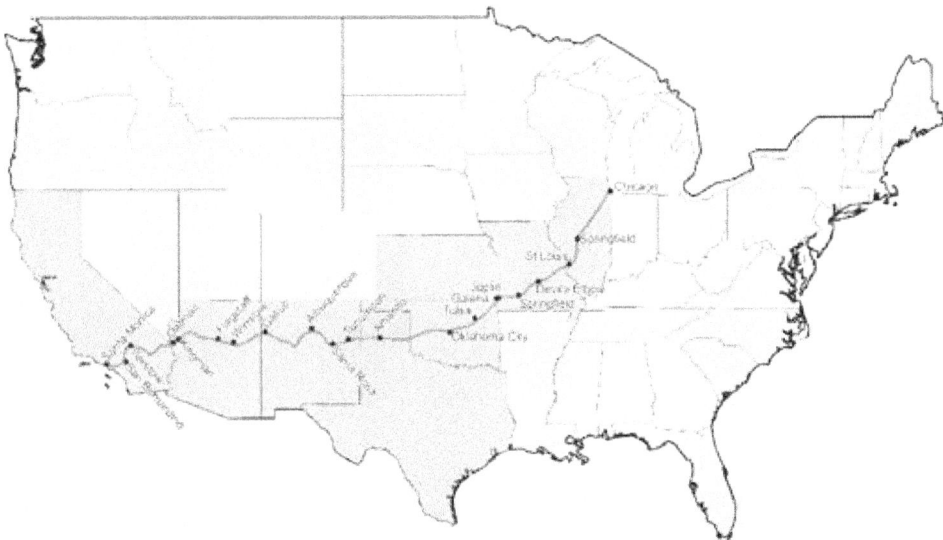

ILLINOIS

Ok, you are ready to start your trip, and Illinois has a lot going on right out of the box.

On your way to the beginning of Route 66 in Chicago on the corner of Adams St and Michigan Ave, you'll be near the Buckingham Fountain that appeared at the beginning of *Married With Children*.

Getting out of Chicago is surprisingly easy. In under an hour, you will be through Al Capone's haunts in Cicero, and on the way you'll see Cindy Lyn's Motel, Henry's Drive-In and the Castle Car Wash. You'll also pass through the town where the Outlaws MC was founded.

Soon you'll see the Giant Rooster at the White Fence Farm, which boasts the world's best chicken dinners, then find yourself in Joliet to see the Rialto Square Theater, Joliet Prison and sculptures of Jake and Elwood Blues atop the Rich & Creamy ice cream stand. On the way out of town you'll pass by NASCAR's Chicagoland Speedway.

After that, you'll be on rural roads with the interstate highway system only an afterthought. You'll see the Gemini Giant holding a rocket, the Bunyon Statue holding a giant hot dog, the Lauderbach Giant that is supposed to hold a Giant Muffler and the world's largest covered wagon with a Giant Abe Lincoln aboard.

There are small towns with proudly restored gas stations from the 1930's, some of them serving as visitor's centers or museums. There are roadhouses that Al Capone frequented and vintage motels with restored neon signs. There are bridges from the 1920's and 1930's and an old brick-paved portion of Route 66.

Springfield is a hot biker town with lots of biker bars and motorcycle clubs. You also can visit Abe Lincoln's home, office, presidential library and tomb.

Twelve Illinois towns starting with Joliet and ending in Towanda participate each May in the Route 66 Red Carpet Corridor. Each of the participating towns puts on an annual festival, many of which feature antique cars and motorcycles.

Route 66 through Illinois is surprisingly rural. Take it slowly and enjoy!

CHICAGO

I ride my bike over 20,000 miles every year, and I've ridden through all of the contiguous 48 states. When I practiced law in New York, I flew over 100,000 miles a year. Still, I've been to Chicago only a dozen times.

A few years ago I was there with my friend Gail. She's an Old School biker babe whose ex husband is a member of the Sons of Silence. We wanted to see some gangland sites. Instead of taking an organized tour, we hired a driver to take us around.

The first stop was the Biograph Theater at 2433 N Lincoln Ave where the Lady in Red ratted out John Dillinger so the G men could gun him down. As we approached the box office, the woman inside disappeared behind the ticket window with a loud bang. We went to get a closer look and found that there was no woman in there at all. It was a mannequin that happened to topple over just as we got there. We had a good laugh out of it because the crash was so loud it startled us and we had been afraid some violent act had taken place.

Buckingham Fountain

The St Valentine's Day Massacre occurred at 2122 N Clark St. As it turned out, the building had been demolished and the bricks from the wall where the seven men were killed had been purchased by a private collector and moved. All we saw was an empty gated lot. However, the house across the street where Capone's men staked out Bugs Moran's North Side Gang was still there.

Dean (pronounced Dee-ahn) O'Bannion and Hymie Weiss were killed in separate shootings at Schofield's Flower Shop at 738 N State St. O'Bannion got it in the notorious hand shake killing. Frankie Yale, John Scalise and Albert Anselm entered Schofield's, and O'Bannion went to shake Yale's hand. Frankie held on tight as Scalise and Anselm each shot Dean.

Hymie Weiss was gunned down outside Schofield's and the chipped cornerstone of the Holy Name Cathedral across the street still bears the scars of the machine gun bullets.

Schofield's also has been torn down.

O'Bannion, Al Capone, the Genna Brothers, Hymie Weiss and other gangland stars are buried at the Mt Carmel Cemetery at 1400 S Wolf Rd.

So much for Chicago's gangland tradition. On to Route 66!

The Outlaws MC is headquartered in Chicago. There are three chapters in Chicago and more chapters in the surrounding towns.

There are few biker bars close to Downtown. The Twisted Spoke at 501 N Ogden Ave is popular. It was busy the night I went, but I was the only one wearing a Club patch, and there were few bikes outside. It has a huge liquor menu with several pages of bourbons alone. Wednesday is half price night. There is an extensive dining menu, and it is open for breakfast, lunch and dinner.

Chicago's Twisted Spoke

Other popular Chicago biker spots include Delilah's at 2771 N Lincoln Ave; Kuma's Corner at 2900 W Belmont Ave; and Hogs & Honey's at 1551

N Sheffield. Austin's Saloon and eatery at 1551 N Peterson Rd in Libertyville also is a popular biker destination about 20 miles out of Downtown.

The Billy Goat Tavern at 430 N Michigan Ave near Route 66 was the inspiration for the Saturday Night Live *Chee Burger-Chee Burger-Chee Burger* skit.

Miller's Pub at 134 S Wabash is a Chicago landmark with hundreds of photos of Chicago athletes. Miller's is known for its ribs. It also is near the Palmer House Hotel, which has one of the great bars in the world.

Everybody talks about Lou Mitchell's at 565 W Jackson. It has been at its current Route 66 address since before Route 66 commissioned. It's a great place to have breakfast before starting your trip. You will not leave hungry. Free Milk Duds are given to the ladies.

On Jackson Ave since 1925

The Congress Plaza Hotel at 520 S Michigan Ave is a solid Route 66 era hotel. The rates are cheap by Chicago standards and there is secure motorcycle parking. The lobby bar has good prices and pool tables. The hotel is within walking distance of the Buckingham Fountain in Grant Park, which was used in the opening credits of *Married with Children*. It's only a few blocks from the corner of Adams St and Michigan Ave, where you will see the *Begin Route 66* sign and start your adventure. The *End Route 66* sign is a block over on the corner of Jackson and Michigan Ave, where Route 66 originally began and ended.

Getting out of Chicago is surprisingly easy even during during peak traffic hours. You'll go through the heart of Downtown Chicago, and wind through some nice tree-lined neighborhoods on your way to Ogden Ave, where you will head toward Cicero.

You are on your way!

West to Cicero

Start at the corner of Adams St and Michigan Ave • Follow Adams St all the way through Downtown Chicago to Ogden Ave • Go left on Ogden Ave and head toward Cicero

East to Chicago

From **Cicero**, follow Ogden Ave • Cross Van Buren • Go right onto Jackson Ave • Cross I-90/94 and the Chicago River into Downtown **Chicago** • Stay on Jackson to the *End Route 66* sign at Lake Shore Drive

CICERO

Cicero on Ogden Ave is an industrial area with lots of hospitals followed by deteriorating neighborhoods. It's not particularly scenic, but the traveling is easy for leaving a major city. There are a few Route 66 landmarks along the way, including the Castle Carwash at 3801 Ogden Ave; Henry's Drive-In at 6021 Ogden Ave with its giant hot dog sign; and Cindy Lyn's Motel and Suites at 5029 W Ogden

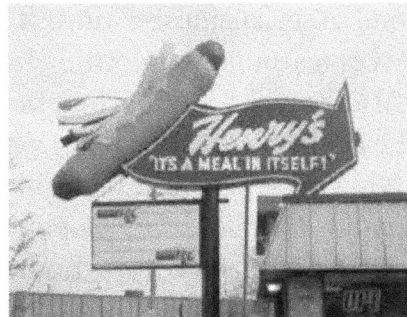

This sign was added to compete with an early nearby McDonalds

Ave. You also can check out the Chicagoland Sports Hall of Fame at 3501 S Laramie Ave.

Henry's opened in 1946 when Bill Henry, who worked in a factory, started selling hot dogs out of the back of a truck. He was so successful that in 1950 he quit his job and opened the current Henry's a few blocks from his mobile location. The ceramic stripes on the building and the distinctive sign were added to compete with a modern McDonalds that had opened down the street. A drive-through window and expanded parking are planned for the summer of 2014.

The Cindy Lyn Motel has been operated by the same family since it opened in 1960. It was the last motel before entering Chicago, and the original rate was $6.18. It had 18 rooms, but now has 65 rooms, including some hot tub suites and a fireplace suite. Be advised: Today you can get hourly or nightly rates.

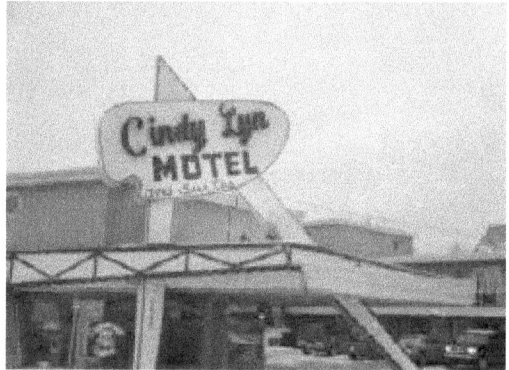

Family operated since 1960

The Castle Car wash dates from 1925, so it pre-dates Route 66. It started as a gas station and housed several other businesses until it closed in about 2004. Restoration rumors have been around but nothing has come of them.

Al Capone's headquarters moved to the Hawthorne Inn at 4833 W 22nd St in in Cicero when Al fled Chicago to avoid the law. On September 20, 1926 (52 days before Route 66 was commissioned), the Northside Gang led a fleet of cars to machine gun the Hawthorne's ground floor restaurant in an attempt to rub out Capone and his senior henchmen. Dean O'Bannion, Hymie Weiss and Vincent *Schemer* Drucci reputedly

On the Endangered Species list

were involved. Nearly 1,000 rounds were fired, but miraculously, no one was killed.

Capone got his revenge. In separate shootings later that year, Dean was shot inside Schofield's Flower Shop, and Hymie got machine gunned outside Schofield's. The *Schemer* was killed in 1927 while riding in the back of a police car after an arrest for kidnapping some supporters of an opposition mayoral candidate.

The Hawthorne Inn closed in 1970. The space is now occupied by a bank parking lot.

West from Cicero to Indian Head Park

From **Cicero**, stay on Ogden Ave to **Berwyn** • Stay on Ogden Ave • Go left on Harlem Ave (Hwy 43) • Go right on 41st St (becomes 43rd St) to **Lyons** • Follow 43rd St until it curves left on Prescott Ave • Go right on Joliet Rd to **McCook** • Stay on Joliet Rd • Pass Hwy 171 • Go right on 55th St • Go left on East Ave • Go right on Joliet Rd to **Countryside** • Follow Joliet Rd to **Indian Head Park**

East from Indian Head Park to Cicero

From **Indian Head Park**, stay on Joliet Rd to **Countryside** • From **Countryside**, follow Joliet Rd across La Grange Rd • Go left on Joliet Ave at the Joliet Ave/E St Sign • Go right on 55th St • Go left back on Joliet Rd in **McCook** • Stay on Joliet Rd • Cross under Hwy 171 • Cross Lawndale Ave • Go left onto Prescott Ave in **Lyons** • From **Lyons,** follow Prescott Ave • Go right onto 43rd St (becomes 41st St) • Go left on Harlem Ave/Hwy 43 • Go right on Ogden Ave to **Berwyn** • Stay on Ogden Ave to **Cicero**

Berwyn, Lyons, McCook, Countryside and Indian Head Park

BERWYN. Berwyn has a reputation as one of the more biker friendly towns in the Chicago area. It has hosted a vintage car show celebrating Route 66 for over 20 years. Berwyn also hosts *Cartopia,* in which car artists from all over the country meet to show their works. The event ends with a spectacular car art parade.

LYONS. Lyons is one of the smaller towns in the Chicago area with a population of around 11,000. It was established on the half mile stretch of land connecting the Chicago River and the Des Plaines River.

Lyons once had a significant mob element and had bunch of strip clubs and bars along Ogden Ave. Lyons has been cleaned up and most of these establishments no longer exist. As B. B. King might say, *The Thrill is Gone*!

MCCOOK. McCook is the smallest town in Cook County. The town is named after former Civil War officer and Santa Fe Railroad director John J. McCook.

The Outlaws MC was founded in McCook in 1935 as the McCook Outlaws. In 1950, following an influx of members after WWII, it moved to Chicago and changed its name to the Chicago Outlaws. In 1963, the Outlaws became the first 1%er Club east of the Mississippi River. Beginning in 1964, it started annexing a series of clubs throughout the mid-west with Chicago being the Mother Chapter. The Florida Chapter came aboard in 1967. The first chapter outside the United States was established in Canada in 1977. The first European Chapter was formed in France in 1993. Today, the Outlaws are all over the world with Chapters in the United States, Canada, Europe, Japan, Australia and Russia.

COUNTRYSIDE. First settled in 1833, Countryside remained mostly farmland until the Great Chicago Fire of 1871. The fire forced people to move out of the city into suburbs like this where land was sold for $2 an acre.

The Marx Brothers had a chicken farm in Countryside. They owned it at the *beak* of their careers. That explains why so many *clucks* live there, although some of them are *good eggs*. Some residents feel *cooped up*. I'll spare you any more puns (cock and pullet jokes might lead me too far astray). Hey, blame Groucho, not me!

INDIAN HEAD PARK. Indian Head Park was incorporated in 1959, but it has been a settled area for a long time. The Congregational Church once was a stop on the Underground Railroad for escaped slaves making their way north to Chicago.

West to Romeoville

From **Indian Head Park**, stay on Joliet Rd • Go under I-294 and get onto I-55 West • Take Exit 268 (S Joliet Rd) • Follow Joliet Rd signs and go under I-55 to Joliet Rd to **Romeoville**

East to Indian Head Park

From Joliet Rd in **Romeoville**, follow the signs to Chicago • Get onto I-55 N • Take the left Exit 267C onto Joliet Rd • Cross under I-294 into **Indian Head Park**

ROMEOVILLE

Romeoville is home to White Fence Farm at 1376 Joliet Rd, which claims to have been serving the world's greatest chicken dinners since it opened in the 1920's. They claim to have had over 40,000 customers in its first four months of operation. Maybe they bought chickens from the Marx brothers in nearby Countryside.

As I walked through the parking lot I had a premonition that it was going to be a giant geriatric gastronomic jihad. There is a huge parking lot with dozens of handicapped spaces. More of them were filled than the regular spots.

Once inside, it looked like a giant Cracker Barrel Restaurant. Turned out it was a family place. There were a lot of children, all well behaved.

The White Fence seats 1,200

I don't think the menu has changed since 1920. There is no bar, but there are cocktail selections on the menu; all classics. You can order a martini, old fashioned, Manhattan, whiskey sour, Rob Roy or other traditional drink. I ordered an old fashioned, and it was pretty good.

Although seafood and steaks are available, it is a chicken place so that's what I ordered. The special is a fried half-chicken. You get four pieces: breast, thigh, drumstick and wing. It is served with pickled beets, creamy bean salad, coleslaw and cottage cheese. You get all of that you can eat (which for me is none). You also get all the fritters you can eat. I wasn't quite sure what a fritter was. Turns out it is fried dough; sort of like a doughnut. They were delicious.

The place is huge. It has been expanded to 12 rooms, only two of which were opened while I was there. They have seating for 1,200, and for Easter, Mother's day and other big weekends, they fill it for several seating's. The whole place is filled with interesting antiques, including several pristine vintage cars and motorcycles.

The staff was pleasant and accommodating. I was given a tour and got answers to all the questions I asked about the history of the restaurant.

The chicken was excellent. They have never-frozen chickens shipped in every day and have their own secret recipe for batter and cooking. I don't know if it is in fact the best chicken anywhere, but I can't recall ever having any better than at the White Fence Farm.

This is a place I can recommend even though it doesn't have a bar.

Romeoville also had the Crazy Rock Gentlemen's Club. You could check out the breasts and thighs at the Crazy Rock after checking out the breasts and thighs at the White Fence. Unfortunately, the Crazy Rock has closed, and the property is being redeveloped.

Since the Crazy Rock is out, you might want to check out the Stone City Saloon at 721 N Independence Blvd. It is a local biker destination with lots of different beers on tap, pretty good food and some nice eye candy.

West to Joliet

From **Romeoville**, follow Joliet Rd (which becomes Broadway) • Go left on Ruby St and follow it as it curves right onto Chicago St • Follow Chicago St as it turns into Ottawa • Go right on Jackson • Go left back on Ottawa into **Joliet** • Follow Ottawa/Hwy 53 heading out of town

East to Romeoville

From **Joliet,** Follow Hwy 53/Columbia to Ruby • Cross the Des Plains River • Go right on Broadway/Hwy 53 • Follow Hwy 53, which becomes Joliet Rd, into **Romeoville**

JOLIET

Joliet claims to be the Gateway to Route 66. The reason is unclear.

The first Dairy Queen opened in Joliet in 1940. It's not there anymore, but check out the sculptures of Jake and Elwood Blues atop Rich & Creamy at 920 N Broadway on the way into town. It's an old fashioned walk up ice cream place.

Across the street is Dick's on 66, a local towing company and Route 66 photo op.

The Rialto Square Theater just off the Square at 102 N Chicago St opened in 1926 (the year Route 66 opened).

The Joliet Area Historical Museum and Route 66 Welcome Center is Downtown at 204 N Ottawa St. It has a nice Route 66 exhibit.

Joliet Prison, which first opened in 1858, is just off Route 66 at 1125 Collins St. It held Leopold and Loeb, who committed a murder in 1924 to try to pull off the perfect crime. Clarence Darrow defended them, successfully arguing that they should not get the death penalty. The prison also was the inspiration for Joliet Jake of Blues

The 1926 Rialto

Brothers fame. Film and TV credits include *The Blues Brothers, Natural Born Killers, Prison Break* and *The Untouchables*. It closed in 2002 and it now is a public park. To get there, follow Ottawa Ave (Hwy 53) and go left on Jefferson. Follow Jefferson as it loops around and becomes Collins, and follow Collins to the Prison. Don't mistake Joliet High School for the Prison. It looks like one (and who knows, maybe the students think it is).

Harrah's Casino is Downtown near the Square at 151 N Joliet St. The Hollywood Casino is off your beaten path at 777 Hollywood Blvd.

Joliet is the eastern most town in *The Route 66 Red Carpet Corridor*. This is a 90 mile stretch

Joliet Prison: Leopold and Loeb and the Blues Brothers

of Route 66 from Joliet to Towanda. Each town plans its own events each May celebrating its Route 66 heritage.

You will pass the Chicagoland Speedway on your way out of town.

Near the Speedway, stop by Boz Hot Dogs at 1601 S Chicago St. It's an old fashioned hot dog stand that has been around for years. Be sure to order the all-beef dog or you will get something akin to Spam.

West from Joliet to Gardner

Follow Ottawa/Hwy 53 out of **Joliet** • Stay on Hwy 53 to **Elwood** • Stay on Hwy 53 through **Wilmington, Braidwood, Godley** and **Braceville** toward **Gardner** • Go right at the Historic Route 66 sign (there is no street sign, but you will be on Washington) • Go left on N Center just before the RR tracks • Take an immediate right onto Depot St • Follow Depot St through Downtown **Gardner**

Elwood, Wilmington, Braidwood, Godley, Braceville and Gardner

ELWOOD. Once you get clear of Joliet, you will begin passing through a bunch of rural towns. It's great to ride out of sight of the interstate highways and get the feel that travelers of the Mother Road must have felt in decades past.

Elwood, which is the namesake of Elwood Blues of the Blues Brothers, is easy to miss. Go several miles past the Chicagoland Speedway and keep a lookout for a Heartland Bank on the right hand side. Take a right and follow it into Elwood. Watson's Pub is there for a few cold ones, but be careful, locals say the police are stringent.

Elwood has *Friday Cruise Nights* from June through August featuring antique cars, music and refreshments.

WILMINGTON. Wilmington is nicknamed *The Island City* after a large island in the Kankakee River.

The Launching Pad Drive-In has the Gemini Giant, which is a 20 foot tall statue of a spaceman holding a rocket. There are three of these Giants in

Illinois. The the other two are the Lauderbach Muffler Man in Springfield and the Bunyon Giant, who moved from Cicero to Atlanta with a giant hot dog.

Unfortunately, the Launching Pad is closed and has been for sale for quite some time. Hopefully, some Route 66 romantic will reopen the place and make a solid go of it.

The Rustic Saloon Downtown is a good biker spot that often has live music.

There used to be a great bar diagonally across from the Rustic Saloon called Freakster's Road House. It catered to bikers and had tributes to military veterans. Check to see if it has reopened when you are in Wilmington.

The Gemini Giant

Wilmington participates in *The Route 66 Red Carpet Corridor* events each May.

BRAIDWOOD. The Polk-A-Dot Drive In at 222 N Front St is a 1950's diner featuring outdoor statues of James Dean, Marilyn Monroe, Elvis Presley and the Blues Brothers. Inside, it is well preserved with period photos. There are some tiny booths designed for children. The wallpaper has old Polka Dot menus. Hamburgers for 30 cents. Yikes! The Men's Room has about 50 Marilyn Monroe photos. No report on the Women's Room decor.

The Korner Keg at 285 E Main St is the local biker spot.

There also are some Burma Shave signs (no doubt reproductions) and a 1939 gas station on Route 129 now housing Lucenta Tire.

Braidwood participates in *The Route 66 Red Carpet Corridor* events each May.

Serving the Mother Road since the 1950's

GODLEY. Godley once was a boom town when coal was mined near there. The Illinois Route 66 Mining Museum opened a few years ago. It features history and artifacts relating to Godley's mining roots. It has been open only in the summer months, but plans are underway to keep it open year round.

Godley participates in *The Route 66 Red Carpet Corridor* events each May.

BRACEVILLE. Braceville once was a bustling town of around 3,500 people. In the 1880's it boasted six general stores, two banks, a hotel and 18 other retail businesses. In 1910, workers at the Braceville Coal Company went on strike and the Company shut down. The town never has fully recovered and today only about 800 people remain.

GARDNER. Take a detour from the suggested route to see the 1906 two cell jailhouse on E Mazon St. Just follow the signs. Unbelievably, it was not closed until the late 1950's.

The 1926 Riviera Restaurant was about two miles outside of Gardner. It was a favorite Al Capone hang-out because he sold them bootleg liquor. The Riviera also offered gambling and

This two cell jail was used from 1906 to the 1950's

prostitution. It had unique architecture that featured stalactites hanging from the ceiling. It burned down in 2010.

West to Dwight

From Depot St, in **Gardner** go right on Jackson just before the RR tracks • Go right on W Parker out of town • Go left on Route 66 (Frontage Rd; there is no Route 66 sign; look for a triangle intersection.) • Go 6.5 miles then left as directed by the Historic

Route 66 sign onto Dwight Rd • At the next Stop sign, intersect with Old Route 66 and go left into **Dwight** • When Hwy 47 goes left, stay straight onto on Waupansie St, which will curve around a bit, but will eventually turn into Old Route 66/Frontage Rd

East from Gardner to Joliet

Follow Hwy 53 out of **Gardner** through **Braceville**, **Godley**, **Braidwood, Wilmington** and **Elwood** • After passing Elwood, stay on Hwy 53 past I-80 • When Hwy 53 hits a T in **Joliet**, go right on Washington then left on Scott • Go left on Columbia

DWIGHT

Beginning in Dwight and continuing on for several miles you will see some of the old Route 66 roadbed that has been replaced by a newer surface. It will give you a feel of how small the old road was.

Becker's Marathon Station at the intersection of Route 66 and Route 17 dates to 1933 and was the longest operating service station pumping gas on Route 66. It originally was Ambler's Texaco. It is open as a Visitors Center during the warm weather months,

The longest operating Route 66 service station is now a Visitors Center

Downtown you can see the 1906 First National Bank of Dwight, which was designed by Frank Lloyd Wright. You also can visit the Dwight Historical Museum at 119 W Main St.

A few old hot dog stands and a set of antique gas pumps and signs next to Route 66 Tire and Auto also are cool attractions.

The Keeley Institute was headquartered in Dwight. It was a world renowned center for the treatment of alcoholism between 1879 and 1965. The four week *Keeley Cure* started off allowing the patients to drink as much booze as they wanted, and was followed by replacement with various tonics developed by Keeley. At its peak, there were over 200 Keeley franchises worldwide, and hundreds of thousands took the *Cure*.

Dwight participates in *The Route 66 Red Carpet Corridor* events each May.

West to Odell

Stay on Old Route 66/Frontage Rd • Go 5.5 miles and follow the Historic Route 66 sign left onto Odell Rd (which turns into West St) to **Odell**

East to Gardner

Follow Frontage Rd out of **Dwight** • Go right on Hwy 53 to a Stop sign in **Gardner** • Go right on Hwy 53 • Go left on Jackson • Go right on Jefferson • Go left on Depot • Go left on Central (which becomes Washington) • Go left on Hwy 53 out of town

ODELL

Odell was a railroad town founded in 1884 that became a major depot for grain transportation in the early 20th century. Its early paved portion of old Hwy 4 became a portion of Route 66.

Odell has a well restored 1932 Standard Oil Station at 400 West St.

There also is an underground passageway that was built in 1947 to make crossing the congested Route 66 safer.

Odell participates in *The Route 66 Red Carpet Corridor* events each May.

1932 Standard Station

West from Odell to Towanda

Follow Odell Rd (West St) through **Odell** • Go left onto Old Route 66 (Frontage Rd) • Go 8.0 miles to Pontiac Rd • Go left just past the North Side Self Storage by the Old Log Cabin Restaurant into **Pontiac** • Bear left following signs with *1926 -30 Route 66* • Cross the RR tracks onto Aurora • Go right on Indiana • Go left on Main • Go right on Water • Go left on Vermillion. • Go right on Reynolds • Go left onto Route 66 and follow it to **Chenoa, Lexington** and **Towanda**

East to Dwight

From **Odell**, follow the Frontage Rd out of town • Go 5.5 miles then go right on Dwight Rd into **Dwight** • Stay on Old Route 66 to the Junction of Hwy 17/Mazone Ave • Go straight onto Waupansie St, which will become Macnamera St • Go straight onto Hwy 47 toward I-55 • After half a mile go right onto Dwight Rd • At the next Stop sign, go right onto the Frontage Rd

Pontiac, Chenoa, Lexington and Towanda

PONTIAC. Pontiac is one of the larger towns in *the Route 66 Red Carpet Corridor* winding from Joliet to Towanda. It is a bit difficult to navigate because Route 66 was rerouted over the years, and the signs for the different routes can be confusing. Also, some of the streets do not have good signs. No matter which route you take, you will have fun traversing Pontiac.

Old Log Cabin Restaurant

As you come into town on Pontiac Rd, you will find the Old Log Cabin Inn at 18700 Old Route 66, which has been in operation since 1926. When Route 66 was rerouted in the 1940's to pass in back of the restaurant, it was jacked up and turned around so the main road still would pass the front door. The food is pretty good and there are lots of old Route 66 photos.

Other attractions include the Route 66 Hall of Fame Museum at 110 W Howard St and the old Division St Bridge with its Hwy 4 marker that predates Route 66. Scotty's Place at 1120 N Division St across from the bridge has a cool old Schlitz beer sign.

Going east to west, I have directed you through Pontiac on the 1930-1939 route. To see the Division Street Bridge, you will have to take the post 1939 route. To do that going east to west, do not bear left past the Old Log Cabin Inn onto Aurora. Instead, bear right following the Post 1939 Route 66 sign. If traveling west to east, take a left onto Ladd St off of Reynolds just before the RR tracks, cross Howard St, and follow the signs to Division.

CHENOA. Chenoa was founded in 1854 to serve as a mercantile center for surrounding agricultural communities. The population is around 2,000.

Chenoa participates in *The Route 66 Red Carpet Corridor* events each May.

LEXINGTON. Lexington was laid out in 1836 and was named for the Massachusetts town of Revolutionary War fame. It was part of the major thoroughfare between Chicago and Springfield.

Today, Lexington is a sleepy but scenic town of about 2,000 residents. It has restored a portion of the 1926 alignment of Route 66 it

Ride down Memory Lane

calls *Memory Lane* with old billboards and Burma Shave signs. *Memory Lane* is only about a quarter of a mile long, and is in rough but passable condition. It's worth a few minutes to go down this skinny concrete slab to see what it was like to drive into Lexington in 1926.

If you take the time to ride through Downtown, you'll find a pleasant community with a Town Square that is residential rather than commercial. Dat Bar on Main Street Downtown is a friendly local pub.

Lexington participates in *The Route 66 Red Carpet Corridor* events each May.

TOWANDA. Towanda has a walking tour through *Route 66 Linear Park*, which follows portions of the abandoned roadway. There also are some Burma Shave signs.

Kick's 66 Bar and Grill at 19578 N 1960 E Rd just outside of town has a nice patio and biker parking.

Towanda is the western most town that participates in *The Route 66 Red Carpet Corridor* events each May.

West to Normal

Stay on Route 66 out of **Towanda** • Go through the Towanda signs and keep following Frontage Rd • Go across Towanda Dr onto Shelbourne Dr • Go left on Henry St, which becomes Pine St • Go left on Linden • Go right on Willow • Go left on Main/US 51 to **Normal**

East from Towanda to Odell

From **Towanda,** follow Frontage Rd to **Lexington** and **Chenoa** • From Chenoa, follow Frontage Rd • As you approach Pontiac, there will be a Hwy 116 sign • Go right onto Reynolds St into **Pontiac** (there is no street sign, so use the Hwy 116 sign as your marker) • Go one block, and just before the RR tracks, go left on Ladd St • Cross Howard St/Hwy 116 • Curve right onto Lincoln • Curve left on Division • Curve right and then left onto Pontiac Rd (becomes Frontage Rd) by the Old Log Cabin Restaurant • Follow Frontage Rd for about 8 miles • Go right onto West St through **Odell** following the Route 66 signs

NORMAL

Normal and Bloomington have grown into a contiguous metropolitan area. Route 66 going into Normal follows a windy path through some old and some relatively new neighborhoods. Be on the look-out for Sprague's Gas Station at 305 Pine St, which has interesting Tudor architecture. Restoration rumors are floating around.

In 1934, Gus Belt converted an old Shell Station into a roadside restaurant featuring steak burgers and milkshakes. Carhops would serve meals on metal trays that hooked onto car doors. There also was indoor dining. This became the first Steak 'n Shake. Gus later replaced the gas station with the Art Deco restaurants Steak 'n Shake customers visit to this day.

The 1937 Normal Theater at 209 W North St is still in operation.

In Normal, you will go past the Illinois State football stadium and take an easy ride into Bloomington.

West to Bloomington

From **Normal** follow Main St/Bus 51 to **Bloomington**

East to Towanda

From Main St/Bus 51 in **Normal**, cross College Ave • Go right on Willow St • Go left at Linden St • Go right on Pine, which eventually will become Henry St • Go right on Shelbourne Dr • Go straight into Old Route 66; do not get on Towanda Drive • Continue to **Towanda**

BLOOMINGTON

The Illinois Republican Party was organized in Bloomington in 1856 at a convention at which Abraham Lincoln spoke.

Illinois State University is in Bloomington, which is a typical mid-west college town. Main Street has a bunch of bars and restaurants, many with live music at night.

Bloomington was home to McLain Stevenson (who played Henry Blake on *Mash*), US Vice President Adlai Stevenson (who was Mclain's great uncle), and Gordon W Lillie (Pawnee Bill).

It has the one and only Beer Nuts factory at 103 N Robinson St.

State Farm Insurance is headquartered in Bloomington.

West to Funks Grove

From **Bloomington,** stay on Main St/Bus 51 as it becomes Center, then Madison, then Center again, through town • Go right on Veterans Pkwy/Bus 55 • Go right on Fox Creek Rd • Cross I-55 and go left onto S Beich Rd (Frontage Rd) to **Funk's Grove**

East to Normal

From **Bloomington**, follow Main St until it runs into East St, then back on Main St • Follow Main St/Bus 51 toward **Normal**

Funks Grove

The Funks have been making maple sirup since 1891. It is open from March through August. The sirup is made in February from the sap of over 3,000 maple trees the Funk family has harvested for over 120 years.

Funk's Grove Store

You'll enjoy chatting with the Funks. The matriarch of the family once admonished me in a friendly way for not wearing my helmet. They are nice folks so stop in if they are open.

The sirup operation gets most of the attention in Funk's Grove but there also is a quaint village that's worth a visit. In addition to relics of an old gas station and café, it features the Funk's Grove Church, which was built by Issac Funk and Robert Stubblefield in 1864. The Funk Prairie Home, built by Marquis de LaFayette Funk in 1864, is available for weddings and other events.

The 1864 Funk's Grove Church

West to McLean

From **Funk's Grove**, continue on Frontage Rd • Frontage Rd will become Carlisle as it approaches town • Go left on Main St in **McLean**

East to Bloomington

From **Funk's Grove** stay on Route 66 • Pass by the Village of Funk's Grove about ¼ mile past the Store and continue on Route 66 (Frontage Rd) to a Stop sign • Go right at the Stop sign • Go left on Veteran's Pkwy • Take the Main St Exit and go left on Main St/Bus 51 into **Bloomington**

McLean

McLean has the Dixie Travel Plaza, which once was the Dixie Truck Stop (opened in 1928) that operated the Route 66 Hall of Fame and claimed to be the country's first truck stop.

McLean is now home to America's Playable Arcade Museum at 107 S Hamilton St. It features restored arcade games from the 1970's and 1980's that visitors are able to play. It sounds like lots of fun!

West to Atlanta

Go right at the Stop sign in **McLean** • Go a few hundred yards and go left back onto the Frontage Rd just before the RR tracks • Go right at the Route 66 sign to NE Arch St through Downtown **Atlanta**

East to Funk's Grove

As you turn off the Frontage Rd from **McLean**, you will see a sign to Funk's Grove in about 100 yards • Go left on Main • Go right on Carlisle • Follow Carlisle as it becomes the Frontage Rd to **Funk's Grove**

ATLANTA

I once got caught in a bad rain storm on my way to Springfield and wound up checking into a motel in Atlanta which will remain nameless. But, I found that Atlanta has a small but cool Downtown. I wound up at Chubby's Bar and Grill, which has been run by the same owner for over 15 years. It has good bar food and a friendly eclectic crowd for a town the size of Atlanta. A group of European bikers visits every year.

That's a big hot dog!

The other Downtown spot is the Korner Bar. It is more rustic than Chubby's.

The Bunyon Giant came to Atlanta in 2003 hoisting a giant hot dog. In 1962, he held an ax in Flagstaff, AZ. In 1965, he was moved to Cicero, IL and traded his ax for a hot dog. It is one of three similar Giants in Illinois. The other two are the Gemini Giant in Wilmington and the Lauderbach Muffler Man in Springfield.

Atlanta also has some Route 66 themed murals, an octagonal library built in 1908 and a 40 foot tall watchtower that is wound by hand.

There is a privately owned museum Downtown called Memories. It features local artifacts, a 1961 Rolls Royce and a 1941 Packard Coupe.

Next door is the Palms Grill, which is in a restored 1940's Greyhound Bus Terminal. It has an extensive menu with over 20 kinds of home-made pie every day.

West To Lincoln

From **Atlanta,** follow SW Arch St to the Frontage Road toward Lincoln • Get on Bus 55 (Lincoln Pkwy) into **Lincoln** • Follow the Route 66 sign to Bus 55 onto Kickapoo St • Go right on Keokuk St • Go across the RR tracks • Go left on Logan • Cross Broadway and go right onto 5th St • Go left on Bus 55 (Lincoln Pkwy) and follow it out of town

East to McLean

From SW Arch St in Atlanta, cross the Junction with Hwy 25 • Continue on NE Arch St • Go left at the first Stop sign (about ½ mile) onto the Frontage Rd to McLean

LINCOLN

Lincoln was the only town to take the name of the 16th president before he became president. It was named for Honest Abe after he prepared the legal documents for the promoters of the site.

C&C Cycles fixes bikes and sells guns

Route 66 does not pass through the Town Square, so be sure to detour through it. It has an impressive court house and a couple of pretty good bars that have friendly locals and reasonable prices. Hallie's on the Square at 111 S Kickapoo St is a good one.

Guzzardo's Italian Villa at 509 Pulaski St on the Square is the local favorite restaurant.

Check out C & C Cycles at 1314 5th St. It's a small bike custom shop housed in a 1921 IlliCo gas station. They service bikes and sell guns, so there is something for everybody

Make sure to go by The Mill at 1555 5th St. It was a 1929 tavern built to look like a windmill. The plans are to restore it to a museum. The windmill currently is not attached to The Mill, but maybe it will be put it back when the restoration is complete.

Also be sure to check out the World's Largest Covered Wagon and Giant Abe Lincoln at 1750 5th St.

West from Lincoln to Springfield

From Bus 55/Lincoln Pkwy leaving **Lincoln,** go left following the Route 66 sign at Frontage Road Entrance • At the Stop sign near town, go left on Frontage Rd through **Broadwell, Elkhart** and **Williamsville** • When entering Williamsville, go left following the Route 66 sign • Go one block to a Stop sign • Go straight and follow Spur Route 66 around a big loop • At the next Stop sign, go left, cross I-55, and get on I-55 S • Get off of I-55 at Exit 105 to Bus 55/Sherman Blvd to **Sherman** • From **Sherman**, follow Bus 55 onto 9th St • Follow 9th St through Downtown **Springfield**

East to Atlanta

From **Lincoln** Bus 55/Lincoln Pkwy, cross Salt Creek (the actual Creek, not a road) • Bear right following the Route 66 sign onto Stringer St (there is no Stringer St sign). • Go straight and past *The Mill* then go right on 5th St/Bus 55 • Bear left onto Logan St • Go right on Keokuk • Go left on Kikapoo • Go right at the Junction with Lincoln Pkwy • Follow the Frontage Rd onto Arch St into **Atlanta**

Broadwell, Elkhart, Williamsville, Sherman and Springfield

BROADWELL. Broadwell had a Route 66 restaurant called the Pig's Hip, which was operated by Ernie Edwards and his family from its opening in 1937 until its closing in 1991. The Pig's Hip once was named *The Best Route 66 Attraction Where the Original Guy is Still There.* After the restaurant closed, it housed a museum until it burned down in 2007. All that is left are some roadside markers.

Die Cast Auto

ELKHART. There has been a settlement in Elkhart since the early 1800's. It became a major shipping point for the C&A Railroad due to large cattle interests in the area. It once was a stop on the route connecting Springfield and Bloomington. Abraham Lincoln frequently stayed there when he was on the Illinois legal circuit.

WILLIAMSVILLE. My directions through Williamsville reference several different street names as you follow Spur 66 to get through town, but that is misleading. It is really one big loop a mile or so long, where the same street takes on different names as the loop makes turns. Don't worry so much about following the street names; you cannot get lost.

Die Cast Auto Sales at 117 N Elm St is the big attraction. It is housed in a converted 1930's gas station and has a large collection of die cast model cars and Route 66 souvenirs.

You also can check out the Williamsville Historical Museum at 104 S Elm St.

SHERMAN. Sherman is the last small town along Route 66 before getting to Springfield. It has a population of about 4,000. There isn't much to do there from a biker perspective, but it is a prosperous looking town that is pleasant to ride through.

SPRINGFIELD. Springfield has a strip with a bunch of biker bars, including Dude's Saloon at 2001 N 11th St and Knuckleheads across the street from Dude's. Weeble's at 4136 N Peoria Rd is a popular biker spot, but it is not as

Old School as Dude's or Knuckleheads. The Cove at 1616 N Dirksen Pkwy stays open later than all the other biker bars.

Guitars and Cadillacs at 2724 N Peoria Rd is a newer spot that is a little more upscale than the other biker joints in Springfield.

Each year over the Memorial Day and Labor Day weekends, the Springfield Fairgrounds hosts motorcycle races around

The original Cozy Dog Sign

a dirt track known as the Springfield Mile. Thousands of bikers attend, and most of the biker bars put on special events with live bands.

Springfield has lots of motorcycle clubs with their own clubhouses. MCs include the Outlaws, Steel Justice and the Black Pistons.

Chief among Springfield's Route 66 attractions is Shea's Gas Station Museum at 2075 N Peoria Rd (9th St). Shea's has been around a long time, but it never seems to be open when I go by. A Shea's neighbor tells me it's rare to find anybody there these days.

The Cozy Dog Drive-In 2935 S 6th St claims to have invented the corn dog. I am a bit of a hot dog snob (Nathan's with skins are the best), so I never had eaten a corn dog before going to the Cozy Dog, but I must admit it was pretty good.

Of course, Springfield has Lincoln's Tomb in the Oak Ridge Cemetery at 1500 Monument Ave, the Lincoln Presidential Library 212 N 6th St; and the Lincoln Home Visitor's Center and the Lincoln Home National Historic Site, both at 426 S 7th St.

Unfortunately, the hotels along the mile of Springfield's biker bars are not very nice or safe. However, when heading out of Springfield at the west end of town, you will find the first Holiday Inn built on Route 66, which now is called the Route 66 Hotel. One wing is the original Holiday Inn and a somewhat newer wing has been added. There is a restaurant, a bar and a Route 66 museum.

When leaving Springfield, I give you two options:

My main route is the old 1926-1930 alignment from Springfield to Staunton, which passes through Chatham, Auburn, Thayer, Virden, Girard, Nillwood, Carlinvile, Gillespie and Benld. This route will take you longer than the alternate route but it is more rural and avoids I-55. If you take this route be sure to check out the Lauderbach Giant at 1569 Wabash on the way out of town. For directions and information about this route, continue reading below.

The alternate route follows I-55 and is quicker but still has a lot to offer. This route passes through Glenarm, Divernon, Farmersville, Litchfield and Mt. Olive before also arriving in Staunton. For directions and information about this route, skip to page 44.

West to Chatham

From 9th St in **Springfield,** go right on Capital Ave • Go left on 2nd St • Go right on S Grand • Go left on Macarthur • Go right on Wabash • Go left on Chatham and follow it until it dead ends at Woodside Rd • Go right on Woodside • Go left on Hwy 4 • Follow Main St/Hwy 4 into **Chatham** • Go right on Walnut • Go left on Church. • At a Stop sign, go right onto Hwy 4

East from Springfield to Lincoln

From 9th St in **Springfield**, go right with Bus 55 to **Sherman** • Cross I-55 and go straight onto I-55 N • Take Exit 109 to **Williamsville** • Go right at the end of the Exit • Go a couple of hundred yards and go right on Spur Route 66 • Follow the road around a big loop until you hit Elm • Go right on Oak (Bypass 66) • Cross Main and go right on Frontage Rd to **Elkhart** • From Elkhart, follow Frontage Rd to **Broadwell** • Follow the Frontage Rd over the I-40 overpass, and go right at Frontage Road Entrance

- At the first Stop sign, go right onto Bus 55 (Lincoln Pkwy) into **Lincoln**

CHATHAM

Chatham hosts the annual *Illinois Champion Cow Chip Throw* (you can't make this stuff up!).

The 1926-1930 route I have given you bypasses Downtown Chatham. You can loop around to the main drag and hit AJs Tavern at 101 E Mulberry St and Fat Willies at 109 E Mulberry St.

On your way to Auburn, you will go over a well preserved portion of Route 66 made of brick. It's a bit bumpy on a motorcycle.

This stretch of road also has a short detour that passes over an old bridge that is closed to traffic. Even so, it is passable easily on a motorcycle.

West from Chatham to Girard

Follow Hwy 4 out of Chatham • Watch for the Route 66 Sign and take a right onto Snell Rd (which will become brick) • Follow Snell, which becomes Curran, back to Hwy 4 • Go right on Hwy 4 to Auburn • Follow Hwy 4 toward Thayer • Just past the *Village of Thayer* sign, go left on Harrison • Follow Harrison back to Hwy 4 • Go left on Hwy 4 and follow it through **Thayer**, **Virden** and onto 6th St in **Girard**

Auburn, Thayer, Virden and Girard

AUBURN. Auburn has a bit fewer than 5,000 residents. You can try Rocky's Bar at 213 W Jackson St.

THAYER. Thayer has only about 1,000 residents. Zip on through to Virden!

VIRDEN. In the late 1890's, Virden was a prosperous mining community. In 1898, there was a strike of the Chicago - Virden Coal Company in which management refused to allow workers to unionize and brought in black workers to operate

Brick 66 near Auburn

the mine. That resulted in a gun battle in which several men on both sides were killed. There is a monument on the Town Square listing the names of those who died.

GIRARD. Girard is a town of under 2,500. There is a Town Square just off of Hwy 4. The Red Bird Café; Pub and Grub; and Andy's Bar all are on the Square.

Doc's Soda Shop is housed in the old Deck's Drug Store, which was established in 1894. The Deck family operated it for three generations until 2001. In 2007, the old soda fountain was reopened for soda and lunch.

The Illinois Terminal System Railroad Depot at 202 N 1st St now is a private home with the old depot preserved.

The Grand Army of the Potomac Soldier's Monument at 629 S 7th St honors Civil War veterans (of the Yankee variety).

The ride to Nillwood winds off of Hwy 4 and follows a long loop in which the street names change with the turns, but it really is one continuous road that ends up back on Hwy 4 by the Iron Sleds MC Clubhouse. It's a bit of a bumpy ride.

West to Nillwood

Follow 6ᵗʰ St out of **Girard** • At the Stop sign at Hwy 4 go straight across Hwy 4 onto Cambridge Rd • Follow Cambridge as it curves around and becomes Wylder, Morean, Pine, and then Morean again

• Follow to the Junction of Hwy 4 by the Iron Sleds MC Clubhouse in **Nillwood**

East From Girard to Springfield

Follow 6th St in **Girard** to Hwy 4 and continue through **Virden** and **Thayer** • Just past the *Village of Thayer* sign, go left following the 1926-30 Route 66 sign • Follow the loop around back to Hwy 4, then go left into **Auburn** • From Auburn, go straight with Hwy 4 at a Stop sign • About one mile out of town go left onto Curran Rd (which is brick) • Get back on Hwy 4 to **Chatham** • From **Chatham,** go two miles out of town on Hwy 4 • Go right on Woodside • Go left on Chatham Rd into Springfield • Go right on Wabash • Go left on Macarthur • Go right on S Grand • Go left on 2nd • Go right on Capitol Ave • Go left on 9th St/Bus 55 in **Springfield**

NILLWOOD

Nillwood is a farming community with only a few hundred people. However, the Iron Sleds MC is from there. The Iron Sleds is a men only family style MC founded in 1976. Visitors are welcome at their Clubhouse.

Our route from Nillwood to Carlinville takes several detours off Hwy 4 that will lead you into the surrounding farmlands. These are interesting segments, but they are bumpy and a bit confusing to follow. You might want to

Iron Sleds MC Clubhouse

check out a few of them and take an easier route bypassing these detours and following Hwy 4 into Carlinville.

West to Carlinville

From the Junction of Hwy 4 by the Iron Sled MC Clubhouse in **Nillwood**, go left on Hwy 4 • Go 1.8 miles and go left on Donaldson Rd • Keep following Donaldson around until it intersects with Hwy 4 • Instead of getting on Hwy 4, stay left with Donaldson • When you next intersect with Hwy 4, go left • Stay on Hwy 4 and go left on Allen. • Follow Allen around until it goes back to Hwy 4 then go left • Go past Hettik and go left on Harvest. • Follow Harvest back to Hwy 4 and go left into **Carlinville**

East to Girard

From **Nillwood**, go right on Morean by the Iron Sleds MC Clubhouse. • Go left on Pine, and keep going as it becomes Morean, Wylder and then Cambridge • Cross Hwy 4 at a Stop sign • Go straight on 6th St into **Girard**

CARLINVILLE

Carlinville is the biggest town along this stretch of Route 66. It has an impressive Town Square with the 1870 Macoupin County Million Dollar Courthouse at 201 E Main St.

The Marvel Theater at 228 W Main St first opened in 1920, but burned down in 1926. It was rebuilt in 1928 and was expanded in 1977. The current marquee is from the early 1960's.

Carlinville's Million Dollar Court House

A river used to run through part of the land that now is the Square. All the buildings on the Square used to be connected by underground tunnels. Some of the tunnels survive but they are not open to the public.

The big biker spot is the Full Throttle at 11578 Shipman Rd about four miles out of town. It has an Old School atmosphere, with a rustic bar and restaurant inside and a large back yard where live bands perform on weekends. Everyone in town (even folks who have never been on two wheels) will tell you that the food is great.

The St George Room at 118 E Side Square is the preferred Downtown biker spot. The juke is loud and the crowd can be bawdy. Oddly, they do not have mixers like club soda or tonic water. So, if you want a gin and tonic on a hot day, you will have to go elsewhere. It is on the ground floor of the 1870 Loomis House Hotel, which once was a whore house. Rumor has it the place is haunted.

Angus Bailey's steak house on the Square has a good bar in the back with several big-screen TVs. Part of the structure once was a grain elevator. Although it is in an historic building, the inside is a bit more modern than the other spots on the Square. The steaks are as good as you are likely to get anywhere.

The Lucky Dog Alehouse is another popular spot on the Square. It gets a late night dance crowd.

West to Gillespie

From **Carlinville**, follow Hwy 4 through the Square • Go left on 1st St/Hwy 4 • About a half mile out of town, bear right staying with Hwy 4 • Go past Evans Rd and go right on Deerfield (be alert; it's a small sign and hard to see) • Follow Deerfield back to Hwy 4 and go right • At the first Stop light, go right following Hwy 4 on Elm St • Go left on Macoupin in **Gellespie**

East to Nillwood

From **Carlinville,** stay on Hwy 4 • Go around the Square and get back on Hwy 4/108 on Route 66 1926-1930 • Go 3.2 miles out of town, go right on Harvest and follow it back to Hwy 4 • Stay on Hwy 4 past Hettick • Two miles past Hettick go right on Allen • Go left on Donaldson and follow it back to Hwy 4 • Go right on Hwy 4 into **Nillwood**

GILLESPIE

Gillespie is the home of actor Howard Keel.

Check out Chief's Bar and Grill.

Each June Gillespie puts on *Black Diamond Days,* which is a three day festival celebrating coal miners.

West to Benld

From Macoupin in **Gillespie**, follow Hwy 4 • Just before town, go left following the 1926-1930 Route 66 sign • Follow the road around until it comes back to Hwy 4, then go left and follow Hwy 4 into **Benld**

East to Carlinville

From **Gillespie,** stay on Hwy 4 • Go right on Pine • Go left on Macoupin • Go right on Elm • Get on Hwy 4 going out of town • Go about 5.5 miles and go left on Deerfield Dr • Go left back on Hwy 4 and follow it to **Carlinville**

BENLD

Benld used to rock out. There was gambling and prostitution. Al Capone operated distilleries there.

The 1924 Coliseum had a 10,000 square foot dance floor. It featured all of Belnd's illicit activities and first rate music. Duke Ellington, Count Basie, Guy Lombardo and Tommy Dorsey played there. More recently, the Everly Brothers, Fats Domino, Ray Charles, Johnny Rivers, Tina Turner and Chuck Berry were headliners. In its waning years it hosted local rock bands. The Coliseum burned down in 2011.

Belnd's other claim to fame is that in 1938, a meteorite went through the roof of Ed McCain's garage and wound up in his 1937 Pontiac coupe. The car and meteorite are on display in the Museum of Natural History in Chicago.

West to Staunton

From **Benld,** follow Hwy 4 • Enter **Staunton** on Edwardsville St • Go right on North St • Go left on Hibbard • Go right on Pearl • Go left on Hackman/Hwy 4

STAUNTON

The pre-1930 and post-1930 alignments of Route 66 meet here. One branch will take you through town, while the other bypasses Downtown.

Be sure to check out the Route 66 Tourist Information Center (AKA Henry's Rabbit Ranch Home) at 1107 Old Route 66, with its mini-Cadillac Ranch and other Route 66 artifacts.

West to Hamel

Follow Hackman/Hwy 4 out of **Staunton** • When nearing Hamel, go right on Worden Rd then take a left onto Old Route 66/Frontage Rd to **Hamel**

East from Hamel to Gillespie

From **Hamel**, follow Hwy 157 through a Stop sign and continue on as it becomes the Frontage Rd • Go to a T and go right (there is no sign, but that will be Wordon Rd) • In a couple of hundred yards, there will be sign showing Historic Route 66 1940-77 straight ahead and Historic Route 66 going left • Go left on Hwy 4 toward Staunton • Enter **Staunton** on Hackman St/Hwy 4 • Go right on Pearl • Go left on Hibbard • Go right on North then left on Edwardsville Rd heading out of town on Hwy 4 • Follow Hwy 4 to **Benld** and **Gillespie**

HAMEL

Hamel was first settled in 1818, but was not incorporated until 1955. Today it has about 400 residents.

Keep an eye out for St Paul's Lutheran Church at 6969 W Frontage Rd outside of town with its distinctive blue neon cross.

Weezy's Roadhouse (formerly Scotty's; before that Earnies; originally the Tourist Haven) first opened in the 1930's and was

An Al Capone hang out

an Al Capone hang-out. It has been redone, and now is more of a family oriented diner with a strong Route 66 theme. It has a small bar. Although it has undergone significant renovation, some of the old road house *feel* remains. It also is a big biker spot and participates in lots of poker runs and other biker events.

West to Edwardsville

From **Hamel**, follow Old US Route 66 to **Edwardsville**

EDWARDSVILLE

The entry to Edwardsville has tree lined and hilly roads that are fun on a motorcycle. It was incorporated in 1818 and is the third oldest town in Illinois. St Louis Street is on the National Register of Historic Places.

Be sure not to Stagger Out of the Stagger Inn

The bar to hit is the Stagger Inn at 104 E Vandalia St.

The movies *The Lucky Ones* and *Stingray* were filmed in Downtown Edwardsville, and Jackson Browne recorded a couple of the songs on his *Running on Empty* album there.

The Edwardsville Route 66 Festival is held in early June each year. It is not really a biker thing, but it is a good biker destination with historical displays, a classic car show and live bands.

Edwardsville is a quaint town, but as you leave, the road gets wider and busier. The feel transitions from rural to suburbia as you get closer to St Louis.

West to Mitchell

Follow Old Route 66 in **Edwardsville** to Hwy 157 through Downtown • Follow Hwy 157 as it bears left on West St • Continue on

Hwy 157 for about 4.6 miles to the Stop light at Siue South Rd • Go straight crossing onto Chain of Rocks Rd • Follow Chain of Rocks Rd to **Mitchell**

East to Hamel

Leave **Edwardsville** on Hwy 157 • At the outskirts of town, bear left staying with Hwy 157 and follow it to **Hamel**

MITCHELL

Mitchell is the last town before passing the Chain of Rocks Bridge on the way to St Louis. There are a few vintage motels that look OK on the outside but are pretty rough inside. The only reason to stay in one of them is to assure a short drive to safety after a night at the Luna Café.

A lit cherry was good news

The Luna Café with its recently restored neon sign has been a stopping off point in Mitchell since 1924 (some sources say 1927), and in its heyday, it had booze and gambling. When the bright red cherry on the sign was lit, customers would know that hookers were available. It is a good biker stop today, but it must have been fantastic when road houses offered one stop shopping!

The bartender told me the Luna Café is a Hells Angels hang-out. I saw some supporters, but no AJs.

The ride from Mitchell to St Louis is complicated. You will go from rural roads to highways and then go back onto rural roads before finally getting on the interstate. Be patient and follow my directions carefully and you shouldn't have too much of a problem.

West to St Louis

From **Mitchell,** follow Chain of Rocks Rd through the Hwy 111 Junction • Go left onto the I-270 West onramp • Exit on Old Alton Rd • Go right and cross under I-270 • Go right onto Frontage Rd • At a light with signs to Route 66 and to Spur Route 66, go right with Route 66 • Go right onto I-270 West • Take Exit 34 (Riverview Dr) off of I-270. • Go left onto Riverview Dr S following the sign toward St Louis and follow it through a Stop light, a Stop sign and four more Stop lights • Go left on Broadway by the Speedie Gas Station (be alert; the Speedie Gas is on the other side of the road on your left and hard to see) • Just past a RR overpass, go right onto Calvary (between two cemeteries • Go left onto Florrisant when the cemeteries end • Get on I-70 East toward Downtown St Louis and follow it to the Junction of I-64/I-55/1-70 • Get on I-55 S and take Exit 207 • Take I-44 Exit 290C (12ᵗʰ St/Gravois) • Go straight through Russell Blvd onto Gravois/Hwy 30 in **St Louis** • Go right onto Chippewa, which will become Watson Rd

East to Edwardsville

From **Mitchell** follow Chain of Rocks Rd • Go past the junction with Hwy 111 and go straight over I-225 to Hwy 157 • Follow Hwy 157 for several miles toward Edwardsville • Go right on St Louis St • Go right at a fork and stay with Hwy 157 (Vandalia St) into Downtown **Edwardsville**

ALTERNATE ROUTE FROM SPRINGFIELD TO STAUNTON

West from Springfield to Farmersville Alternate Route

Follow 9th St/Bus 55 through **Springfield** • Go right on Spruce • Go left on 5th • Follow Bus 55 to I-55 • Get on I-55 S • Exit I-55 at Exit 88 and take the Frontage Rd S through **Glenarm** • From Glenarm, follow Frontage Road S and get on I-55 at Exit 82 • Get off I-55 at Exit 80 to **Divernon** • From Divernon get on Old Route 66/ West Frontage Rd south to **Farmersville**

East from Farmersville to Springfield

From **Farmersville** follow Old Route 66/West Frontage Rd • At the Stop sign cross I-55 into **Divernon** • Get on I-55 and get off at Exit 82 • Go to Hwy 104 and cross under I-55 • Go right on West Frontage Rd to **Glenarm** • In Glenarm get on I-55 and Exit on Bus 55 in Springfield • Stay on Bus 55 onto 6th St • Go right on Myrtle • Go left on 9th St/Bus 55 in **Springfield**

Glenarm, Divernon and Farmersville

GLENARM. Glenarm is an unincorporated community south of Springfield. Not much happening, but don't worry, St Louis is coming up!

DIVERNON. Divernon was founded in 1887 and was

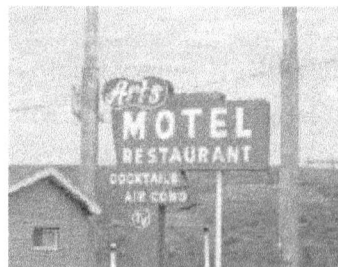

Art's once had booze, broads and gambling

named for a character named Di Vernon in Sir Walter Scott's book *Rob Roy*. Divernon's main businesses were the Madison Coal Mine No 6 and the Illinois Central Railroad. Both are closed.

FARMERSVILLE. Farmersville has an old boarded up Opera House that's kind of cool.

Art's Motel has a restored Route 66 sign. Art's was started when Art McAnrney and Marty Gorman opened a tavern on Route 66 after prohibition was repealed. A dance hall and casino soon were added. The business passed hands between Art and Marty several times, and the business was moved a couple of times. The business survived a fire in 1952. It may or may not be open.

West to Litchfield Alternate Route

From **Farmersville**, stay on Old Route 66/West Frontage Rd through Waggoner and past I-55 Exit 60 • When the Frontage Road ends, go left and pass over I-55 at N 16th Ave • Go right on the other side of the overpass onto the Frontage Road, which will be Old Route 66 (there is no Historic Route 66 sign) • Cross the RR overpass and go left on 1930-40 66 into Downtown **Litchfield** • Go right at N 10th St then take an immediate left onto Old Route 66

East to Farmersville Alternate Route

From Route 66 (Frontage Rd) in **Litchfield,** go three miles then go left and cross over I-55 (there is no sign, but the street will be N 16th Ave) • Go right on Old Route 66 (West Frontage Rd) • Go straight at the Stop sign just past Lisa's Antique Mall and continue on the Frontage Rd • Go straight at the Stop sign at Hwy 148 and continue on the Frontage Rd past Waggoner to Art' s Motel in **Farmersville**

LITCHFIELD

The three miles of Route 66 through Litchfield passes by the Ariston Café at 413 Old Route 66, which is in the Route 66 Hall of Fame. The Ariston was founded in 1924 in Carlinville, but later was moved to Litchfield.

The Ariston opened in 1924 in Carlinville

The Route 66 Café at 318 S Old Route 66 first opened in 1935 as the Belvedere Café and Motel.

The Sky View Drive-In Theater at 1500 N Old Route 66 has been operating since 1951.

West to Mt Olive Alternate Route

From **Litchfield**, follow 1930-40 66 out of town for a couple of miles • At the End 1930-40 66 sign, go right onto Route 66 • Cross St John Rd • Go left on Old Route 66 St into **Mt Olive**

East to Farmersville Alternate Route

From Hwy 138 in **Mt Olive**, go right by the Dollar Store onto Old Route 66 to see Soulsby's Service Station on your immediate right • Turn around and go straight on Route 66 • Go right at the first Stop sign following Route 66 (there is no sign directing you to Litchfield) • When approaching Litchfield, go right following the 1930-40 Route 66 sign onto N 10th Ave then bear left onto 1930-40 66 and follow it all the way through **Litchfield** • At the Stop sign showing the end of 1930 -1940 Route 66, go right on Route 66 1940-1977 (Frontage Rd) to **Farmersville**

Mt Olive

The Soulsby Station at 710 W 1st St sold gas on Route 66 for 65 years beginning in 1926, when Russell Soulsby and his father quit coal mining to start a gas station along the soon to be built Illinois Hwy 16. It claims to be the oldest gas station on the Mother Road.

The oldest Route 66 station

Mother Jones' Grave is located just off Route 66 in Mt Olive. Mary Harris Jones was a community organizer and labor activist primarily for miners. She was co-founder of the Industrial Workers of the World, and once was called *The most dangerous woman in America* because of her success in organizing miners' unions. She is buried in a miners' cemetery with miners killed in the Battle of Virden that occurred during a strike in the early 20th century.

West to Staunton Alternate Route

From **Mt Olive**, follow Old Route 66 out of town and continue for a few miles • Go left on US Hwy 66 • Cross under a RR overpass and go right on Old Route 66 • Cross I-55 and keep going • At Staunton Rd cross onto Historic Old Route 66 St and follow it to **Staunton**

East to Mt Olive Alternate Route

From **Staunton**, take Madison and follow Old Route 66 by going right at a fork • Go to the Junction with Staunton Rd • Cross onto Old Route 66 • Cross I-55 • Go left on East Frontage Rd • Go right on Hwy 138 into **Mt Olive**

STAUNTON

If you have taken this Alternate Route from Springfield to Staunton, return to page 39 to pick up our suggested route through the rest of Illinois.

MISSOURI

St Louis is the first Route 66 town in Missouri. The most interesting parts are on the western outskirts where you will find well maintained neighborhoods with older stone and brick homes. Be sure to stop by Ted Drewes Frozen Custard on the way out of town.

Once out of the St Louis metropolitan area, you will be treated to some of the most beautiful tree lined rides on the Mother Road. Most of the ride will be away from interstate highways, and even when you are on or near them, the riding is wonderful.

You will see well preserved motels like the Munger Moss in Lebanon and the Rail Haven in Springfield. The Boots Motel in Carthage is being restored. Nearby is a reputed Bonnie and Clyde hideout.

In Stanton you can visit the Jesse James Wax Museum where they will tell you Jesse lived until 1952. The Meramec Caverns are just a few miles down the road.

On the way to Devil's Elbow, you'll get to travel on some rare concrete four lane Route 66 roadway, and when you get there, you'll find the Elbow Inn, which is one of the best biker destinations anywhere.

In Springfield, you can see the site of a Wild Bill Hickok shootout.

From Springfield to Joplin, you will pass through a dozen rural towns, most of which are all but gone. Halltown, Paris Springs and Spencer, although ghost towns, have some of the coolest Route 66 relics in Missouri.

In Carthage, you can visit the site of the first Civil War battle between Northern and Southern ground troops.

For the bikers along this stretch, there is the Route 66 Tavern near Albatross and the Route 66 Café in Avilla, which are visited by bikers from all over the world.

Joplin is rebuilding from the 2011 tornado. The destruction cannot be understood without seeing it in person. Still, much survived, and there are serious biker spots there like Hogs and Hot Rods and the Undercliff, which is built into the side of a cliff.

So, enjoy Missouri. It is a great motorcycle riding state.

St Louis

The 630 foot tall Gateway Arch dominates the St Louis skyline. It is the tallest man made monument in the United States. Rides to the top are available, but it looks pretty confining.

St Louis used to be accessible by crossing the Mississippi River on the 1929 Chain of Rocks Bridge, which has a 22 degree turn in the middle.

The tallest US man made monument

The bridge has been closed to vehicles for decades, but it is open to hikers. It was used in *Escape from New York*.

The ride from Mitchell, IL to St Louis is complicated and takes a long time. You will alternate between rural roads and interstate highways, double back on yourself, and navigate confusing roadways around the city. Once inside the city, however, getting through St Louis is pretty easy.

Many St Louis Route 66 attractions have vanished in the last few decades. The 1941 Coral Court, which started as a fine motel but later became a house of ill repute, was torn down in 1995. One of the rooms was preserved and is on display in the Museum of Transportation in St Louis at 3015 Barrett Station Rd. The 1946 Crystal Court, across the

Frozen custard on '66 since 41

50

street from the Coral Court, was torn down in 1988. The 1937 White Castle on Chippewa was lost in 1983. The 1945 66 Auto Court was demolished in the 1980's, and the 1948 66 Park-In Theatre flickered its last flick in 1996.

But some old places have survived. Most notable is Ted Drewes Frozen Custard at 6726 Chippewa. Ted and his family started selling frozen custard out of a truck in 1929. By 1935, the business was so popular Ted built a permanent stand. In 1941, he opened a second stand on Route 66, which is the current Route 66 location. They serve dozens of flavors of *Concretes*, which are frozen custards so thick that they will not spill out of the cup when turned upside down. Forget your diets and enjoy.

Don't forget the Anheuser-Busch Brewery at 1127 Pestalozzi St. Clydesdales and free beer.

West From St Louis to Crestwood

Follow Chippewa/Hwy 366 past the St Louis City Limits sign • Chippewa will turn into Watson Rd • Follow Watson Rd to **Shrewsbury** then through **Marlborough** and **Webster Groves** to **Crestwood**

East to Mitchell Illinois

From **St Louis**, stay on I-70 West (that's right, you are going to get on I-70 West to wind up going east) • Take Exit 245B (Florissant Ave) • Go straight on Florissant to Calvary, then go right through the cemetery • Go left at the fork to a Stop light at Broadway • Go left on Broadway • After going through four Stop lights and a Stop sign, continue on to Riverview • Go right on Riverview by Speedie Gas and follow it to I-270 • Get on I-270 East and cross over the Mississippi River into Illinois • Get off at Exit 3A, get on Hwy 3 S and take an immediate left on to Chain of Rocks Rd • Go to the Stop sign at Old Alton Rd • Go left, then take another left on to the I-270 East on ramp • Go over the overpass and take the next off ramp to Hwy 203 (Granite City) • Go right and go under I-270 and get back on Chain of Rocks Rd into **Mitchell**

Shrewsbury, Marlborough, Webster Groves and Crestwood

SHREWSBURY. Shrewsbury was settled in about 1889. It starts out as a bunch of strip malls, but gets a bit less congested as you pass through town. Traffic can be bad during business hours.

MARLBOROUGH. Marlborough mostly is strip malls and fast food restaurants and doesn't have an Old Route 66 feel, but there is a Farmers Market with a Giant Farmer and his son that would do the Gemini Giant proud.

The now demolished Coral Court and Crystal Court Motels were in Marlborough.

WEBSTER GROVES. Webster Groves originally was a fur trapping region. Family Circle Magazine once ranked it 9th in its list of the *10 Best Family Cities in America.*

CRESTWOOD. Crestwood has the biker themed Club 277 at 10701 Watson Rd. The food is good and there is live music every night. It is attached to a Holiday Inn that has good rates.

I stayed at that Holiday Inn last summer. I got in at about 7:00. My friend Heidi was driving in from Nashville to meet me for a few days

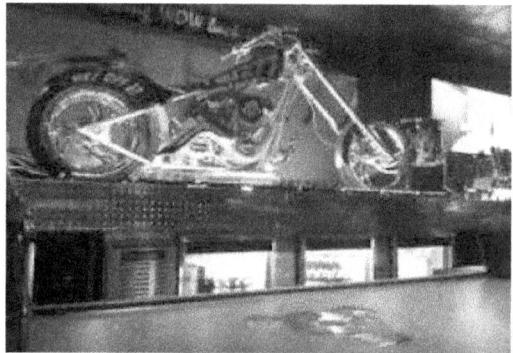

A hot custom bike inside Club 277

of riding, and was scheduled to get in by 10:00. So, I worked out a bit and headed to Club 277 for some dinner and a couple of cold ones.

I started off with a few Miller Lites. I ordered some chicken noodle soup and pot roast, and washed it down with some pinot grigio. After dinner, I ratcheted up to double Turkey and sodas and settled in to listen to the band and wait for Heidi.

Heidi got in a little over an hour late, but by the time she arrived, I was only on my third Turkey, so I was reasonably sober and in an excellent mood.

Heidi ordered a mojito, and while she was on her second one, an unordered double Turkey showed up. Some guy at the bar I didn't know had bought it for me and he came over to chat. I don't know why he bought one for me and not for Heidi. She's 4'11" tall and has a set of natural 44G's (that's not a typo; check out the photo nearby). By the way, she also has an MBA and works for one of the biggest real estate companies in the country.

The guy had weird hair. Less than Richard Nixon but more than Don Rickles. Well, I drank the Turkey and I reciprocated by buying him a drink. Courvoisier, if you can believe that! I should have known I was in trouble.

Closing time crept up, so I ordered one more and asked for my tab. The guy insisted on picking up my entire bill, and over my protestations, the bartender let him do it.

Then the shooters started arriving.

We started with a Jaeger. Then the bartender bought us all a star burst. Then there was some Rumplemintz, followed by a strait Turkey shooter. After that, we had a Gran Marnier shooter. I don't remember if there were any more shooters, but the bartender gave me a double Turkey and soda to go, and Heidi and I went to the room.

I woke up in the middle of the night with dry mouth and decided I needed a Coke, so

When Heidi moves it registers on the Richter Scale

I walked to the vending machine by the elevators. Unfortunately, I forgot to put my clothes on, so I didn't have any money. I also didn't have my room key.

That was a bigger problem than you might expect, because I forgot my room number. I went to the room I thought I was in and knocked on the door. It turned out to be the wrong room. Fortunately, the guy who answered the door didn't seem too impressed. Anyway, he must not have been gay because he didn't invite me in.

The implications of my situation started to set in. I was going to have to keep knocking on doors in the hope that I would find the right room, and then hope Heidi would hear me and open the door. The prospect of knocking on more wrong doors and getting arrested as a pervert or being invited in for a reaming was not too appealing. The other alternative was calling the front desk, which also was not very appealing.

Fortunately, the next door I tried was the right one and Heidi let me in. I got in bed and fell asleep immediately. The next morning, I had forgotten the whole episode until I saw my half-finished Turkey and soda on the night stand.

There is a moral to this story. Always keep some emergency Coke in your hotel room.

****

When leaving Crestwood, I give you two options:

My suggested route is the pre-1932 alignment passing through Manchester, Ballwin, Ellisville, Pond, Hollow and then Gray Summit. For directions and information about this route, continue reading below.

The alternate route follows I-44 through Allenton and Pacific before also arriving in Gray Summit. For directions and information about this route, skip to page 85.

West to from Crestwood to Gray Summit

From Watson Rd in Crestwood, follow 1926-33 Route 66 • Get on Kirkwood/US 67 N to Manchester Rd/Hwy 100 in Des Peres and follow it to **Manchester, Ballwin** and **Ellisville** • Stay on Hwy 100, cross Hwy 340, and in about two miles go left onto Manchester Rd • Stay on Manchester Rd through Grover, cross Hwy 109 and remain on Manchester Rd to **Pond** • Stay on Manchester Rd, cross Hwy 100, then take an immediate left onto Old Manchester Rd • At the Melrose Rd sign, bear left then take an immediate right onto Hwy 100 into **Hollow** • From Hollow, stay on Hwy 100 and go right on Old Manchester Rd • At the Junction of Hwy OO, go right on Hwy 100 to **Gray Summit**

East from Crestwood to St Louis

From Watson Rd in **Crestwood**, follow Watson Rd/Hwy 366 through **Webster Groves, Marlborough** and **Shrewsbury** • Watson Rd will become Chippewa • Follow Chippewa to Gravois • Go left on Gravios • Follow Gravois across I-55 and follow the signs to I-55 North • Follow I-55 North to I-70 West and continue past Downtown **St Louis**

Manchester, Ballwin, Ellisville, Pond, Hollow and Gray Summit

MANCHESTER. There has been a settlement in Manchester for over 200 years. Manchester Rd through here is one strip center after another. But thee is a nice *Historic Manchester* sign with a small covered bridge.

BALLWIN. Money Magazine includes Ballwin on its list of *Best Places to Live.*

ELLISVILLE. Ellisville was founded in about 1847 by Captain James Harvey Ferris, who brought slaves with him. The slaves constructed his house, known as The Brick House, out of bricks they made by hand. The house was razed in 1969.

When leaving Ellisville, you finally will leave the strip centers of suburban St Louis behind and go into some beautiful rural countryside as you head toward Pond. You will go through some residential developments, but don't worry; you will be heading in the right direction.

POND. Pond is so small it doesn't have a Wikapedia page. However, just outside of Pond is B Donovan's Steak House, which is in the old Big Chief Motel at 13572 Manchester Rd. This is a modern place inside a historic building built in 1928 by William Clay Pierce of the Pierce-Pennant Oil Company. It originally had a main office, a café, a motor court and a gas station, and was intended to be one of a chain of motor courts between Springfield, IL and

B Donavan's is a modern steak house in this vintage building

Tulsa, OK that would feature Pierce-Pennant gas stations. Pierce sold it to Henry Sinclair of the Sinclair Refining Company, who later resold it after Route 66 was realigned. This place is a cut above most of the spots you will find in old buildings along Route 66.

HOLLOW. Stovall's Grove Dance Hall and Saloon has a nearby Wildwood address at 18721 Stovall Lane. It is a country music place with live music.

GRAY SUMMIT. Gray Summit is where the 1926-33 alignment of Route 66 meets the newer post-1933 alignment.

Gray Summit has the Gardenway Motel and the Diamond Restaurant sign, each at I-44 and Hwy 100.

The Gardenway was named for a 30 mile portion of Route 66 that was landscaped in 1937 by the Missouri Botanical Garden, the National Park Service and the Missouri State Highway Commission. The Diamond was a restaurant that catered to both families and truckers. The truckers were relegated to a dining room segregated from the families. Shower and lodging facilities were provided for the truckers. Families were directed to the Gardenway for lodging.

The Gardenway was named for a 30 mile landscaped section of Route 66

Outside of Gray Summit you will find the 1943 Sunset Motel in Villa Ridge at 427 Hwy AT with its recently restored neon sign. The motel itself is being restored and some rooms already are available.

The Roadhouse Café at 2763 Hwy 100 offers food and booze. It gets modest reviews from the locals.

West to St Clair

From **Gray Summit**, follow Hwy 100 • At the Junction of Hwy 100 and Hwy AT, go straight onto Hwy AT • Cross Hwy 50 and get on N Outer Rd • Follow N Outer Rd several miles through and past a residential neighborhood • Just past the Indian Harvest Trading Post, go left across I-44 and take S Outer Rd into **St Clair**

East from Gray Summit to Crestwood

From **Gray Summit**, follow Hwy 100 across I-44 • Go 5.5 miles and go left on Old Manchester Rd to **Hollow** • Stay on Hwy 100 through Hollow and go left on Old Manchester Rd • After about two miles, go left on Melrose Rd, then take an immediate right onto

Old Manchester Rd • Cross Hwy 100 and follow Old Manchester Rd into **Pond**, and continue on Old Manchester Rd /Hwy 100 into **Ellisville** • Stay on Hwy 100 to **Ballwin** and into **Manchester** • From Manchester, follow Hwy 100 across I-270 through Des Peres and onto Kirkwood Rd/US 67 • Go through Downtown Kirkwood • Cross I-44 • At the Hwy 366/Watson Rd Junction, take the off ramp and go left onto Watson Rd and follow it into **Crestwood**

St Clair

The ride from Gray Summit passes through Union, MO, where you will find Bourbouise Harley-Davidson and Stout's Motorcycle Apparel.

Stout's is a flee market kind of place owned and operated by Mike Stout. Mike worked in a factory for 30 years and was in the flea market business on the side. He wishes he had gone flea market sooner. It has nice apparel, and the prices on things like motorcycle jackets and chaps are great. There are lots of vendors in the parking lot on the weekends. Bikers from all over the world stop by.

Stouts is an Old School Biker spot

You also will pass the Indian Harvest Trading Post. The folks who run it are nuts. When I tried to take a picture and tell the owners about my Route 66 project, I was met with a

Beware! Travelers report bad experiences here

violent shouting outrage that nearly came to blows. I have never experienced anything so hostile on Route 66, or anywhere else for that matter. I have come across Internet postings from people reporting similar experiences. Mike Stout won't recommend it to travelers for fear they will have the same kind of experience I had.

West to Stanton

From **St Clair** stay on S Outer Road, and get on Hwy 47/Commercial Ave • Stay on Commercial Ave and go right with Hwy 30 • Take another right following Hwy 30 and cross I-44 • Go left on Hwy WW/N Outer Road • Stay on N Outer Rd past the Hwy WW turnoff • Cross I-44 at Hwy W and JJ and follow into **Stanton**

East to Gray Summit

From **St Clair**, stay on Commercial Ave • Keep going straight through several Junctions as Commercial Ave becomes to S Outer Rd • Cross I-44 just before the Hwy AH sign and go right on N Outer Rd East • Go across Hwy 50 to Hwy AT • Keep going straight, get on Hwy 100, and follow it into **Gray Summit**

STANTON

Meremec Caverns advertised on billboards and with ingenious paintings on the sides of barns and the like. Some of these signs survive.

The Caverns are about three miles out of town off of Exit 230. The ride to the Caverns follows a beautiful tree-lined path along the Meremec River. It is a large privately-owned facility with plenty of parking, even for RV's. There is a restaurant and a gift shop with all the tacky stuff you could want.

To view the Caverns you must take a guided tour that lasts about an hour and twenty minutes. Tours leave about every twenty minutes, so you don't need to worry about waiting around. The tour guides are entertaining and informative.

There is spot in the Caverns that the James Gang used to divide loot then sneak out through an underground river. The authenticity of this spot is based on recovered artifacts from known James Gang robberies.

Jesse James lived until 1952!

I bypassed this stop off for years but I shouldn't have.

The Jesse James Wax Museum off Exit 230 claims Jesse died in 1952 under the name J. Frank Dalton.

There is a movie in which Mr. Dalton claims to be Jesse James, along with interviews and affidavits from folks who claim Mr. Dalton was Jesse James. DNA evidence appears to have discredited this story. Nonetheless, the movie presents a fairly compelling argument, and whether J. Frank Dalton was Jesse James or not, the Jesse James Wax Museum is an entertaining half hour.

West to Sullivan

From the I-44 cross-over in **Stanton,** follow S Outer Road, which becomes Springfield Rd • Cross the Junction with Hwy 185 staying on Springfield Rd • At the next Junction with Hwy 185, go left staying on Springfield Rd to **Sullivan**

From **Stanton**, cross I-44 at the Stop sign at Exit 230 • Go right on N Outer Rd, which eventually becomes Hwy WW • Cross I-44 on Hwy 30 • Go left on Hwy 30 then left on Commercial Ave/Hwy 47 into **St Clair**

Sullivan

Sullivan was founded in the late 1850's and early on had a railroad station. The main Route 66 attraction seems to be the Sullivan Antique Mall at 201 N Service Rd W, which is in the old Snell's café building.

From **Sullivan,** stay on Springfield Rd (which was S Outer Rd) to **Bourbon** • Get on Old Hwy 66, which becomes S Outer Rd, to **Cuba** • Follow S Outer Rd, which becomes Washington St and then Hwy ZZ out of town to **Fanning** • Stay on Hwy ZZ to Hwy KK into **Rosati** • Stay on Hwy KK, which becomes St James Blvd, into **St James**

From **St James**, follow St James Blvd/Hwy KK past Hwy U into **Rosati** • Follow Hwy KK to Hwy ZZ to **Fanning** • Stay on Hwy ZZ past Hwy KK into **Cuba** on Washington St • Go through Cuba on Washington St, which becomes S Outer Rd • Go straight across the Hwy U Junction and continue into **Bourbon** • Stay on Old Route 66 through several intersections and enter **Sullivan** on Springfield Rd • Stay on Springfield Rd past the I-44 Junction • At a three way

Stop, go right staying on Springfield Rd • Go straight at the Junction of Hwy 185 and follow the Outer Rd to **Stanton**

Bourbon, Cuba, Fanning, Rosati and St James

BOURBON. This Bourbon is in the wrong state, but it claims to be the only town in the country named for bourbon whiskey.

Bourbon is home to the Circle Inn at 171 S Old Route 66, which has been a family owned diner since 1955. The prices and food are good.

Outside of town you will pass by the now closed Bourbon Lodge. It once had a

The Bourbon Lodge now is a private residence

restaurant, cabins and a Phillips 66 Station. The restaurant was in a stone building that now serves as a private residence.

Bourbon is near Skippy's at 247 Hwy H in Leesburg, which is a biker bar of the Old School variety.

CUBA. Between Bourbon and Cuba, Route 66 passes through residential neighborhoods with only fleeting contact with I-44. Cuba is a good stopping point if you want to stay in an authentic Route 66 town that has nice amenities.

Cuba is known as the *Mural City* because of the murals on the historic buildings through town. Check out www.cubamomurals.com to see them.

There is a 1932 Phillips Station Downtown at the *4-Way*, which is a four way stop at the corner of Route 66 and Hwy 19.

The East Office Bar and Grill at 406 E Washington is a popular watering hole. It has food, pool tables and other games. The juke box is Classic Rock. The food is bar fare, but it is done well.

The Rose Bar at 1109 E Washington on the edge of town also is good.

The most popular places to eat are the Missouri Hick Bar B Q at 913 E Washington and Frisco's at 121 S Smith St. I went to the Missouri Hick thinking it would be run of the mill, but boy was I wrong. I live in Texas where folks are proud of their Bar B Q (although they smoke the wrong animal). I had the best pulled pork and ribs I have ever eaten.

Frisco's is billed as a steak place, but it has lots of other offerings. The bar dates to the early 20th century, and the restaurant was added about 15 years ago. It is very bright and has a family atmosphere

The Rose and Frisco's are the only late night spots in town. If you want something laid back, go to Frisco's. If you want something more lively, go to the Rose.

The Wagon Wheel Motel at 901 E Washington is the oldest continuously operated motel on Route 66. It was purchased by its current owner in 2009, and since then, the wonderful neon sign and the stone bungalows have been restored. Each room has nice furniture and bedding, a flat screen TV and a modern bathroom and shower. It has covered bike parking. This is an authentic Route 66 experience, and one of the nicest motels you will find along the way.

The oldest motel on Route 66

FANNING. Fanning is a bump in the road outside of Cuba. It has the Route 66 Outpost and General Store at 5957 Hwy Z that boasts of the World's Largest Rocking Chair, which is over 40 feet tall.

ROSATI. Rosati is a small unincorporated village known for its vineyards. It is sometimes called *The Little Italy of Missouri* because of the Italian heritage of its founders.

St James. Like Rosati, St James is known for its wineries.

Jonnies Bar at 225 N Jefferson St has been serving booze over 50 years. It has a distinctive three-sided *Stag* beer sign at the front door. As you enter, there is a sign with about 20 names of people who have been barred from entry. I asked the bartender what you have to do to get banned, and she said "Quite a lot, actually." No further explanation was given.

Inside, it's a smoky old fashioned joint, with nicotine stained walls and ceiling. There are lots of antiques, like an old cash register, old liquor bottles and that kind of thing. There also are a bunch of arrowhead displays. The crowd is a bit eclectic. Everybody smokes (except me). A lot of the women had pierced noses and lips, and the bartender had a tattoo on her face. Even so, it has more of a good old boy atmosphere

Don't get banned from Jonnies!

than a punk atmosphere. It is a biker spot for sure. The prices are super cheap ($3.50 for Wild Turkey).

Between St James and Rolla, be on the lookout for the Murdon dripping water sign.

West to Rolla

From **St James**, follow St James Blvd, then go right on Jefferson St/Hwy 68 • Cross I-44 • Go left on N Outer Rd West • Go left at the Junction with US 63 • Cross I-44 and follow US 63/Bus 44 (Bishop St) into **Rolla**

East to St James

Cross I-44 outside of **Rolla** • Go less than a mile then turn right on Route 66 just past the *Northywe* sign near the KIA Kingdom store • In a quarter mile be careful to bear left with Route 66 (if you accidentally go right you will come to a dead end) • Go through the Stop sign by the Love's Truck Stop • Follow N Outer Rd into **St James**

ROLLA

The ride between St James and Rolla is entirely on the I-44 Frontage Rd. It has a hilly and curvy terrain that is a lot more fun to ride than the Interstate. Plus, the ride into town passes through a nice rural neighborhood. Don't try to make up time by taking the highway. You'll miss a lot!

A Rolla Route 66 survivor

Rolla is half way between St Louis and Springfield. It has lost some of its old Route 66 atmosphere, but the Totem Pole Trading Post at 1413 Martin Springs Dr still operates on the Outer Road along I-44. Zeno's Motel and Restaurant is gone. The site has been leveled and is for sale. *Another one bites the dust!*

Downtown features the 1860 Phelps County Jail on Park St between 2nd and 3rd, which was used by Union forces during the Civil War for both military and civilian prisoners. This stone structure remained in use as a jail until 1912.

Downtown also has the 1857 Dillon Log House at 302 3rd St, which was the area's first courthouse.

The Trail of Tears, in which Cherokees were forced to relocate from their homes in Georgia to reservations, passed through Rolla.

Keep a lookout for the Mule Trading Post at 11160 Dillon Outer Rd with its Giant Hillbilly with swinging arms. The Hillbilly originally was at a gift shop in the Hooker Cut, near Devil's Elbow.

West to Doolittle

Follow Bus 44 in **Rolla**, and go right continuing on Bus 44 at the Junction of Kings Hwy (be careful, it is an easy turn to miss) • Before I-44 Exit 184, go around the traffic circle onto Martin Springs Drive/ Outer Rd • Cross the Hwy T Junction • Outer Road will become Eisenhower St into **Doolittle**

DOOLITTLE

Doolittle is so tiny it has a Rolla, MO address. It originally was called Centerville. In 1944, residents decided to rename the town after a World War II hero, and they ultimately selected Medal of Honor winner Jimmy Doolittle, who commanded the Doolittle Raid bombing of Tokyo. Doolittle could not personally accept the honor until the war ended, and on October 10, 1946, he flew his own B-25 in for the ceremony renaming the town for him.

The only place to go is the Back Road Grill & Bar (shouldn't it be Bar and Grill?) at 195 Doolittle Outer Rd. It is so new it smells new. There is live music on the weekends.

The ride from Rolla through Doolittle to Devil's Elbow is rural. There is a small stretch on I-44, but overall this is one of the better short hops between towns. There even is a stretch of original four-lane Route 66.

West to Devil's Elbow

Follow Eisenhower St out of **Doolittle** • At Exit 176 get on I-44 • Get off at Exit 172 (Jerome/Dixon) • Go left on Outer Rd West • At Exit 169/Hwy J, cross I-44 and go right on Hwy Z • Go left on Teardrop Rd into **Devil's Elbow** (be alert, the sign is small; if you get to a bridge you have gone too far)

East to Rolla

From **Doolittl**e, follow Eisenhower St/Historic 66 as it becomes Martin Springs Outer Rd, then Martin Springs Dr into **Rolla** • Go right on US 63/Bus 44 • Go right at the Stop light staying with US 63 • At a Stop light go left staying with US 66 • Cross I-44 to leave Rolla

DEVIL'S ELBOW

Devil's Elbow is at a sharp turn along Route 66. As you approach the Elbow, you will be going over a four lane portion of the roadway.

A great biker joint on '66

Once you make the turn, you will come to the Elbow Inn at 21050 Teardrop Lane, which is a road house dating from 1929. It is one of the great biker destinations anywhere. It has Bar B Q and all the other food you usually find in biker joints.

All you biker chicks be ready to give up your bras, sign them and get them stapled to the ceiling. If you are too timid for that, sign a dollar bill and put that up instead.

The Munger Moss Sandwich Shop originally was at the site of the Elbow Inn. When the town was bypassed in the 1940's the owners moved to Lebanon and opened the Munger Moss Motel.

Sheldon's Market also is in Devil's Elbow. It opened as Miller's Market in 1954 and later became Allman's Market. It also serves as the local post office.

West to St Robert

From **Devil's Elbow**, follow Teaardrop Rd to the intersection of Hwy Z • Go left on Hwy Z, and continue on it past Hwy 28 into **St Robert**

East to Doolittle

From **Devil's Elbow** follow Teardrop Rd across the bridge • Go right on Hwy Z and follow it to the Junction of Hwy J and I-44 • Go left across I-44 • Go right on Outer Rd East • Get on I-44 at the first opportunity • Get off I-44 at Exit 176/Sugar Tree Rd • Go right onto Historic 66 and follow it onto Eisenhower Rd into **Doolittle**

ST ROBERT/FT LEONARD WOOD

Ft Leonard Wood was established in 1940 as a training center for the US Army in preparation for the United States entering into World War II. As a result, Ft Leonard Wood thrived while other business along Route 66 suffered. Lodging was so scarce that some farmers converted chicken coops into housing. Italian and German prisoners of war were interned there during the war.

The Fort is named for Major General Leonard Wood, a Congressional Medal of Honor winner who began his military service as a contract surgeon during the Apache Indian wars of the 1800's. He later was Teddy Roosevelt's commanding officer during the Spanish American War.

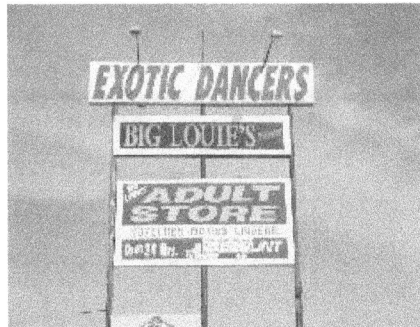

Big Louie's has it all

Today, Ft Leonard Wood covers nearly 63,000 acres, and is one of the largest military facilities in the country. The US Army Engineer School, the US Army Military Police School, and the US Army Chemical, Biological, Radiological and Nuclear School all are at Ft Leonard Wood.

Big Louie's at 14400 Hwy Z is in St Robert, which is next to Ft Leonard Wood. Big Louie has it all, from restaurants to adult toy stores, to strip clubs to tattoo parlors.

For less risqué fare, there is Judy's Place at 21754 Teardrop Lane, which has proudly been serving Budweiser for 24 years. It's a good biker stop on the way to or from the Elbow Inn just down the road.

West to Waynesville

Follow Hwy Z though **St Robert** • Go straight across Missouri Ave • At a Stop light, get onto Bus 44, and follow it out of town • Cross I-44 onto Bus 44 in **Waynesville**

East to Devil's Elbow

From **St Robert**, follow Bus 44 straight through the Spur 44 Junction onto Hwy Z • Go past Big Louie's then stay straight on Hwy Z at the I-44 Junction • After one mile, bear right onto Teardrop Rd into **Devil's Elbow** (be alert; it's a right turn at a bend in the road, and the Teardrop Rd sign is small; there is a Route 66 sign)

WAYNESVILLE

Just past the sign showing you are entering Waynesville, keep a lookout on the right up a hill for a rock painted like a giant frog (known locally as W H Croaker).

There is an 1850's stagecoach stop at 106 Lyn St on the Town Square. It is the oldest building in Waynesville.

W H Croaker

Waynesville used to be a big stomping ground for GIs from Fort Leonard Wood. It apparently had a bunch of rowdy bars. The current bars are OK, but they are not too rowdy.

Try Hopper's Pub at 318 Historic Route 66. Steve's Place just west of town at 202 Glenda Dr is another biker friendly place.

West from Waynesville to Hazelgreen

From **Waynesville**, follow Bus 44 through Downtown • Bus 44 will join Hwy 17 • Follow Hwy 17/Historic 66 to **Buckhorn** • Stay on Hwy 17 past Hwy P • At the Hwy 17 fork, bear right onto Hwy AB • Pass Hwy AA and go to the Junction of Hwy 133 • Go straight on S Outer Rd to **Hazelgreen**

Buckhorn and Hazelgreen

BUCKHORN. Buckhorn was named for the long gone Buckhorn Tavern, which was a stage stop.

There is not much in Buckhorn today. There is a Giant Bowling Pin advertising some lanes next to an Adult Superstore sign. Route 66 has lost some of its innocence.

HAZELGREEN. It's quite a long ride between Buckhorn and Hazelgreen, and there is not much out there except a long windy rural road that crosses the 1923 Gasconade River Bridge.

Home of the Gutter Ball

West to Lebanon

From **Hazelgreen**, go over the Gasconade Rive Bridge · Pass the Hwy S Turnoff · Go straight on the S Outer Road at the Hwy T Junction · Go right at Hwy F and cross I-44 · Go left onto the N Outer Road West/Route 66 into **Lebanon**

East from Lebanon to St Robert

From Bus 44 in **Lebanon**, go left on Historic Route 66 just before the Wyota Inn · Go about five miles to Hwy F and go right · Cross I-44 and wind down to Historic Route 66/Pennington Rd · Go left and follow Route 66 for several miles until you cross the Gasconade River Bridge to **Hazelgreen** · Follow the Outer Rd, which will become Hwy AB · Pass the Hwy AA Junction and go straight onto Hwy 17 into **Buckhorn** · Follow Hwy 17 over I-44 to Bus 44 into **Waynesville** · Stay on Hwy 17 to Bus 44 in **St Robert**

LEBANON

On the way into Lebanon you will pass the Lebanon I-44 Speedway at 24069 Route 66. This is a 3/8 mile asphalt oval raceway. It was opened in 1983 by Bill Willard as a dirt track. It was paved in 1988, went back to dirt in 2003, then went to asphalt in 2009. They claim that in any year over a quarter of the Daytona 500 field once raced there. Daytona 500 winner Jamie McCurray began his racing career at this small track.

Get your kicks in the Route 66 Room at the Munger Moss Motel

The 1946 Munger Moss Motel is at 1336 E Route 66.

The Munger Moss has a complicated history (having moved there from Devil's Elbow), but it has been at its present location since 1946. It has a distinctive sign that is a knock-off of the original Holiday Inn sign. There are several renovated rooms with Route 66 themes, including a *Route 66 Room* with nostalgic photos and mementos, a *Pretty in Pink Room* dedicated to the now defunct Coral Court Motel, and a *Texas Room* with prints of the renowned Route 66 historian and artist Jerry McClanahan. You cannot get all the kicks on Route 66 unless you visit the Munger Moss.

There also is the Forest Manor Motel at 1307 E Route 66 and the Starlite Lanes bowling alley across the street from the Munger Moss.

The Lebanon Route 66 Museum is at 915 Jefferson St.

Wrink's Market at 1336 E Route 66, which was opened in 1950 by Glen Wrinkle, was operated until recently by Glenn's son Terry. It was closed the last time I passed by.

The Bell Restaurant on E Route 66, a long time Route 66 staple, is gone. Until recently, the sign and building remained, but they have been torn down.

West from Lebanon to Springfield

From **Lebanon,** follow Bus 44 to I-44 Exit 127 • Go right on Hwy W • Stay on Hwy W to I-44 Exit 118 • Cross I-44 and take Hwy C to **Phillipsburg** • Go right on Hwy CC and follow it to **Conway** • Stay on Hwy CC through the Junctions with Hwy J and Hwy M into **Marshfield** • Stay on Hwy CC and merge into Hwy 38 • Turn left onto Hwy OO • Stay on Hwy OO past Hwy B to the Junction with Hwy 125 in **Strafford** • Go through the Hwy 125 Junction staying on Hwy OO into **Springfield** on Hwy 744/Kearney St

East from Springfield to Lebanon

From the Junction of Hwy 744/Kearney St in **Springfield** go right, cross US 65, and go several miles to Hwy OO • Follow Hwy OO to **Strafford** • Stay on Hwy OO through **Marshfield** • At the Junction with Hwy 38, bear right onto Hwy 38 • Go left on Hwy CC • Stay on Hwy CC to **Conway** and **Phillipsburg** • Continue on Hwy CC to the Junction with Hwy C • Go left on Hwy C • Go right on Hwy W/N Outer Rd • Go left on Bus 44 into **Lebanon** and follow it through town

Phillipsburg, Conway, Marshfield, Strafford and Springfield

PHILLIPSBURG. Hwy W from Lebanon to Phillipsburg starts off hugging I-44, but eventually veers off to be a pleasant country road. Even where it follows I-44, it is a fun ride, which is a good thing, because there is not anything to stop and do on this portion of your trip.

CONWAY. It's only five miles from Phillipsburg to Conway, and again, Route 66 follows near I-44 but stays rural enough to make you feel like you are in the country. There are rolling hills, easy turns, grasslands and lots of ponds.

You can visit the Conway Route 66 Welcome Center at 726 W Jefferson Ave.

If you are getting hungry or thirsty and can't make it the 14 miles to Marshfield, there is a nice country store called Summer Fresh, which has an excellent deli.

Between Conway and Marshfield, you will come across Sorrell's Trading Post, which used to be Luthy's Buzz Inn. It sells liquor, beer and rudimentary groceries and snacks.

MARSHFIELD. Edwin Hubble, inventor of the Hubble Space Telescope, is from Marshfield. A replica of the telescope is in the Town Square in front of the Webster County Museum at 219 S Clay St.

Nearby you can stroll the *Marshfield Walk of Fame* honoring people of note, including George Bush, Dred Scott, Bob Barker, Robert Cummings, Edwin Hubble and George *Goober* Lindsey. What a Motley Crew!

Luthy's is now Sorrell's Trading Post

STRAFFORD. Despite its diminutive size, Strafford has a proud Route 66 heritage, and each year hosts *Route 66 Cruise* and *Route 66 Days*, which features a classic car show.

Getting through Springfield Going West

Enter Springfield on Hwy OO from Strafford • Merge with Hwy 744/Kearney St • Go left on Bus 44/Glenstone • Cross Chestnut Expressway, go over a tall overpass crossing some RR tracks and go right on St Louis St • Go past Jefferson St onto Park Central East • Follow the

Park around to Park Central West (this is a tricky route to follow because the streets off the Park do not have clear signs; basically, you will be coming in from the east and going out the west end of the Park about half way around the circle) • Go straight onto College St and follow it to Bus 44/Chestnut Expressway • Go left on Bus 44/Chestnut Expressway and follow it to Hwy 266 heading out of town

Getting through Springfield Going East

Follow Hwy 266 from from Halltown into Springfield • Cross the Junction of W Bypass/US 160 • Bear right onto College St • Go straight through Kansas Expressway and Campbell St • Go right around the Square and go right on the opposite side onto Park Central E • Go straight through Jefferson • Park Central becomes St Louis after crossing Jefferson • Go left onto Glenstone • Glenstone becomes Bus 44 • Go right on Hwy 744/Kearney, and follow it to Hwy OO out of town

Springfield

As you enter Springfield you'll see the Rest Haven Court Motel at 200 E Kearney St with a sign that looks a lot like the sign at the Munger Moss Motel in Lebanon.

There is a Route 66 loop that will take you past Springfield's interesting sites, including the Rail Haven Motel (now a Best Western) at 203 S Glenstone, the 1926 Gillioz Theater at 325 Park Central E, a

Does this look familiar?

vintage Steak-N-Shake at 1158 E St Louis, the College Street Café at 1622

W College St, and the College Street Body Shop at 2136 W College St, all with wonderful Route 66 era signs. You also will see an interesting Route 66 mosaic along a wall.

Don't miss the 1945 Rock Fountain Court (now called the Melinda Court Apartments) on College Ave. There are nine original cabins with stone veneers set in a semi-circle. It no longer is a motel.

Your Springfield tour of Route 66 also will take you past a Town Square that was the site of a Wild West shoot out. Wild Bill Hickok and Dave Tut had a dislike for each other because they both were after the same girl. Tut stole Wild Bill's watch and bragged he would wear it on the Town Square at an appointed time. When that time came, Wild Bill was waiting. Tut drew on Bill and Bill

Entertaining Springfield since 1926

shot him dead. There is a marker on the square commemorating the event.

Most of the rides through Missouri are terrific, but the ride between Springfield and Webb City is exceptional. You will pass through several ghost towns that have fun photo ops. You will not see any interstate highways. This ride is what Route 66 and motorcycles are all about.

West from Springfield to Carthage

Follow Hwy 266 out of Springfield through **Halltown** • At the Junction of Hwy 96, stay straight on Hwy 266 to **Paris Springs** • Follow Hwy 266 to the Junction with Hwy 96 • Go across Hwy 96 and get on Hwy N • Take the first right and cross the bridge into **Spencer** • Go straight to the Junction with Hwy 96 • Go left on Hwy 96 and follow it through **Heatonville, Albatross, Phelps, Rescue, Plew** and **Avilla** • Go past Hwy BB and in about four miles go left on Route 66 Bypass/Hwy 118 • When it 'again intersects with Hwy 96, go left and follow it into **Carthage**

East from Carthage to Springfield

From Garrison St in Carthage, go past the Hwy 96 and Route 66 signs that will take you through the Square, go right on Hwy 96/Central Ave and follow it out of town • Go to the Junction of Hwy 96 and Hwy V • Go right on Old Hwy 66/Hwy 118 just before the Best Budget Inn (be careful, the Old 66 sign is hard to see) • Follow Old 66/Hwy 118 until it intersects with Hwy 96 • Go right and follow Hwy 96 through **Avilla, Plew, Rescue, Phelps, Albatross** and **Heatonville** • Half a mile past Hwy M, go right on Farm Rd 2059 and follow it through **Spencer** • Cross the bridge after Spencer and go left on Hwy N • When Hwy N intersects with Hwy 96, cross the road and follow Old 66 to **Paris Springs** • From Paris Springs, merge into Hwy 266 and follow it through **Halltown** and into **Springfield**

Halltown, Paris Springs, Spencer, Heatonville, Albatross, Phelps, Rescue, Plew, Avilla and Carthage

HALLTOWN. Tiny Halltown is only 0.2 square miles in area, but has been a community since 1833. In the late 1940's, it had over 20 establishments, including gas stations, cafés, antique shops and other stores. Today about the only thing left is Whitehall Mercantile, which is now an antiques place.

Whitehall Mercantile

PARIS SPRINGS. Paris Springs was founded in 1855. Nearby Paris Springs Junction was established with the commissioning of Route 66 and died with its decommissioning. Today, the main attraction is the Gay Parita Station, which is a replica of an early 20th century Sinclair station. The original station was built in the 1930's and the stone ruins of the garage are on the property.

SPENCER. You will enter Spencer over a 1922 Pony Bridge.

Spencer has been a ghost town twice. It was founded the 1870's when a post office opened there, but it was a ghost town by 1912. It experienced a resurgence when Route 66 came through, but it became a ghost town again after Route was realigned to bypass the town. There is nothing left of Spencer but the stone Phillips 66

The Spencer ghost town

Spencer Garage. There once was a barber shop, a café and a feed store. If you look in the windows, you will find that they all are clean, and there even is an old barber chair in the barber shop.

Check out the gasoline prices still displayed: $0.12 for Regular!

The road out of town is narrow and gives an old time Route 66 experience.

HEATONVILLE. Once you leave Spencer you will go through a string of ghost towns or near ghost towns. The first of these is Heatonville, which was founded in the 1880's. Today, there are a few homes and a Friendship Assembly Church, along with a few old Route 66 relics, including the abandoned stone D L Morris Garage and Station.

ALBATROSS. Albatross was founded after Route 66 was established. It started as a stop for the Albatross Bus Lines, and at one time, it had six gas stations. It may be in the middle of nowhere today, but it has the Route 66 Tavern, which is an Old School biker destination. It sometimes has bands, poker runs and other biker events.

PHELPS. Phelps has several interesting buildings including an abandoned church and a boot shop.

RESCUE. Rescue had a school until 2003 when it was closed due to lack of enrollment.

PLEW. Plew has erected some Burma Shave style signs with a fire and brimstone religious theme. Don't think I want to break down there!

AVILLA. As bumps in the road go Avilla is a pretty big one.

Avilla is home to the Route 66 Café (not to be confused with the Route 66 Tavern in Albatross), which is a major Route 66 biker spot. Bikers from all over the world make a point of stopping there.

There also is a 1915 bank building now housing a US Post Office.

Avilla had a tumultuous Civil War record. Confederate raider Bloody Bill

Bikers from around the world visit the Route 66 Café

Anderson, who rode with Quantrill's Raiders, led an attack on Avilla's Union supporters and killed dozens of them. The Union army later took control of Avilla and based a headquarters there. Avilla prospered during reconstruction, and had many businesses and tradesmen in the 1870's. Prosperity continued well into the 20th century, but after I-44 bypassed Avilla, it went into quick decline and was a ghost town by the 1970's.

On your way between Avilla and Carthage, you will pass the Red Rock Apartments, which used to be a motel under another name. Local legend has it that Bonnie and Clyde once stayed there.

CARTHAGE. Just before you come into Carthage, you will pass by the Crapduster sculpture, which is a flying manure spreader created by local artist Lowell Davis. It is outside a gas station and convenience store at 13011 Hwy 96. This sculpture reportedly was dedicated to a local businessman who was full of...., well, you know!

Foxfire Farm Sculpture on the edge of town features more Lowell Davis artwork.

Davis has erected a replica ghost town called Red Oak II a few miles northeast of

The Crapduster

Carthage. Davis grew up in the real Red Oak, which is a real ghost town. He moved and restored buildings from the original Red Oak, and he has added other buildings, including a Phillips 66 Station, an old school house, a feed store, a diner, a town hall and a blacksmith shop. Davis lives in a house where notorious female outlaw Belle Starr once lived.

Carthage has an impressive Town Square featuring the Jasper County Courthouse, which was built in 1894. Belle Starr, whose maiden name was Myra Belle Shirley, grew up in her father's hotel on the north side of this Square. She supposedly fought with Quantrill's Raiders after her brother Bud was killed. She later married Sam Starr from Oklahoma

Newly restored Boots Court

Territory and became a notorious woman outlaw.

The Boots Court at 107 S Garrison Ave opened about a block off the Town Square in 1939. It was a big deal because it had a radio in every room. For years, the Boots had a false roof that was not original, and a sign that said "Boots Motel" that was not original. The false roof has been removed, and the new "Boots Court" sign is a replica of original. There are five restored rooms from its 1946 annex. The plan is to restore the entire motel.

Jim's Bar off the Square at 325 E 4th St has been in operation for 33 years and is in a 120 year old building. Plus, it is haunted. Employees tell stories of plates flying around in the kitchen and other unexplainable incidents. Go to You Tube, then search "ghost orb you tube best", and a video of an orb at Jim's will come up. A bunch of ghost hunter type TV shows have been there, and they all claim that there are spirits in Jim's. *Who you gonna call...Ghost Busters!* It has liquor and beer, but is not open on Sundays.

The Route 66 Drive-In Theater is on the way out of town at 17231 Old Route 66. It has been named the best drive in theater in America. It is open only for the summer season.

The Battle of Carthage Civil War Museum at 205 Grant St features a mural depicting the Battle of Carthage, which was fought on July 5, 1861. Supposedly, it was the first Civil War battle that pitted Northern and Southern land soldiers against each other.

Boomer Sooner Rib Brothers Bar B Q at 1220 Oak St on the way out of town is terrific. I was there the day of the 2011 tornado that hit Joplin.

West from Carthage to Joplin

From **Carthage**, follow Hwy 96/Central Ave • Go left on Garrison • Go right on Oak St • Cross US 71 and go left at the fork onto Old 66 Blvd to **Brooklyn Heights** • Follow Old 66 Blvd to the Junction with Bus 71/Hwy 171 • Stay on Bus 171 crossing Hwy 171 to Old 66 Blvd • Go left on Old 66 Blvd • Go left on Pine St • Go right on Main St into **Carterville** • Follow Main St out of town • Just after some concrete ruins, bear left on Broadway into **Webb City** • Go left on Webb then take an immediate right back on Broadway • Go left on Madison and follow it all the way past the *Joplin* sign • Go right on Zora • Go left on Florida • Go right on Utica • Go left on St Louis • Go right on Broadway • Go left on Main into Downtown **Joplin**

East from Joplin to Carthage

From Main St **Joplin**, go right onto 2nd St and follow the *Missouri 66 Byway* signs • Jog from 2nd St onto Broadway • In a half a mile, go right on St Louis • Go left on Euclid • Go right on Utica • Go left on Florida • Go right on Zora • Go left on Range Line Rd, which will become Madison • Follow Madison through the Hwy 71 sign and go right on Broadway, which has a small sign; it is a block before a Stop light • Follow Broadway until it ends on Webb St • Go half a block and go right back on Broadway into **Webb City** • Broadway becomes St Louis • Curve left on Carter and go right on Main • Go through Downtown • Go left on Pine St • Take the first right over the RR tracks onto Old 66 Blvd • Follow the *Historic 66* signs to **Carterville** • Cross over Bus 171 and go left onto Old 66 into **Brooklyn Heights** • Take Old 66 Blvd through **Brooklyn Heights** • Old 66 turns into Oak St into **Carthage** • Go left on Garrison Ave

Brooklyn Heights, Carterville, Webb City and Joplin

BROOKLYN HEIGHTS. Brooklyn Heights is so small that there is no sign on Route 66 telling you that you are there (although there is a Brooklyn Heights Exit off Hwy 71).

CARTERVILLE. At one time, Carterville was a major mining community, but it went into decline after WW I when lead and zinc mines were closed. By the mid-1940's it was a near ghost town.

For some refreshing summer fun, stop in at the Supertam on 66 Ice Cream Parlor at 221 Main St.

WEBB CITY. When you are coming into Webb City, you will pass by Fat Head's Hogs and Hot Rods Bar at 660 E Daugherty. It has been in a dispute about its name with another bar called Hogs and Hot Rods that is just outside the other side of Joplin near the Kansas border. They both are biker bars and both fun.

There is a cool neon sign directing travelers to the Business District. Near that sign, you will find a monument to local miners and some Giant Praying Hands.

JOPLIN. The Joplin police are notorious. They are all over town all of the time, and they will pull folks over for any minor infraction (real or manufactured), including things like loud pipes. Be careful!

I was in Joplin on the morning of May 11, 2011. I headed out of town in dicey weather and by the time I got to Carthage just 20 miles down the road, it was raining so hard I had to stop. I went to a Bar B Q place, ordered up some food and fired up

It will take decades to rebuild Joplin

my computer to get a bit of work done. A couple of hours later, it was still raining, but I decided to gut it out to Springfield. It was a hard ride but I made it OK.

Later that afternoon, the tornado hit Joplin. I saw the damage on TV and it looked bad. I have a friend named Jackie who lives there. She once flew to New York to meet me, and we rode to through New England to the most northern point in Maine, then back to Joplin with stops at the Antietam and Fredericksburg Civil War Battlefields and a run through the Tail of the Dragon in the North Carolina Smokey Mountains. I tried to call to see if she was OK, but I couldn't get her.

I was back in Joplin about a week later. I found Jackie, who was fine, and she drove me around to see the destruction. Parts of town were leveled for as far as the eye could see in every direction. In some neighborhoods, the locations of the streets could not be identified. The smell of decaying flesh was unmistakable.

I've been back to Joplin several times since then. Most of the rubble has been removed and Joplin is getting back on its feet, but it will take years to rebuild.

Wilder's at 1216 Main St is a former speak easy and steak house that survived the tornado. The original owner had a painting of his wife and him hanging in the restaurant. When he found that she was cheating on him, he had the painting redone to cut her out. The painting still hangs in the bar. The current owners found some postcards in perfect condition showing Wilder's in the 1930's. Ask to see one, and if you are lucky, you may get to keep it.

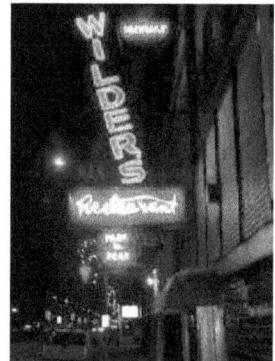

A 1930's speakeasy

Next door, the Kitchen Pass is the best Downtown bar with live entertainment.

Frank's Lounge at 2112 Main St was not so lucky. This smoky Old School bar was completely destroyed by the tornado, but it has been rebuilt, complete with a new neon sign just like the original featuring a green martini glass. It has more of a sports bar atmosphere than the original but Frank's still is a great place.

Turtle Head's is a good bar with live bands most nights on a patio out back. Thursday is Bike Night.

The Undercliff Grill and Bar is built into the side of a mountain. It's a nice ride out there and the food is good, especially the home made chili.

Route 66 going west out of Joplin follows 7th St. Check out Guitars Rock N Country Night Club, which is a biker friendly bar that features outdoor murals of ZZ Top and other Rockers along with a motorcycle graveyard out front.

On the Kansas border you will find Hogs and Hot Rods. The building is from 1928, and the patio out back features a 1934 bus that is being remodeled to be a bar. The owner plans to renovate an old gas station next door. Hogs and Hot Rods tries to have biker events every weekend, like wet T-shirt contests, chocolate pudding wrestling, and weenie bites. It also is involved in poker runs and charitable benefits. This is an Old School place. Unfortunately, it serves only beer and wine.

This Old School biker joint is on the Kansas-Missouri border

If you are in Joplin on a weekend and want to do something a bit different, ride out to the Gallows Bar in Lamar, MO. It is about a half hour ride from Joplin, but it's so unique that it's worth it. It is owned by a custom motorcycle builder who created a bike with a real double barrel shotgun barrel for pipes. The owner always rides his bike through the back door and out the front door before closing time. Don't worry about a designated driver. They have a school bus to drive everybody who needs a ride home.

MISSOURI ALTERNATE ROUTE
West from Crestwood to Grey Summit

From **Crestwood**, follow Watson Rd to I-44 West • Take Exit 261 to **Allenton** • Cross under I-44 to Bus 44/Osage St and follow it to **Pacific** and **Gray Summit** • Resume Main Route

East from Gray Summit to Crestwood

From **Gray Summit**, at the Junction of Hwy 100, follow Bus 44/Osage Rd to **Pacific** and then on to **Allenton** • Follow Bus 44 onto I-44 toward St Louis • Take Exit 277A/Watson Rd and follow it to **Crestwood** • Resume Main Route

Allenton and Pacific

ALLENTON. Allenton is about 30 miles outside of St Louis. It was a stop on the Union Pacific Railroad that once had over 70 homes and several businesses, including a canning factory. Nothing remains of the original businesses but ruins.

Pacific's 1933 speakeasy

PACIFIC. Pacific has a sleepy Downtown with 19th century buildings, some of which have been restored. There are some striking rock formations outside of town that have large caves where silica was mined.

The Red Cedar Inn opened in 1933 as a speakeasy and restaurant. It was one of the oldest restaurants along Route 66 and was operated by the same family until it closed in 1973. In 1987, other family members reopened the restaurant. It closed a few years ago. For a while, it housed a used car dealership. Now it is up for sale as a historic Route 66 site.

Great Pacific Pub & Grill at 220 S 1st St is located in an early 20th century brick building. The Third Rail Bar & Grill at 564 Old Route 66 looks like a good spot. Whiskey River Saloon appears to be closed, but I'll check it out again next time I'm through there. Who wouldn't like a river of whiskey!

Gray Summit. If you have taken this Alternate Route from Crestwood to Gray Summit, return to page 57 to pick up our suggested route through the rest of Missouri.

West to Galena, Kansas

From Main St **Joplin** go right on 7ᵗʰ St and follow it out of Joplin • After the *Old 66 Next Right* sign go right onto Old 66 Blvd • Cross some RR tracks and go left into **Galena**

KANSAS

There are fewer than 20 miles of Route 66 through Kansas, but they are a satisfying 20 miles passing through Galena, Riverton and Baxter Springs. You should explore each one.

In Galena, you will find a Main Street that looks like it must have been 80 years ago.

Riverton has the Eisler Bros Store (now called The Old Riverton Store), which has been in continuous operation since 1925. On your way to Baxter Springs, you'll cross the 1923 Rainbow Bridge.

Baxter Springs once was known as the most robbed town in Kansas and you can see a bank that fell to Jesse James.

Have fun in Kansas. It is an enjoyable 20 miles of rural road that won't take you Over the Rainbow, but it will take you back in time.

The last remaining Marsh Arch Bridge on the Mother Road

GALENA

Galena is the first of only three Route 66 towns in Kansas. Hopefully you will have stopped for a couple of cold ones at Hogs and Hot Rods on the Kansas border.

Galena once was a mining boom town with a population of over 15,000. It was the site of a violent strike by the International Mine, Mill and Smelter Workers Union in which several men were killed, including nine men at the Union's offices.

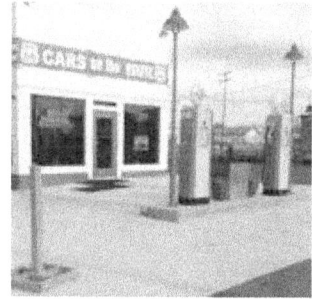

Meet the new boss. same as the old boss

Main Street has Cars on the Route Snack Shack, which is in a restored Kan-O-Tex gas station that features nice artifacts including some antique gas pumps. This used to be called "Four Women on the Route." It recently was sold. One of the original owners and most of the staff remain. As of April 2014, the store was opened, but the kitchen is not scheduled to open until later in the summer.

The Galena Murder Bordello, which is an abandoned whore house that was operated by serial killer Ma Staffleback, opened for guided tours and special events in October 2013. Ma, her husband and two sons supposedly robbed and killed over 50 *Johns* during the 1890's. The first was Frank Galbraith in 1897. Their *modus operandi* was to drug the target, whack him on the head with an ax, strip the poor guy of his valuables and dump him in a mine shaft. *Galena's Bloody Madame* died in 1909.

West From Galena to Riverton

From Main St **Galena**, go right on 7ᵗʰ St/Hwy 66 and follow it to **Riverton** • From Riverton, go right to the Junction of US 400 & 69A • Go straight on Beasley Rd • Follow the sign painted on the road telling you to jog right (there is no Route 66 sign; the road will become 50th St then Willow) • Curve left onto 3rd St • Go right at the Stop sign onto US 69A/Military Ave through **Baxter Springs**

East to Joplin

From Main St **Galena** go right on Front St • Stay on Old 66 Blvd into Missouri • Get on MO 66 toward Joplin • Go left at the Junction of Hwy 66 • Go left on Main St/Hwy 43 through Downtown **Joplin**

RIVERTON

Nelson's Old Riverton Store (formerly Eisler's) at 7109 SE Route 66 has been in operation since 1925. It is a grocery store and deli that serves lunch. They also have a good collection of Route 66 souvenirs.

As you head toward Baxter Springs, you can jog over and cross the restored Brush Creek Bridge, which dates from 1923, and purports to be the only remaining Marsh Arch Bridge on Route

Serving Riverton since 1925

66. Marsh Arch Bridges were designed by James *Barney* Marsh, who patented this form of concrete reinforced bridge in 1911. Hundreds of them were built through the 1930's. They were called Rainbow Bridges because of their distinctive rainbow-shaped arches. Country singer Brad Paisley performed the song *Get Your Kicks on Route 66* on the bridge for the TCL Special *Route 66: Main Street America*.

BAXTER SPRINGS

Baxter Springs has been known as the toughest town in Kansas, the first cow town in Kansas and the most robbed town in Kansas.

Baxter Springs was the site of an infamous Civil War massacre. Quantrill's Raiders attacked a contingent of Union forces. The Union soldiers surrendered and then were gunned down. Over 110 Union Soldiers were killed.

This 1930's gas station is the Baxter Springs Visitors Center

After the Civil War, Baxter Springs prospered as a cattle town. It later prospered as a resort community and later as a mining town. Mickey Mantle, whose father was a miner in nearby Commerce, Oklahoma, played ball for the Baxter Springs Whiz Kids.

Today, Baxter Springs has well preserved 19th century brick buildings, several of which have painted advertisements or murals on them. There is a Visitors Center in an old Phillips 66 Station and several restaurants if you are hungry.

The Café on the Route and the Little Brick Inn (a B&B) are in a former bank building that Jesse James robbed. The former Murphy's Restaurant also was a bank that was robbed in 1914.

West to Quapaw

From **Baxter Springs**, follow US 69A to the Oklahoma state line
• Hwy 69A will becomes Hwy 69 into **Quapaw**

East to Galena

From US 69A/Military Ave in Downtown **Baxter Springs**, turn left onto Third St (there is no Third St sign, so take the next left past 4th St) • Third St will become Willow Ave, then 50th St then Beasley Rd • Keep going to a traffic circle, and follow the signs to stay on Route 66 into **Riverton** • From Riverton, follow Hwy 66 to 7th St in Galena • Go left on Main St in Downtown **Galena**

OKLAHOMA

Oklahoma has more drivable miles of Route 66 than any other state, and almost all of them are a treat.

When you come into Oklahoma from Kansas, you will be on the Quapaw Reservation. The short ride from Quapaw to Commerce, Mickey Mantle's hometown, is through beautiful rural grasslands.

Miami is a well preserved mid-western town filled with well-maintained early 20th century buildings, including the 1929 Coleman Theater.

The ride to Tulsa passes through rural towns on a well maintained roadway that will allow you to make good time. You will pass by the world's largest totem pole near Foyil; Will Roger's hometown of Claremore; and Catoosa's Blue Whale, which has been named as one of the 50 best roadside attractions in the United States.

The ride into Tulsa on 11th St passes vintage motels and restaurants. The 11th St Pub and the Hurricane Lounge are two Old School biker bars along the route. The newly restored Campbell Hotel is one of the nicest hotels along Route 66. Downtown Tulsa is an art deco museum in its own right.

The ride from Tulsa to Oklahoma City is even better. The countryside gets a bit more rural, and the roadway has the turns and hills that bikers enjoy. You'll see the 1939 Rock Café and the Skyliner Motel in Stroud, several restored gas stations and the 1898 Big Round Barn in Arcadia.

Oklahoma City is an oil town and a cowboy town with vintage motor courts, restaurants and theaters.

The ride from Oklahoma City to Weatherford is along miles of roadway out of sight of any interstate highway. You'll go through Garth Brooks' hometown of Youkon; Ft Reno, which was established to protect settlers from Indian attacks; Lucille's Roadhouse near Hydro; and the Thomas P Stafford Air and Space Museum in Weatherford, where you can see moon rocks.

The last section of Oklahoma's Route 66 will take you to Route 66 museums in Clinton and Elk City; the Trade Winds Motel in Clinton where Elvis stayed; and Roger Miller's hometown of Erick.

Have fun in Ohhhhhhhhh - Kla - Homa, where the wind wind comes sweepin' through your mein!

West from Quapaw to Catoosa

From **Quapaw**, follow Hwy 69 to Mickey Mantle Blvd in **Commerce** • Go right on Commerce St through Downtown, and at the T, go left onto Main St/Hwy 69 and follow it to through **North Miami** and **Miami** • Go right on Hwy 10/Steve Owens Blvd • Keep going straight on Hwy 69 through **Narcissa**, **Afton** and **Vinita** • In Vinita, go left on Wilson St and follow it out of town to **White Oak**, **Chelsea** (Hwy 69 becomes Route 66), **Foyil** and **Claremore** to **Catoosa**

East from Quapaw to Baxter Springs

From **Quapaw** follow US Alt 66 into Kansas • Follow US 69 Alt, which becomes Military Ave into Downtown **Baxter Springs**

Quapaw, Commerce, North Miami, Miami, Narcissa, Afton, Vinita, White Oak, Chelsea, Foyil, Claremore and Catoosa

QUAPAW. Somehow Bobby Troup forgot to mention Quapaw (pronounced O-Gah-Pah) when he wrote *Get Your Kicks on Route 66*. Even so, there is some action at the Quapaw Casino at 58100 E 64 Rd in Miami and the Downstream Casino at 69300 E Nee Rd in Quapaw. You can eat at Dallas' Dairyette at 103 S Main St or at Hemi's Café across the street at 104 S Main St.

COMMERCE. Commerce is a mining community that was Mickey Mantle's hometown. You can see his boyhood residence at 319 S Quincy St. There is a plaque on the front door with some interesting information.

Surprisingly, although there is a Mickey Mantle Blvd and a statue of *The Mick* at Mickey Mantle Field, Commerce has not seemed to capitalize on his fame. There was a

Mickey Mantle's boyhood home

movement to build a Mickey Mantle Museum, but it apparently was decided it needed to be in a bigger town (aka, it would have been too expensive to build and operate in Commerce).

There is a 1925 Marathon Station at 101 S Main St, and across the street, a vintage Dairy King at 100 N Main St.

In April 1934, Bonnie and Clyde killed Commerce police officer William Campbell at present day E 60 Rd and Tahoe Drive. Former Commerce resident Doyle Alsbury saw it happen when he was a boy and later painted a sign on the road to mark the spot. Bonnie and Clyde were were killed a month after the shooting.

The local motorcycle shop is Bike Go at 108 Commerce St.

NORTH MIAMI. On the way from Commerce to North Miami, you will pass by PMI Performance Machine, which specializes in building high performance engines for Harley-Davidsons and other motorcycles and cars.

The nine foot wide Ribbon Road

MIAMI. The ride into Miami is lined with strip malls and used car dealerships, but once on Main St, Miami has character. The Coleman Theater at 103 N Main St is especially impressive. It opened to a sell-out crowd of 1,600 in 1929.

In the summer of 2013, my friend Tracie and I got invited to visit friends in Jackson Hole, Wyoming. We hopped on the bike and made a 150 mile detour by taking a one day 575 mile ride to Miami to get a picture of the last surviving section of the nine foot wide *Ribbon Road,* which is a National Landmark. On the way to Miami, a bunch of Mongols passed us and checked out my patch as they passed by. Later that night she told me that the *Mongrels* (like the dogs) looked scary. Indeed they are!

To get to the Ribbon Road from Downtown Miami, go south on Main St and straight out of town past the Route 125 turnoff. Eventually you will come to a T. Go right and follow it to the Ribbon Rd. It will be obvious when you get there. You can ride it all the way through to Hwy 69 and head to Narcissa, but it is rough going.

Don't miss the restored Marathon Service Station at 331 S Main St.

At the south end of Downtown, you will find Route 66 Custom Cycles. Across the street is the Route 66 Vintage Iron Motorcycle Museum.

For a quick bite to eat, try Waylon's

Miami's 1929 Coleman Theater

Ku Ku Burgers at 915 N Main, with its distinctive Ku Ku Bird popping out the front of the building like a Ku Ku clock. They have been serving burgers since 1961. Make sure to order the biggest burger they have because the regular size is small. This is the last survivor of a chain of Ku Ku Burger restaurants.

The Kick-Off Bar and Grill is not an old Route 66 establishment, but its the best bar in town and has great food. I had some deep fried mac and cheese. It goes directly from you fingers to your arteries. You can feel your heart slowing down!

For you gamblers, there is the Buffalo Run Casino at 1000 Buffalo Run Blvd; the High Winds Casino at 61475 E 100 Rd; and the Stables Casino at 530 H St.

Tracie and I left Miami, and spent the next two days on Route 66, making stops in Weatherford, Oklahoma and Santa Fe. After leaving Santa Fe, we didn't hit Route 66 again until we got to Amarillo on the way home. In between we rode through Cheyenne and Jackson Hole, Wyoming; Yellowstone, where we weathered a violent thunder and hail storm (God bless Tracy; she laughed it off) and across Bear Tooth Pass into Montana; then on to Deadwood and the Black Hills. The whole ride was just under 5,000 miles.

NARCISSA. As you are leaving Commerce toward Narcissa, you will begin a long stretch of Route 66 (now Hwy 69) that passes through several small towns on the way to Tulsa. The road is good and you will be able to make good time. Narcissa is a bump in this road with a few abandoned Route 66 buildings.

AFTON. Afton began as a farming community, but gained prosperity as a railroad center and later as a Route 66 town.

In 1956, Russell and Arlene Kay opened the Buffalo Ranch at the confluence of four US highways, including Route 66. The Kays lured travelers to their gift shop and restaurant by showing their heard of seven buffalos. The heard grew to about 40 head. Other animals, like llamas and yaks, along with a petting zoo, were added. The Buffalo Ranch finally closed in 1997 and the structure

DX Station and old Packards

was torn down in 2004 to make way for a convenience store.

Main St Afton is crumbling; however, there is a gem. The restored DX Station at 12 SW 1st St has a private collection of Packards next door.

VINITA. The original entrance to Vinita was over a narrow bridge with sidewalks. The bridge has now been bypassed with a modern bridge but the old one still is there.

Clanton's Café at 319 E Illinois Ave has a giant EAT neon sign. The restaurant has been owned by the same family since 1927.

Downtown Vinita has some character. There are lots of Route 66 era buildings, some still in use and some abandoned. There are plenty of motels and restaurants.

The infamous Ma Barker and her gang are buried in the nearby Williams Cemetery. Of Ma, George, Herman, Doc and Fred, only Herman has a grave marker.

As you get a bit out of town, check out the Western Motel and the HiWay Café (*Small enough to know you but big enough to serve you*).

WHITE OAK. Not much in White Oak. Keep on going to Chelsea.

CHELSEA. The Chelsea Motel has a vintage sign. The motel appears to house some unfortunate down and out folks. There also is the Chelsea Motor Inn.

When entering town follow directions to the 1926 Pryor Creek Bridge.

Also check out the Hill Top Bar at 25062 E Hwy 66.

FOYIL. Ed Galloway's Totem Pole Park is four miles off Route 66 at 21300 Hwy 28a. It has a 90 foot tall totem pole, claimed to be the world's largest. Foyil hosts the *Totem Pole Bar B Q & Music Fest* each October.

The Tin Foyil Café at 123 Main St and the Top Hat Bar at 12215 S Andy Payne Circle are next to each other on Route 66.

CLAREMORE. Claremore is Will Rogers home town, and half the town is named for him. Claremore gained popularity in the early 20th century through the discovery of so called medicinal waters. It later gained popularity as Will Rogers gained fame. Still later, Claremore became a prosperous Route 66 town.

The Will Rogers Hotel was built in 1930 and had 68 rooms and seven apartments. It still is the tallest building in Claremore and houses apartments for Seniors.

The Will Rogers Memorial Museum is located at 12720 Will Rogers Blvd.

The JM Davis Arms and Historical Museum at 333 N Lyn Riggs Blvd has the world's largest

Still Claremore's tallest building

privately owned firearms collection. It has guns owned by Cole Younger, Emmett Dalton, John Wesley Hardin, Bonnie and Clyde, Pretty Boy Floyd and Pancho Villa.

When you leave town toward Catoosa, you will go over the Twin Bridges. One dates to 1936 and is 24 feet wide. The other dates to 1957 and is 28 feet wide. The bridges are being replaced by new bridges that will not keep the arches. One of the arches now is the entrance to Molly's Landing Restaurant and another is at the entrance of Rogers Point Park. What a shame.

Claremore hosts the Route 66 Car Show and Swap Meet each June.

One of the 50 best roadside attractions in the United States

CATOOSA. Time Magazine named The Blue Whale one of the 50 best roadside attractions in the US. It was built in 1972 by Hugh Davis as an anniversary present for his wife Zelda, who owned Zelda Davis's Alligator Farm, which was next door. On the other side of the the Alligator Farm was Chief Wolf Robe's Trading Post. Zelda Davis was the Chief's sister in law.

The Blue Whale is in need of repair, but it's still one of those places that turns out to be as good as anticipated.

Downtown Catoosa has the Catoosa Historical Museum and the D W Correl Museum at 18834 E Pine St, which displays rocks and gems in one building and vintage cars in another building.

Zelda Davis's Alligator Farm

As you head out of town, you will come across the Hard Rock Casino with its Toby Keith's *I Love This Bar*.

West to Tulsa

Go about half a mile past the Blue Whale, cross Spunky Creek and bear right onto Ford St (be careful, there is no sign) • Follow Ford St to Downtown Catoosa and go left on Cherokee St • Go left on Hwy 167/193rd St • Go past the Hard Rock Casino, go under I-44 and past Admiral St • Go right on 11th St and follow it all the way to Downtown **Tulsa** • At the Stop light just before Elgin, go through the traffic circle exiting onto 10th St • At Boulder St, go straight past the First Church of Christ Scientists and rejoin 11th St, which will become 12th St • Follow 12th St to Southwest Blvd out of town

East from Catoosa to Quapaw

From Cherokee St in **Catoosa** go right on Ford St just past the Police Station • Go left on Hwy 66, go past the Blue Whale and on to **Claremore** • Continue on Hwy 66 through **Foyil**, **Chelsea** and **White Oak** to **Vinita** • Go from Hwy 66 to Hwy 69 • Go left on

Wilson St and follow it out of town • Go through the Junction of Hwy 69 and Hwy S • Go straight at the Hwy 66 Junction into **White Oak** • Stay on Hwy 69 into **Afton** and then **Narcissa** • Continue on Hwy 69, which will become Steve Owen Blvd as you approach **Miami** • Go left onto Main St Miami at the *Business District* sign • Follow Main St/Hwy 69 to **North Miami** • At the Y at the edge of town just past the *Quapaw Nation* sign, go left following the Route 66 signs into **Commerce** • At the Stop sign by the Dairy King, go right onto Commerce St • Follow Commerce St through town then go left on Mickey Mantle Blvd • Follow Hwy 69 into **Quapaw**

TULSA

The ride from Catoosa into Tulsa follows 11th St. Eleventh St starts in a rural neighborhood and is lined with old buildings that once housed thriving businesses. Someone should do one of those *Then and Now* books showing photos of the old businesses and what is in them today.

Ed's is an Old School Biker Bar

You will pass by the 1961 Rose Bowl Lanes at 7419 E 11th St, now the Rose Bowl Event Center.

As you get closer to Downtown, you will pass still operating motels, like the Desert Hills Motel, The Brookline Motel, the Berkshire Motel and the American Value Inn with its *He's Not Here* bar.

The best of these hotels is the Campbell at 2636 E 11th St. It opened in 1927 as the Casa Loma Hotel inside the Max Campbell Building. The building originally housed the hotel, a barber shop, a beauty shop, a drug store and a grocery store. It was abandoned for years, but now has been restored as a hotel with 26 rooms, each with a separate theme, including a *Route 66 Room.* Care has been taken to preserve as much of the original architecture as possible. The rooms are nicely appointed, and some have original sky lights. The bar is open every day, and a restaurant is on the way. The space that will be used for the restaurant currently has some well preserved antique cars on display. Secure bike parking is available in the back.

The Rancho Grande since 1950

There are good restaurants like Tally's Café at 1102 S Yale St, the Corner Café at 1103 S Peoria and the El Rancho Grande' at 1629 E 11th St, all with nice Route 66 signs.

There are biker bars like the 11th Street Pub at 6119 E 11th St; Ed's Hurricane Lounge at 2216 E 11th St; the Blues City Bar & Grill at 3156 Mingo; the Grey Snail at 1334 E 15th St; the Crow Creek Tavern at 3534 Peoria Ave and McNellie's at 409 E 1st St.

Be on the lookout for an old 1950s Tastee-Freeze building that now houses an automotive business.

Also be on the lookout for the Medal Gold Milk Ice Cream sign. It should be viewed at night.

Downtown Tulsa is like being in an Art Deco museum, and there are guided tours available. The Blue Dome District around 2nd St and Detroit Ave now is a hub of Tulsa night life. The Blue Dome at E 2nd St was a 1920's gas station with a distinctive Art Deco dome. This area hosts the Blue Dome Arts Festival each May.

Cain's Ballroom at 423 N Main St provides live music from a garage built in 1924.

A bit farther afield at the Tulsa Fairgrounds at 4145 E 21st St stands the Golden Driller, a 76 foot tall statue of an oil worker built in 1953 by the Mid-Continent Supply Company of Ft Worth for the International Petroleum Exposition. It was

A great Tulsa biker spot

moved to Tulsa in 1963. It is the tallest free standing statue in the world and the third largest statue in the United States.

West from Tulsa to Oklahoma City

Follow Southwest Blvd out of **Tulsa** to **Red Fork** • Continue on Southwest Blvd to **Oakhurst** and into **Bowden** (Southwest Blvd becomes Frankhoma) • Follow Frankhoma under I-44 • Go right on Dewey Ave through Downtown **Sapulpa** • From Dewey Ave get on Hwy 66 and follow it to **Kelleyville** and **Bristow** • Follow 66/Roland St out of Bristow • After about seven miles, look for a small sign taking you left into **Depew** • Follow the road back to Hwy 66 and go left to **Stroud, Davenport** and into **Chandler** • Route 66 will become 1ˢᵗ St and then Manvel through Chandler; follow it through town and continue on Hwy 66 to **Warwick** • Cross I-44 and go right on Hwy 66B through **Wellston** until it re-intersects with Hwy 66, then go right on Hwy 66 to **Luther** and **Arcadia** to **Edmond** • Hwy 66 will become 2ⁿᵈ St • Go left on Broadway toward **Oklahoma City**

East from Oklahoma City to Catoosa

Follow Broadway in **Oklahoma City** to **Edmond** • Go right on 2ⁿᵈ St in Edmond, which will become Hwy 66, toward **Arcadia** and **Luther** • Go left on Hwy 66B through **Wellston**, and when it re-intersects with Hwy 66, go left to **Warwick** and on to **Chandler** • In Chandler, go left on Manvel through Downtown and bear right onto E 1ˢᵗ St/Hwy 66 • Follow Hwy 66 to **Davenport** and **Stroud** • Look for a Route 66 shield directing you to **Depew** • Go right through Depew until you re-intersect in Hwy 66 • Go right and follow Hwy 66 to Roland St, which will become 4ᵗʰ St, in **Bristow** • Stay with Hwy 66 to **Kelleyville** and into **Sapulpa** • Follow

Dewey Ave/66 until it ends at Mission and go left • Follow Hwy 66 then go left on Frankhoma Rd • Follow Frankhoma Rd to **Bowden** and into **Oakhurst** (Frankhoma becomes Southwest Blvd) • Follow Southwest Blvd through **Red For**k, then across the river into **Tulsa** • Immediately after crossing the bridge into Tulsa, go right on 12th St • 12th St will become 11th St then 10th St • Go past Detroit St and go through the traffic circle back onto 11th St (ignore the Route 66 sign pointing left; that's an east to west direction) • Follow 11th St 11.5 miles to 193rd St • Go left, and pass under I-44 • Go through four Stop lights then go right on Cherokee in **Catoosa**

Red Fork, Oakhurst, Bowden, Sapulpa, Kelleyville, Bristow, Depew, Stroud, Davenport, Chandler, Warwick, Wellston, Luther, Arcadia and Edmond

RED FORK. As you leave Tulsa on Southwest Blvd you will go over the Arkansas River to Red Fork. The 11th St Arkansas River Bridge (now called the Cyrus Avery Route 66 Memorial Bridge), which was built in 1917, is being restored.

Stryker's is an Old School Biker beer joint just outside Tulsa

You will come across Stryker's at 3748 SW Blvd, which has a new sign with its original name, the *Route 66 Lounge*. The new sign was put up by a Route 66 Historical Society. The thing to remember is that Stryker's and the Route 66 Lounge are the same place. By either name, it's an Old School biker joint owned by a local motorcycle club that didn't want to be named. It is not an Outlaw place. I met several of the MC members and they were good guys. Unfortunately, it's beer and wine only.

Stryker's/Route 66 Lounge frequently has weekend bashes with live music during the summer. The first Friday of the month is Veteran's Night, and Vets get a free drink. Also, an ordained minister is on standby so biker weddings can take place on 45 minute's notice. Too bad they don't have a judge on standby so bikers can get a divorce on 45 minutes' notice! They also are involved in Toys for Tots, as well as fund raisers for veterans and healthcare related causes.

Ride in Lube Up and Ride Out Smooth at Gears and Beers

Drop by Gears and Beers Bike Shop at 3908 SW Blvd, where you can *Ride in Lube Up and Ride Out Smooth*. This is a cool little Old School bike shop and beer joint (Panheads out front!). According to owner Marty Brown, "Who wouldn't like to have a cold beer while getting their oil changed?" This place has the Scavenger Total Oil Change System that gets every drop of old oil out in each oil change.

Marty used to be a mechanic for the Yamaha Motocross Racing Team. He is a meticulous guy who designed his own pistons for high performance racing. These days, he wants to focus on service, and he and his wife Jennel are there all the time. Sunday afternoons are busy.

Route 66 Park at 3700 SW Blvd is being constructed by the cities of Tulsa and Red Fork. It features the Frisco Meteor locomotive, which is so big you can almost feel the power it must have had. A giant oil derrick stands nearby.

You also will go by Ollie's Station Restaurant at 4070 SW Blvd, which has model trains in the ceiling.

OAKHURST. The ride to Oakhurst goes through some industrial areas following I-44 on the left and some railroad tracks on the right. A few abandoned Route 66 relics are identifiable, but there is nothing special. It is not a pretty ride, but at least there are few stop lights and little traffic.

BOWDEN. As you ride from Oakhurst to Bowden the road gets away from I-44 and becomes more rural, leaving the industrial complexes behind in favor of country neighborhoods. There is not much to see along here but it is a pretty ride on a good road.

SAPULPA. Sepulpa hosts the *Route 66 Blowout* each year in early June.

Creek County Cycles is at 619 N Mission St and the Hickory House Bar B Q and Grill is across the street at 626 N Mission.

Sepulpa has a Trolley Museum and a 1921 Bridge with a brick surface that goes over Rock Creek.

KELLEYVILLE. You will pass through Kelleyville in a blink, but there are a few attractions. There is an antique shop with a boat sticking out the front of the building. There also is the Creek County Speedway and a rodeo arena.

Kelleyville hosts the *Kelleyville Heritage Days Rodeo* each June.

BRISTOW. Bristow has the headquarters of the Route 66 Rallies that are held in Milfay, Oklahoma. The rally site is a large camp ground with RV hook ups. There appear to be several events a year, but advertising is sparse and it's hard to find out what's going on.

As you head out of town on Roland St, look in the Chrysler Dealer lot for a Giant Penguin.

DEPEW. Depew was founded in 1901 and became a thriving oil town on the original 1926 alignment of Route 66. The roads around Depew were dirt, but the Route 66 portion through town was paved. The oil business dried up during the Great Depression and so did the town.

The 500 or so residents are sprucing the town up with murals and other artworks.

Find this guy just west of Bristow

To see Depew be careful to follow the signs off of the newer alignment of Route 66 you were following. There are no signs to guide you through town, but you should be able to figure it out. Once in the village you will find Spangler's Store at 322 Main St and an old bank building. Just keep following the loop around until you get back to the main road.

STROUD. Between Depew and Stroud you will pass the Route 66 Biker Rally and RV Park. There is nothing going on there except during the rallies.

In Stroud, you will find the 1939 Rock Café at 114 Main St, which was built from stone mined from the construction of Route 66. It burned in 2008 but has been rebuilt and is doing fine.

Serving Route 66 since 1939

The Skyliner Motel at 717 W Main St is well preserved. Around the corner is Vellarta's Mexican Restaurant at 315 N 8th Ave, whose sign welcomes bikers.

For a few pops, there is the Cue and Brew at 417 W Main.

DAVENPORT. Davenport has Guy Wooly's Food and Fun at 1025 Broadway. It's a small place with a few tables and a counter with soda fountain stools. I found a review by a group that showed up 21 bikes strong without a reservation. The reviewer said the staff was great, the service quick and the food good.

CHANDLER. Chandler hosts *The Hog Wild BBQ and Chrome Fest* each June.

Chandler has a 1930 Phillips Station on Manvel Ave that currently is being restored. There also is the 1939 Lincoln Motel at 740 E 1st St, which has a distinctive neon sign and nice bungalows.

Chandler claims to be the site of the last wild west shoot out, when in 1924 retired Dodge City Marshall Bill Tilghman was killed by a corrupt prohibition officer.

Jerry McClanahan's Art Gallery is in Chandler at 306 Manvel Ave. His artwork can be found all over Route 66, including in a specially redone room at the Munger Moss Motel in Lebanon, Missouri. He wrote *EZ 66 Guide for Travelers,* which is one of the best Route 66 guidebooks.

Chandler also has the Route 66 Interpretive Center-Oklahoma Route 66 Association at 400 E 1st St.

WARWICK. The 1924 Seaba Station originally was a machine shop and later became a service station. The building is listed on the National Register of Historic Places.

Today, Seaba Station houses a motorcycle museum. It has dozens of vintage bikes, including a 1923 Pope. There are antiques and accessories for sale. The ruins of a two holer stone out house is in the back.

Seaba Station Motorcycle Museum has a stone two-holer outhouse

WELLSTON. Wellston was bypassed in 1933, but a 1933 iron bridge remains. You will pass the now closed stone Pioneer Bar B Q. It originally was part of a tourist spot called Pioneer Camp.

LUTHER. Luther has Sherry's Country Line Bar at 21940 E Hwy 66 and the Boundary Restaurant at 16001 E 66, both of which are biker destinations.

The Boundary got its name from being on the eastern boundary of the 1889 Land Run. It was first claimed by an African American family named Treat who got the property in the Land Run. They farmed, raised cattle and mined sandstone before opening Treat's Grocery and Gas Station in 1926 and its restaurant in 1935. The current restaurant is in the restored Treat's gas station.

There also is an unidentified gas station relic between Luther and Arcadia.

ARCADIA. Arcadia has the restored 1898 Round Barn. There is a good Route 66 exhibit and a gift shop. You can buy a commemorative brick engraved as you like. The proceeds go to the upkeep of the Barn. I bought one over 20 years ago, and it's kind of fun to go back and find it from time to time.

Across the street from the Round Barn are a bunch of biker related businesses, including the Biker

The 1917 Arcadia Round Barn

Shak Leather and Apparel. It is located in a run-down series of buildings that includes the Hillbilly Bed and Breakfast. These places may or may not be open at any given time.

Next door to the Round Barn is the 1917 Tuton Drug Store Building at 201 N Main St. It housed the First State Bank of Arcadia. By 1919, the bank sold the building to Thomas Tuton, who operated a drug store there until 1934, and his wife continued in the business until 1941. The building currently houses a real estate office.

OK County 66 features miniature replicas of Route 66 attractions, including Twin Arrows, the Blue Whale, the Wigwam Motel and the Cadillac Ranch.

Pop's' at 66 W Hwy 66 is a popular Oklahoma City area biker destination. It is a gas station and roadside restaurant that features a giant wire sculpture of a soda pop bottle. It has hundreds of different kinds of soda (but I couldn't find birch beer, which is big in the New England town where I grew up).

EDMOND. Edmond is commercial and doesn't have the Route 66 flavor of some of the towns to the east. However, it has the Harley-Davidson World Shop.

On the way into Edmond you'll find Freddy's Frozen Custard at 1925 E 2nd St. It is not as quaint as Ted Drewes in St Louis or Andy's in Springfield, Missouri, but unlike those places, Freddy's has a full menu in addition to its terrific frozen custard.

Getting through Oklahoma City Going East to West

Enter Oklahoma City from **Edmond** on Broadway · Take the Memorial/Kelly St Exit · Go left on Kelly and follow it to Britton Rd · Go right on Britton Rd to Western Ave · Go left on Western Ave (be careful, its a tricky turn across some RR tracks) · Go right on 23ʳᵈ St · Go right on N May Ave · Get in the left lane as you approach I-44 · Go left on 39ᵗʰ St before a Shell Station (be careful, there is no sign; it will look like you are getting on I-44, but you won't be · Follow the Route 66 signs to 39ᵗʰ St in **Warr Acres**

Getting through Oklahoma City Going West to East

From **Warr Acres** follow 66/39ᵗʰ St and merge into I-44 toward Oklahoma City · Get off at Exit 126/May Ave · Go right on May Ave · Go left on 23ʳᵈ St · Go left on Western Ave · Follow Western Ave past the I-44 interchange and past 90ᵗʰ St · Go right on Britton Rd and follow it to the Stop sign at Kelly · Go left on Kelly · Go right on Memorial then take an immediate left on the Frontage Rd · Follow the Frontage Rd until it intersects with Broadway/77 · Go right on Broadway to **Edmond**

OKLAHOMA CITY

Oklahoma City is an oil town. There are wells pumping on the Capitol grounds. The dome on the Capitol building is new, being added in 2002.

Collectibles and live music

OKC also is a cowboy town, and has the National Cowboy & Western Heritage Museum (aka the National Cowboy Hall of Fame) at 1700 N 63rd St.

Oklahoma City is a biker town too. Locals think the Thunder Roadhouse at 900 W Memorial Dr is the best biker spot in the OKC metro area. The restaurant is open late. There's off track betting from Remington Park, which is a premier horse racing facility. They also have the Big Dog and used Harley-Davidson Dealership where you can browse and watch the mechanics.

Hobo's at 3500 W 29th St is another Old School biker bar. On weekends there are bands and poker runs. Bring cash, because Hobo's doesn't take anything else.

Vick & Tim's at 1001 N Western Ave is just west of Downtown Oklahoma City. The Oklahoma City Police love the bikers because the homeless dope addicts who used to gather at the vacant strip across the street have now found a new location. There is plenty of bike parking. Cages have to park on side streets. The parties on the weekends get pretty wild but it's all in good biker fun. The ceiling is covered with hanging bras donated by partying biker chicks. There usually is food on weekends from a huge smoker in the backyard.

Since 1930

Downtown Oklahoma City features Bricktown, which has lots of restored warehouses that now have restaurants and bars. The minor league baseball Oklahoma City Red Hawks play in Bricktown Park.

Mickey Mantle's Steak House at 7 S Mickey Mantle Dr has pricey but good food and lots of Mantle memorabilia.

There are several good hotels within walking distance, including the Bricktown Hotel at 2001 E Reno Ave; the Sheraton at 1 N Broadway; and the Renaissance Hotel at 10 N Broadway. The Skirvin Plaza Hilton at 1 Park Ave is expensive, but it is a great early 20th century hotel.

At 742 W Britton Rd, you will find the Owl Court, which has a 1934 gas station that is being restored, and an adjacent restaurant that will have a Route 66 museum.

The Western Trails Trading Post at 9100 N Western Ave is a cool old structure that still sells Route 66 antiques. There is live music on weekends. You also will pass the Will Rogers Theater at 4322 N Western Ave.

Just after you turn off of Western Ave onto 23rd St, you will find the Braum's Giant Milk Bottle at 2426 N Classen. It sits atop a 350 square foot building constructed in 1930 to house Milk Bottle Grocery. The giant milk bottle was added in about 1948. Today, the Saigon Baguette Restaurant is in this small building.

The Owl Court

West from Warr Acres to Ft Reno

From **Warr Acres**, follow Hwy 66/39th St to **Bethany** and **Youkon** • Stay on Hwy 66 • Go through the Junction of Bus 40/US 81 into **El Reno** • Go left on Wade • Go right on Choctaw • Go left on Sunset • Follow Bus 40 out of town • Follow the *Ft Reno Next Right* sign to **Ft Reno**

East from Ft Reno to Warr Acres

From the entrance of **Ft Reno,** go left on Route 66 for 100 yards to the intersection of Route 66/Bus 40 · Go left and follow Bus 40 into **El Reno** · Go right on Choctaw · Go left on Wade · Go right on Bus 40/Rock Island and follow it to **Youkon, Bethany** and **Warr Acres**

Warr Acres, Bethany, Youkon, El Reno and Ft Reno

WARR ACRES. Warr Acres has Ann's Chicken Fry House at 4146 NW 39th St, which features a 1950's nostalgia look complete with vintage cars and Route 66 artifacts.

Jack's BBQ at 4418 NW 39th St has a distinctive neon sign. The food is terrific, especially the pulled pork sandwiches and ribs.

On Route 66 since the 1940's

Biker wise, there is the Hideaway at 228 W Harmon Dr, which is a small smoky biker bar, and the Route 66 Roadhouse at 4328 NW 39th St, which has live music.

The Carlyle Motel 3600 NW 39th St claims to be a 1943 Route 66 original. The sign looks like the sign for the original motel, but the motel doesn't seem to be of the original motor court style. There must have been reconstruction along the way.

BETHANY. Bethany was founded in 1906 by members of the Nazerene Church, which

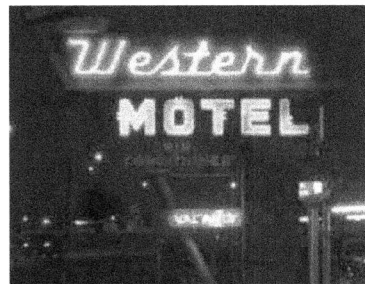

Vintage Bethany

started a college there. That influence lingered at least into the mid-1940's, at which time no alcohol or tobacco products were allowed, and there were no theaters.

The most distinctive Route 66 site is the Western Motel at 7600 NW Expressway.

Between Bethany and Youkon there is the restored 1919 Lake Overholser Bridge. There is concrete from the old road that now is accessible. This is a neat little detour off the main road to an alternate part of Route 66 along Lake Overholser. It is only a few minutes out of the way and is worth the ride. Just follow the signs.

Bethany hosts the *Bethany 66 Festival* each May.

YOUKON. Yukon is Garth Brooks' home town, although he no longer lives there.

Grady's 66 Pub at 444 W Main St is the local biker hang out. It's beer only.

Across the street from Grady's you'll find the Horseshoe Bar at 445 W Main St, which is a beer joint that has been in operation since 1906. They have some vintage photos of Youkon, and signed photos of Mickey Mantle, undefeated heavyweight champion Rocky Marciano and legendary Oklahoma football coach Barry Switzer.

The big site is the brightly lit Yukon's Best Flour sign at 1020 W Oak.

There are several Chisholm Trail sites, including a Chisholm Trail Wall Mural and a Chisholm Trail Historic marker at 2200 S Holly Ave.

Yukon also is proud of its Yukon's Best Railroad Museum at 1020 W Oak St.

Youkon is home to the Express Clydesdales, which is rare black version of this breed. There are over 40 Clydesdales and one touring company. There is a Welcome Center, and viewing these magnificent horses is free.

EL RENO. Don't miss the WW II bomber on Bus 40 on the way into El Reno.

The first weekend in May El Reno hosts *The Onion Burger Festival*, where they cook a 750 pound onion burger that is served to the public while it lasts.

Gilmore's Pub at 112 S Choctaw is the big biker destination. It has an Old School biker atmosphere, but also caters to local families. They have a good big rib eye. Unfortunately, they only serve beer and wine.

Bombs away!

Also check out Charlie B's Bar at 1701 E Hwy 66. It's small but a good biker destination.

FT RENO. Ft Reno was established in 1875 to support the US Army after a Cheyenne uprising in 1874. After the Indian wars concluded, Ft Reno operated to protect the so called Five Civilized Tribes (Cherokee, Chickasaw, Choctaw, Creek and Seminole) from the Plains Indians. The Ninth Cavalry of Buffalo Soldiers was stationed there.

Ft Reno Chapel

Ft Reno was abandoned in 1908 after Oklahoma was admitted as a state in 1907. It remained a Cavalry remount station until 1949.

It was used as a prisoner of war camp during WW II and some of the prisoners are buried there.

The US Department of Agriculture's Grazinglands Research Laboratory is in Ft Reno.

It doesn't take long to go through the Fort. If you get there outside of its business hours, you can edge your bike past the gate and ride around. You just won't be able to get into any of the buildings.

West from Ft Reno to Weatherford

From **Ft Reno**, follow Route 66 to the first Stop sign, which will be Hwy 270 (there is no sign) • Go right on Hwy 270 to **Calumet** then **Geary** • From the Stop sign at **Geary** by the Diamond Supper Club sign, go left onto Hwy 270/281 • Go about four miles and look for the Spur 281/281 S sign and go right • Go down a long hill and cross the South Canadian River across a long *Pony Bridge* • At a curve going left by a roadside Rest Stop, go straight instead of following the curve and get on Route 66 to **Hydro** • Follow Route 66 past the original Lucille's and on to **Weatherford** • At the Stop sign by the new Lucille's Roadhouse, go straight across Airport Rd onto East Main St • At the end of East Main St, go left on Washington, then take an immediate right onto Main St through Downtown **Weatherford**

East from Weatherford to Fort Reno

From Main St in **Weatherford**, go left on Washington then take an immediate right onto East Main St (Frontage Rd) and follow it past the original Lucille's to **Hydro** • At the Stop sign at Hydro go straight staying on Route 66 • Cross the South Canadian River across a long *Pony Bridge* • Continue up a long hill, and at the Junction go left onto Hwy 281 to **Geary** • Go right on Hwy 270 by the Diamond Supper Club sign to **Calumet** • Follow Hwy 270 through Calumet, and go left at the Stop sign about five miles out of town to **Ft Reno**

Calumet, Geary, Hydro and Weatherford

CALUMET. The ride from Ft Reno to Calumet follows a narrow ribbon of road mostly out of sight of I-40. The landscape is dominated by farms and grasslands along with occasional businesses. You have the feel that you are in the middle of nowhere, and for the most part, you are. It's easy to imagine what it must have been like to travel Route 66 along this beautiful but lonesome stretch of road on the way to better times in the west.

Calumet is a sleepy farming community with a few restaurants and markets. Rumors Bar at 103 N Calumet Rd is recently opened and is alive and kicking. Davidson's Saloon next door to Rumors seems to have seen better days. Jonnies Grill at 224 S Calumet Rd is one of the main hang outs. You can smell the grease from your bike as you ride by.

Jesse Chisholm's Grave

The longest *Pony Bridge* on 66

GEARY. The landmark you will see on Route 66 is the abandoned Diamond Supper Club sign. To see Downtown, go right at the Diamond Supper Club sign instead of going left following my directions. There is a 1893 wooden jail that doesn't look very comfortable.

Jesse Chisholm, who blazed the Chisholm Trail, is buried nearby. It's not on Route 66, but if you are a western history buff, this is a remote must stop spot. It's hard to find because the signs are somewhere between non-existent and incorrect. It took me an afternoon, but here's how I got there:

Go about a mile out of Downtown on N 281. Go right at a red sign pointing the way to the grave site and cross some RR tracks. Go about a quarter mile to a Stop sign. There will be a blue sign for the grave site. Go left to a four way stop. Go right following the paved road. Go until you cross a bridge and take a left onto a dirt road. Go about two miles and go left on another dirt road at a blue Jesse Chisholm Grave Site sign. This is a rough road, but you will find the grave site after about a quarter of a mile.

Jesse Chisholm should not be confused with John Chisum, the New Mexico rancher who participated in the Lincoln County War that brought Billy the Kid to fame. John Chisum never sent a cow up the Chisholm Trail. Instead, he sent his cattle over the Goodnight Loving Trail for sale in San Antonio.

HYDRO. The ride from Geary to Hydro will take you across the South Canadian River over a distinctive narrow 1933 *Pony Bridge*.

On Route 66 for 70 years

To see Hydro, take a right at the Stop sign at Hydro Junction. Between Hydro and Weatherford you will pass the original Lucille's. It was built by Carl Ditmore in 1929. In 1934, it was bought by W.O. Waldrop. In 1941 Lucille and Carl Hammons bought it and operated it as a service station, restaurant and motel for 59 years.

WEATHERFORD. There is a new Lucille's on the edge of town built in 2006. One wing has a 1950's diner motif and another wing is a casual steak house with a country music flair.

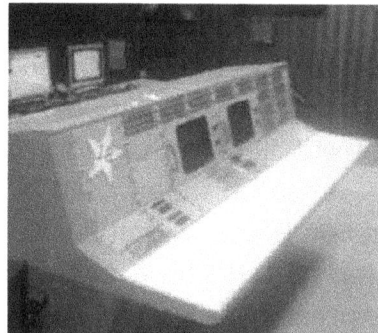

The Apollo Control Console

The Thomas P Stafford Space Museum is at 3000 Logan Rd in Weatherford. Some of the exhibits are replicas, like reproductions of the Spirit of St Louis and the Wright Brothers' plane. Perhaps the coolest authentic exhibit is the actual control console used during the Apollo missions. Compared to modern equipment it looks like a toy. But it got our astronauts to the moon and back.

There also are several real rocket engines and fighter planes, including a Russian MiG.

Jerry's Restaurant at 1000 E Main St serves breakfast all day. It has photos of old diners from all over the country, including to my surprise, the long gone Garden Restaurant in Middletown, Connecticut near where I grew up. If you stop in, you might find a photo of one of your own lost childhood favorites.

Fort Sill is south of Weatherford. Geronimo is buried there.

West to from Weatherford to Clinton

Follow Main St in **Weatherford** going out of town. • As you get to the edge of town, go straight instead of following the curve going left • Go about a quarter mile, then go left on 4th St and follow it onto the Frontage Rd • Stay on the Frontage Rd • At the T, go left across I-40, then go right onto S Rt 66 • Go two miles and cross I-40 again • Go left and get on Bus 40 into **Clinton**

CLINTON

Clinton hosts the *Annual Clinton Route 66 Festival* each May. This is a big time biker event featuring a poker run, burn outs, car and motorcycle shows and live music.

Be sure to visit the Oklahoma Route 66 Museum at 2229 W Gary Blvd. It costs a few dollars, but you will have a fun self-guided tour through six decades of Route 66 history. There are vintage cars and exhibits focusing on road construction,

This diner is an Exhibit at the Route 66 Museum in Clinton

transportation, lodging, restaurants, garages, curio shops, attractions and other artifacts, and it's all set to music. Outside is a tiny Route 66 diner that operated on Route 66 in Shamrock, Texas from 1956 to 1964. Dozens of these diners were manufactured by the Valentine Manufacturing Company of Wichita, Kansas.

Elvis liked to stay in Room 215 at the Trade Winds Motel at 2128 W Gary Blvd across the street from the Museum.

The Glancy Motor Hotel at 217 E Gary Blvd still operates, and the newest owners are reported to have spent $250,000 for renovations. It was built in the 1950's and was operated by Chester and Gladys Yancy. After that it was a Best Western until the late 1970's. It offers nightly, weekly and monthly rooms.

The Glancy's neighbor was Pop Hick's Restaurant, which was open 24 hours a day. Pop Hick's burned down in August of 1999. The foundation is still there.

You also can visit the 1892 Mohawk Lodge Indian Store at 22702 Route 66 N, which was the first trading post in Oklahoma.

The family-owned 1950 Dairy Best at 301 S 19th St is the oldest restaurant in Clinton.

The Cheyenne Cultural Center at 22724 Route 66 N is located on the original Red Wheat allotment of the Cheyenne-Arapaho Indian Reservation. There also is the Lucky Stars Casino at 10347 N 2247 Rd.

The Y was bypassed in 1956

On your way out of town you will pass the "Y", which served Clinton as a service station and café from 1937 until it was bypassed in 1956. It now is a used car lot.

Nearby, you will see the 1934 Neptune Court, which was a motel, bar and gas station.

West from Clinton to Canute
(You aren't going to believe you have to do all this for a 10 mile ride!)

Follow Bus 40 through **Clinton** • As you get to the west end of town, be careful not to get back on I-40 • Go left at the "Y" onto Hwy 183 S • Go 0.6 miles and bear right onto Opal Ave (the sign is small and hard to see; look for a beat up Texaco Station) • Go left on 10th St • Follow 10th St under I-40, where it becomes Neptune, and follow it out of town • Stay on S Frontage Rd • Look for Exit 57/Stafford on I-40 • Go under I-40 and then go left onto the Frontage Rd • At the first Stop sign at the ruins of Michael's Place, go straight and follow the signs toward a KOA Campground • Stay on that road to I-40 Exit 50 • Go left and cross I-40 • Go right on S Frontage Rd • Cross I-40 again and go left on N Frontage Rd • Go left and cross I-40 at I-40 Exit 47, get on N Frontage Rd • Cross I-40 and go right on Route 66 at the **Canute** Heritage Center

East from Clinton to Weatherford

From **Clinton**, follow Bus 40/Gary Blvd out of town • Cross Turtle Creek and go left across Bus 40 at the first opportunity, which will be Turtle Creek Rd (there is no identifying street sign at this left hand turn) • Take an immediate right onto Route 66/N Frontage Rd • Cross over I-40 at the first chance (by the Cherokee Trading Post), then go left onto S Frontage Rd • At the next Stop sign, go straight across Hwy 54, and stay on S Frontage Rd to the next Stop sign • Go straight, stay in the right lane, and follow Bus 40 onto Main St and through **Weatherford**

CANUTE

After all of the complicated turns to get to Canute following as much of the Old Road as possible, you'll find that Canute is little but relics. The highlights are the Canute Cultural Center (in the former 1928 Holey Family Church); the Cotton Boll Motel sign; the abandoned Uniroyal Station; and the Washita Motel sign.

Another lost Route 66 Motel

On the other hand, I always seem to come across motorcycles in Canute. It must be because of Wild J's Strip Club on 9th St. It's a friendly enough place, but the girls are a bit rough and it's beer only.

Canute has some history. In 1541, the Spanish explorer Coronado passed through present day Canute in search of the Lost City of Gold. Three hundred and fifty years later, hundreds of thousands of cattle were driven to northern markets over the Great Western Trail, which passed about a mile and a half east of present day Canute. The town wasn't founded until 1902 near the long gone Rock Island Railroad. The first oil wells in west Texas were drilled on the C. H. Wilcox farm just north of town in 1917. Canute was a big Route 66 stop until it was bypassed in 1970. Despite the town's decline, The Canute National Bank remains the oldest State chartered bank in Oklahoma still in operation.

West from Canute to Texola

Follow Route 66 through **Canute** • Go 0.4 miles past the RR overpass and go right under I-40 (be careful; this turn is hard to miss) • Go left on N Frontage Rd • Go straight through the first Stop sign and stay on N Frontage Rd to a second Stop sign past I-40 Exit 41 • Go left and take a quick right onto Bus 40 into **Elk City** • Follow Bus 40 through

Elk City • Go past Hwy 6, go past the Hwy 34 Junction and jog onto N Frontage Rd (there is no Route 66 sign) • When the road dead ends, go left across I-40 then go right onto S Frontage Rd • Cross Timber Creek Bridge, go right at the first Stop sign and cross I-40 (at Exit 40/Cemetery Rd) • Go left under I-40 onto the Frontage Rd and follow it to a Stop sign • Go right into **Sayre** • At the next Stop sign, go left onto Bus 40/4ᵗʰ St/US 183 • Go over the river and take a right at Sayer Creek Park • Go left at the T • Go right at the Y then go right onto N Frontage Rd • Follow the Frontage Rd, go under I-40 and follow Bus 40 into **Erick** • Stay on Bus 40/Route 66

East from Texola to Clinton

From **Texola**, follow Bus 40, which becomes Roger Miller Memorial Hwy, to **Erick** • Stay on Bus 40 through town • Follow the signs to Sayre • When approaching Sayre, a few hundred yards before the American Lodge and Suites, go left onto US 66 (be alert, the sign is small and hard to read) • Follow alongside the brick wall by the Park on the right, and when the wall ends, go right and follow the road through the Park • Once through the Park, go left (there is no sign, but you will be on Bus 40/US 283/4th St) into Downtown **Sayre** • Stay on Bus 40 past Main St and keep going straight on 4th St • Go right on Bus 40 • Just past Western Technology Center, go left on N Frontage Rd • At the Stop sign, cross I-40 then go left just before the TA Travel Center onto S Frontage Rd • Cross Timber Creek Bridge, then at the Stop sign go left, cross I-40 and go right on N Frontage Rd • At the Stop sign, go left on Route 66 into **Elk City** • Follow Route 66 through Elk City • At the Junction with Hwy 34, go left then take a quick right onto N Frontage Rd • At the first Stop sign, go straight staying on N Frontage Rd • Go right at the dead end • Cross under I-40 then go left onto Hwy 66 into **Canute** (there is no Route 66 sign) • From Route 66 in Canute, go to the first Stop sign and go left • Cross I-40 and go right on N Frontage Rd • Follow N Frontage Rd over I-40 onto S Frontage Rd • Cross back over I-40 at Exit 50 going toward the KOA Campground and go right onto N Frontage Rd • Go straight at the first Stop sign (by the abandoned Michael's Store) • Go 3.8 miles and cross under I-40 at the first opportunity • Go left and follow S Frontage Rd (which will become Neptune Dr) • Go to the Stop sign at Neptune Dr • Go left and follow Neptune under I-40 • At the first Stop sign (at Jaycee Lane near Route 66 Miniature Golf) go straight then immediately bear right onto Opal • Go left at the next Stop sign onto US 183/4th St to Bus 40 in **Clinton.**

Elk City, Sayre, Erick and Texola

ELK CITY. Elk City hosts *Route 66 Days* in late May or early June every year.

The National Route 66 Museum with its giant neon Route 66 shield is at 2717 W 3rd St.

The Old Town Museum is adjacent to the Route 66 Museum. This museum is an expanding collection of historical and replica period buildings, railroad cars and similar exhibits.

The National Route 66 Museum

On your way through town, you will pass by the 179 foot tall Parker Drilling Company Rig at the Anadarko Basin Museum of Natural History, located at 204 N Main St. It is one of the tallest drilling rigs in the world.

The big biker joint is Knucklehead Red's at 2417 W Broadway. There is no food and they only serve beer.

Also check out the Longhorn Bar at 514 N Van Buren. They sometimes have wet T-Shirt contests. Again, only beer, but they put out simple food like hot dogs and chili, for free.

SAYRE. Sayre has the Western Motel at 315 N Hwy 66, which has a terrific neon sign. There also is the Route 66 Pub at 2405 S El Camino, which has a nice Route 66 mural. Owl Drugs at Main and 4th St has

Sayre City Hall

the largest antique soda fountain in Oklahoma. City Hall is in an early 20th century bank building.

The Beckham County Courthouse at 302 E Main St was featured in *The Grapes of Wrath*.

On the corner of 4th and Elm, there is a passageway that was built so pedestrians could walk under the street to avoid heavy Route 66 traffic.

You also can check out the R S & K railroad Museum at 411 6th St.

A few miles from Sayre (not on Route 66) you can visit the Washita Battlefield Historic Site. Washita is where George Custer and the 7th Cavalry attacked a camp of Cheyenne Indians consisting mostly of old men, women and children. Black Kettle was killed. This battle, which was Custer's only victory in the Plains Indian wars, was viewed by some of Custer's contemporaries as an unjustified massacre of peaceful Indians. Others defended Custer, claiming it was not a massacre because some of the old men and women were armed and because he didn't kill everybody.

Between Sayre and Erick, be on the lookout for the old roadbed that is being reclaimed by trees and other overgrowth.

ERICK. As you come into town you will be greeted by the crowned Cabana Motel sign. Alas, there is no motel.

Erick is Roger Miller's home town, and everything in town is named for him. Old Route 66 is The Roger Miller Expressway. You will be on two lanes next to two now abandoned lanes of the original roadway.

The other celebrity from Erick is Sheb Wooley. He wrote the 1950's hit *Purple People Eater* and the theme song for the television show *Hee Haw*. He was more notable for his acting career. He was in *High Noon*, *Giant*, and *The Outlaw Josey Wales*. He also was on TV westerns, including playing Pete Nolan on *Rawhide*.

The Roger Miller Museum is at 101 Sheb Wooley. Across the street is the 100th Meridian Museum in the 1907 First National Bank building, which features an exhibit about the disputed boundary between Texas and Oklahoma and a Route 66 exhibit.

Just a few feet away is the Brandin' Iron at 204 Roger Miller Ave where you can get a cold beer.

Erick is home to The Sandhills Curiosity Shop at 201 S Sheb Wooley, which

The Sand Hills Curiosity Shop

claims to be the most unique roadside establishment along Route 66. It is run by Harley and Annabelle Russell, who entertain customers with their own music and humor. There are thousands of artifacts to enjoy. Locals tell me it's rarely open these days, and the phone has been disconnected. Still, give it a try.

The ride from Erick to Texola goes through flat grasslands. Be ready for some tumble weeds.

TEXOLA. Texola is the last town in Oklahoma before the Texas State Line. There are a few people living there, and there is a restaurant along I-40, but it pretty much is a ghost town along Route 66.

Ruins in Texola

The buildings that remain are abandoned relics that once housed bars and beer joints. The feel you get is that Texola must have been some kind of border town where Texans in a dry county could come to get booze and party, but that's just a guess. In any event, Texola looks like it once Rocked Out.

A new addition to the Texola Ghost Town is the Tumbleweed Grill, housed in the 1930's Water Hole No. 2, which lets Tumbleweed's owner declare that it is the oldest working café on Route 66. It has been wonderfully restored using lumber from local abandoned buildings for the interior trim. The Tumbleweed features home cooked food from 7:00 am to 7:00 PM, and breakfast is served all day. If you are passing

1910 Territorial Jail

Texola on I-40 rather than following the old road, you will have to exit and wind your way to the Ghost Town to find this oasis.

On the west side of town you can view a 1910 one cell Territorial Jail. It has a small display inside featuring articles about notorious outlaws like Belle Star, Billy the Kid, Jesse James and Black Bart. None of the featured outlaws ever was in that jail. The jail is not much to see, but it definitely would deter someone from a life of crime.

West to Shamrock Texas

From **Texola**, follow Route 66, which becomes Frontage Rd, to Bus 40/Route 66 in **Shamrock**

TEXAS

When you cross the Texas State Line, somehow it feels like Texas rather than Oklahoma, even though Oklahoma will be just behind you.

Route 66 through Texas crosses the Panhandle, so remarkably, Texas has less of Route 66 than any state except Kansas. Be ready for a lot of Frontage Roads, grasslands and near ghost towns.

You might get tempted to save time by staying on I-40 to each town. Avoid this temptation. The Frontage Roads may be slower, but they have terrain and curves not found on I-40, and they are more fun to ride.

In Shamrock you'll find the U Drop Inn, a restored 1936 service station now functioning as the offices of the Chamber of Commerce. It has two steeples and a restored neon sign. Shamrock also has a piece of the True Blarney Stone from Ireland.

McLean has the first Route 66 Museum ever opened. There also is a large museum dedicated to the history of barbed wire that has photos from Old West ranch life. It is a lot more interesting than it may sound, and is one of the less heralded but interesting spots along Route 66. The oldest Phillips 66 Station on Route 66 also is in McLean.

Amarillo has the Cadillac Ranch, the Big Texan Steak House and a restored Route 66 district with several good biker bars and restaurants. It is the largest Route 66 town in Texas.

Just before Amarillo, you will pass through Conway, which is home to the tilted Britten water tower and the largest Christian Cross in the Western hemisphere. Don't miss the Bug Ranch, which is a take-off on the Cadillac Ranch but made out of VW Beetles.

In Vega, you can rest up at one of the coolest Old West style bars in the middle of nowhere, and in Adrian, you'll hit the mid-point of Route 66 between Chicago and LA.

In addition to all this, there are ghost towns and other remnants of bygone days not to be missed.

Have fun over the 178 miles of Texas Route 66!

SHAMROCK

Shamrock has the restored U-Drop Inn/ Tower Conoco station in the heart of town. It was opened by in 1936 by J.M. Tindell as the Tower Station and Café. The U-Drop Inn got lots of business from passengers on busses that stopped there, and it became known as the best place to eat between Oklahoma City and Amarillo. The Art Deco building now houses the Chamber of Commerce,

The U-Drop Inn/Conoco Tower

and there are some nice Route 66 artifacts to view inside. The building is especially impressive at night when its neon lighting is ablaze.

Shamrock has hosted its *St Patrick's Day Festival* since 1938. There is a related *Motorcycle Rally and Poker Run*, as well as a carnival, nationally known live entertainment, a beard growing contest and a Miss Irish Rose contest.

Shamrock has a piece of the original Blarney Stone, which is at Blarney Castle in County Cork, Ireland. If you kiss the Blarney Stone, you magically get the gift of gab, thus the term *Blarney*. As they tell it in Shamrock, it got its fragment of the true Blarney Stone in 1959 when a Shamrock public official brought it back from Ireland, claiming it accidentally fell off of the original stone. Right! Sounds

Shamrock's piece of Blarney

like the guy who stole it must have kissed the original in Ireland to get the gab needed to try and pass off that story as believable.

Anyway, to get there, go down Main St then go left just before a water tower. It is a hundred yards down the road in a small park.

There is a fake Blarney Stone Downtown between 3rd and 4th Streets. Don't fall for the fake Blarney!

The Pioneer West Museum is located at 204 N Madden St in the 1925 Reynolds Hotel. It has a variety of exhibits ranging from Native American culture to space exploration.

The Silver Creek Sports Bar at 1800 N Main St is newly opened.

West from Shamrock to Alanreed

From Shamrock, follow Bus 40/Route 66, which becomes S Frontage Rd toward **Lela** (be careful to bear left on the Frontage Rd at the end of town and avoid going the wrong way onto the I-40 Exit ramp) • From Lela, stay on S Frontage Rd • At the third Stop sign, cross I-40 and go left on N Frontage Rd • At the dead end, go left onto Route 66 • At the Y, head onto 1st St in **McLean** • From McLean, follow 1st St out of town • Pass the Cactus Motel • Cross Hwy 273 • After about one mile, go left at the One Way sign just before the entrance ramp to I-40 • Follow around a sharp curve and go left under I-40 at the first opportunity • Go onto N Frontage Rd (Hwy 291) and follow it to Alanreed • Follow Loop 271/3rd St into **Alanreed**

East to Texola

From Shamrock, follow S Frontage Rd to Texola

Lela, McLean and Alanreed

LELA. In the mid-1940's, Lela was small, but getting along. It had five gas stations, a café and a post office, but no motels. It once had a rattlesnake exhibit with a *Rattlesnakes Exit Now* sign on I-40. That sign now is at the entrance to McLean.

McLEAN. In 1984, McLean became the last town in Texas bypassed by I-40. The Texas Route 66 Museum at 100 Kingsly St claims to be the first Route 66 museum anywhere. It was opened in 1991 by Delbert Trew, who says he knows all the artifacts are real because

This Cobra came from Alanreed

he stole them himself. Exhibits include the original statue of a steer that was at the Big Texan Steak House in Amarillo and the Giant Yellow Cobra that once was outside the Regal Reptile Ranch in Alanreed.

The Devil's Rope Museum is in the same building as the Route 66 Museum. It has exhibits about the history of barbed wire and photos of old Texas ranches and their operation. It is a delight for western and cowboy history buffs.

The 1928 Phillips 66 Station two blocks west of Main St was the oldest in Texas and operated for over 50 years.

The 1930's Avalon Theater theater on Main St has a nicely preserved Art Deco facade.

The McLean-Alanreed Area Museum at 116 N Main features exhibits about Texas Panhandle history and about a nearby WW II prisoner of war camp.

The Cactus Motel at 101 Pine St on the west end of town has a great neon sign.

ALANREED. Alanreed began in the 1880's as a farming community along the stage line from Mobeetie to Clarendon. In days gone by, it was called Prairie Dog Town (for a prairie dog town that was nearby), Spring Town or

Spring Tank (for a large spring fed pond, which Texas ranchers would call a tank) and Gouge Eye (for a bar room fight). The name Alanreed is based on the contracting firm Alan and Reed, which laid the tracks for the Oklahoma and Texas Railroad that once went through the site of the current town.

Alanreed's 1932 Super Station

A 1932 66 Super Station is near the village, where you also will find a Visitors Center with a small motel.

West from Alanreed to Amarillo

From **Alanreed**, follow Loop 271/3ʳᵈ St · Go left on S Frontage Rd · Get on I-40 at Exit 132 · Take Exit 124/Hwy 70 and cross I-40 · Take S Frontage Rd (be careful not to accidentally cross I-40; there is a sharp jog left to stay on the Frontage Rd) · Go onto Bus 40 into **Groom** (again, be sure not to go under I-40) · Follow Bus 40 to a Stop sign · Get on S Frontage Rd · At the Junction with Hwy 207, go straight to get on Hwy 2161 into **Conway** · From Conway, stay on Hwy 2161 · Go about 11 miles and keep a lookout for Exit 89 on I-40 · At I-40 Exit 89, follow Hwy 2161 across I-40 and get on the Frontage Rd · Go straight at the Stop sign at Randall Rd · At the next Stop sign, go straight across four lanes of roadway · At the Junction with Hwy 1912, go straight onto 8ᵗʰ St · Go all the way to the end and go right on Ave B · Go to the end of Ave B past an underpass and go left onto Bus 40/Amarillo Blvd · Stay on Bus 40/Amarillo Blvd through the Junction with US 287 · Go through Fillmore and take a left on Taylor · Go a few miles and take a left on 6ᵗʰ Ave through the heart of **Amarillo's** Route 66

East from Amarillo to Shamrock

From **Alanreed**, follow Loop 271/3rd St to a Stop sign at the intersection with Hwy 191 • Go straight across Hwy 291 onto S Frontage Rd • At the first Stop sign, go straight and continue on S Frontage Rd • At the second Stop sign (after crossing under I-40) go left onto N Frontage Rd (it's going to feel like you should turn right, but the correct turn is left) • At the next Stop sign, go right onto Bus 40, which will become Railroad, and follow it to Downtown **McLean** • Follow Railroad out of town to a Stop sign • Go straight at the Stop sign onto N Frontage Rd • At the next Stop sign, go right onto County Line Rd and over I-40 • Go left on S County Rd to **Lela** • From Lela, follow S Frontage Rd to **Shamrock**

Groom, Conway and Amarillo

GROOM. Groom has two Route 66 attractions; one is old and one new.

The older attraction is the tilted Britton Water Tower, which was built at an angle to attract attention. It may be my imagination, but it seems to be more tilted that it used to be. Anyway, the rear legs do not have any contact with the ground.

The newer attraction is the Cross of Our Lord Jesus Christ built in 1995, which is open 24 hours a day. It is 191 feet tall and is claimed to be the tallest Christian cross in the western hemisphere. More than 1,000 people visit per day. There are ancillary exhibits, including life size sculptures of Jesus and the two thieves and a monument to aborted babies since the Supreme Court's decision in *Rowe v. Wade*. It is inspiring or creepy, depending on your viewpoint.

Built on a tilt

At the Blessed Mary Restaurant at 701 Front St Downtown you pay what you want and the proceeds go to charity.

CONWAY. Conway was founded in 1882 when the Lone Star School was established. It was the first school of substance in the Texas Panhandle.

When Route 66 was commissioned, Conway had only about 25 residents. By 1939, it had about 125. Route 66 must have helped things along, because it ultimately had about 175 residents, two grain elevators, four service stations, three cafés and a general store. Today, the population is under 20.

The Bug Ranch in Conway is a group of buried VW Beetles lampooning the Cadillac Ranch outside of Amarillo. To get there, go right on Hwy 207 and follow it for a couple of hundred yards. Look to the left by the large *Motel/Café* sign.

Not much left of the Bug Ranch

AMARILLO. When you come into Amarillo, you will loop around the perimeter of the airport before getting into civilization.

Starting when you get on Amarillo Blvd on the east side of town, there are motels with colorful neon signs. None of them look very nice or safe.

Amarillo's biggest biker hang out

As you get into Downtown, you will be on 6th Ave, which has a well preserved section of Route 66. There are lots of bars and restaurants, including several that cater to bikers.

The best of the biker bars is Smokey Joe's at 2903 SW 6th Ave. It has cold beer and good food of the biker bar variety, but no whiskey. A lot of Texas and Oklahoma biker bars are like that (what's that about?).

There also is Skooters down the street at 4100 Bushland Ave and the Broken Spoke at 3101 SW 6th Ave (no affiliation with the Broken Spokes in Sturgis, Daytona and Laconia).

Everybody always talks about the Big Texan Steak House at 7701 E I-40 as a Route 66 attraction, even though it's on I-40, not on Route 66. If you can eat a 72 oz steak, a salad, a baked potato and a shrimp cocktail in an hour, you get it for free. The record used to be something like 16 minutes until Joey Chestnut, the professional eater and world record hotdog eating champion, recently did it in eight

The very strange Cadillac Ranch

minutes and fifty-two seconds. If you meet the challenge, your name goes in a book with your name, age, date, weight and the time it took you to finish, plus you get to add some commentary about your experience.

There are regular sized meals for the mortals and you can get a cold draft beer in a glass shaped like a cowboy boot.

For hotels, your best bet is to stay somewhere along I-40 or Downtown. I've stayed at a Marriott Courtyard Downtown a few times. It is modern and a bit avant-garde. The rates can vary and sometimes it's a little expensive, but there are a lot of good bars, nightclubs and restaurants within walking distance. There is safe bike parking. But beware, it's Deadsville on Sunday nights because everything Downtown is closed.

West from Amarillo to Glenrio

Follow 6th Ave in **Amarillo** until it turns into Bushland Ave then 9th Ave • Go left onto Bus 40/Amarillo Blvd • Go past Loop 335 and Helium Rd • Go right on Indian Hill Rd • Go several miles to a Stop sign at S Hill Rd, go left, then take an immediate right onto N Frontage Rd to **Bushland, Wilderado** and into **Vega** on Bus 40 • From Vega, follow Bus 40 to N Frontage Rd to **Adrian** • From Adrian, stay on N Frontage Rd to I-40 Exit 18 · Get on I-40, go 18 miles and get off at Exit 0 · Go left over I-40, then right on Route 66 into **Glenrio**

East from Amarillo to Alanreed

From 6th St in **Amarillo**, go left on Fillmore St to Amarillo Blvd · Go right on Amarillo Blvd through the Junction of US 287 · Take the Amarillo College East Campus Exit, which will put you onto Ave B · When Ave B dead ends, go left on 8th St · Follow 8th St past two Stop lights · At the second light, go straight across Hwy 192, and 8th St becomes Hwy 2575 · Stay on Hwy 2575 to a Stop sign at the entrance to I-40, and cross over Bus 40 onto N Frontage Rd. · Go straight at the Stop sign at the Junction with Hwy 2373 · At the Junction with Hwy 2161, go straight and follow Hwy 2161 to **Conway** · From the Junction of Hwy 2161 and Hwy 207 in Conway, go straight on the Frontage Rd · When Hwy 207 turns right at a Caution light, stay straight on the Frontage Rd, which will become Bus 40 into **Groom** · From Groom, stay on S Frontage Rd to the Stop sign at the Junction of Hwy 70 · Go right and stay on S Frontage Rd · Follow S Frontage Rd to the next Stop sign at the Junction with Hwy 70 and go straight onto I-40 · Get off I-40 at Exit 132 · Go right at the end of the off ramp · Go left on S Frontage Rd · Go right on Loop 272, which becomes 3rd St in Alanreed

Bushland, Wilderado, Vega, Adrian and Glenrio

BUSHLAND. As you leave Amarillo on Indian Hill Rd, you will be just off the I-40 Frontage Rd. If you look to your left through the trees, you will see the Cadillac Ranch, the sculpture erected by Stanley Marsh in 1974 out of 10 Cadillacs buried in a field at an angle (supposedly the same angle as the Great Pyramid of Giza). The 10 cars represent each of the 10 tail fin styles

Cadillac produced. You can walk out to the cars if you go to Bushland and double back on the Frontage Rd on the far side of I-40.

Bushland is at the eastern edge of the Llano Estacado, or Staked Plains, which is one of the largest natural grassland in the world. Legend has it that when Coronado was searching the west for the Lost City of Gold in 1541, the grass was so thick he had to plant stakes into the ground to find his way out. For you *Lonesome Dove* fans, this is where Blue Duck escaped after Gus McCrae saved Lori from having been kidnapped.

WILDERADO. Wilderado was founded in about 1900 and is named for nearby Wilderado Creek. It was a camp where travelers could get rest, shoe their horses and repair their equipment.

Route 66 originally went down Main Street Wilderado. When I-40 was built, a 300 foot right of way caused all the businesses on the south side of Route 66 to be relocated. This was a raw deal for those businesses, which included a bank, a couple of service stations and restaurants, a mercantile store and a car dealership.

If you love the smell of manure in the morning, today's Wilderado is the place for you. There is a 20,000 head cattle feedlot that is smellible for miles in all directions.

Wilderado also has a huge wind farm. There must be some way to have the windmills blow the aroma out into the plains.

VEGA. What happens in Vega stays in Vega.

Vega has a 1920's Magnolia Gas Station that has been partially restored.

Dot's Mini Museum at 105 N 12th St once was a Route 66 staple. It has a few small rooms filled with Route 66 artifacts and a Cowboy Boot Tree on which cowboy boots are tied. It is not always open, and when open,

Get good food and booze at this Old West style saloon in Vega

not always attended. Apparently Dot's daughter Betty is in charge. You may want to call before you visit.

Of more recent vintage, Vega has the Boot Hill Saloon at 909 Vega Blvd. It is a good spot with an ambitious menu that they pull off well. It is new construction, but it has an old saloon feel, complete with a long solid wood bar, a patterned tin ceiling, oak tables, and chairs with red velvet upholstery. The selection of beer and liquor is good and the staff is friendly. There is a sign at the bar that says anyone who is overly aggressive will be banned for a month. Apparently, the Boot Hill Saloon has some interesting clientele! It's worth staying over night in Vega to party at this cool bar in the middle of nowhere.

The 1947 Vega Motel was put up for auction in 2009. Last time I checked (in February 2014) it didn't appear to be open.

ADRIAN. Adrian claims to be the midpoint between Chicago and LA on Route 66. You can stop at the 1928 Midpoint Café and Gift Shop if it's opened. Everyone talks about the *ugly crust* pies. This place has not been open during any of my trips through Adrian, but when I called recently they claimed to be open from 8:00 to 4:30 seven days a week.

Don't miss the Fabulous 40 Motel sign.

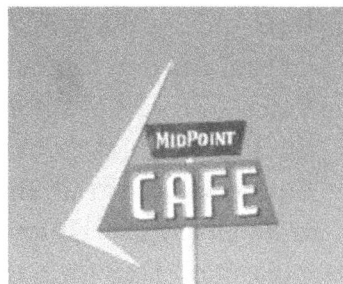

Midway between Chicago
and LA

GLENRIO. Glenrio is a ghost town. It was first settled as a farming community in about 1905. In 1906, the Chicago, Rock Island and Gulf Railway established a station there to ship cattle and other freight.

By 1920, the town had a hotel, a hardware store, a post office, a land office, several grocery stores and service stations and a newspaper. Route 66 helped Glenrio prosper; however, when I-40 bypassed Glenrio, it went into rapid decline. The railroad depot closed in 1955, and by the 1980's, only two residents remained.

Part of *The Grapes of Wrath* was filmed in Glenrio. Poignantly, Glenrio was an actual stopping point for Oakies traveling west during the Great Depression.

After you see the Glenrio ghost town, turn around and follow my directions to San Jon. Stop by Russell's Travel Center (in present day Endee NM). It is a modern store that will have any provisions you might need. There also is a museum with antique cars and Route 66 memorabilia.

There is an optional route to San Jon through the now defunct Endee. It is a bumpy 20 miles on a dirt road, so I suggest you skip this option if you are on two wheels, especially in wet weather.

East from Glenrio to Amarillo

From **Glenrio**, get on I-40 at Exit 0 · Get off I-40 at Exit 18 · Cross I-40 and get on N Frontage Rd · Follow N Frontage Rd to **Adrian** · From Adrian, follow N Frontage Rd, which will become Bus 40 to **Vega** · From Vega, follow Bus 40 through town and continue on to the Frontage Rd to **Wilderado** and then on to **Bushland** · From Bushland, go strait through the Stop sign just past the Bushland grain elevators · Follow the Frontage Rd for about two miles · Keep a lookout on I-40 for Exit 60/Arnot Rd · Take the next left, which will be S Hill Rd (be alert, the sign is small) · Take an immediate right on Indian Hill Rd · Follow Indian Hill Rd to Bus 40 · Go left on Bus 40/ Amarillo Blvd · Keep going past Loop 335 then go right on 9th Ave · Follow 9th Ave through the Stop light at the intersection of Western Ave and Bushland Ave · Follow Bushland Ave, which will become 6th St into the heart of Route 66 in **Amarillo**.

NEW MEXICO

The first things you will notice when you head into New Mexico are that you can see forever, and that the orange and black Burlington Northern Santa Fe Railroad is everywhere. There are trains all over Route 66, but they just seem more numerous in the west. In many New Mexico towns you can hear and feel the trains roll by all night long.

Tucumcari is 50 miles from the eastern border of New Mexico. It has one of the best remaining collections of Route 66 motel neon signs, including the Blue Swallow sign advertising its *100% Refrigerated Air*. Be sure to tour Tucumcari at night to see these signs lit up.

In Santa Rosa, you can see the Blue Hole, which is a 60 foot wide 80 foot deep pond with crystal clear water in the middle of the New Mexico Desert. There also is the Fat Man Sign that used to adorn the now closed Club Café.

Santa Fe is one of the oldest towns in the United States. The Palace of the Governors is on the Plaza (never the Square!). It is the oldest government building in the Country. Santa Fe also has the oldest house in the United States, which dates from about the year 1200. Santa Fe is full of old Spanish missions. It also has prosperous vintage Route 66 motels.

Albuquerque is the biggest town in New Mexico. Route 66 follows Central Ave, which at 18 miles, is the longest Main St in the country.

Grants hosts the Fire and Ice Motorcycle Rally each July.

Gallup is another New Mexico town with lots of well-preserved vintage motels. The best of these is the El Rancho, where dozens of Hollywood stars stayed when filming in New Mexico. The El Rancho has a lobby you must see even if you are staying somewhere else.

There are lots of ghost towns. Still, following the old road is worth it. There are twists and turns and some beautiful vistas that you will miss if you just follow I-40.

A word of caution: Flash floods and muddy roadways are common along the Old Road between towns when it rains. So, in bad weather, stick to I-40.

West to Tucumcari

From **Glenrio**, get on I-40 and get off at Exit 369 • Go right, then left in front of Russell's Travel Center onto N Frontage Rd • Go left at I-40 Exit 356, and cross under I-40 into **San Jon** • Go right on 469/S Frontage Rd through town and continue until it dead ends and curves onto Bus 40 in **Tucumcari**

East from San Jon to Glenrio

From the S Frontage Rd in **San Jon**, go left on Hwy 469 just before the Post Office (there is no Hwy 469 sign going east, so be alert) • Go under I-40 and go right on N Frontage Rd just before the D Hillon Fuel sign (be alert, there is no sign designating the N Frontage Rd) • Follow the N Frontage Rd until it dead ends • Go right and get on I-40 • Get off I-40 at Exit 0 into **Glenrio**

San Jon and Tucumcari

SAN JON. San Jon (pronounced San Hone) is almost completely abandoned, but it once was was the largest town in eastern New Mexico and was a major ranch and farm supply center. As late as the mid-1940's, it was a favorite spot for cowboys to let off steam on Saturday nights.

Some friends of mine stayed at the San Jon Motel at 715 E Main Ave for under $30, and the owner bought beer and grilled burgers in the parking lot for everybody. They tell me it was a fun deal at a cheap price.

TUCUMCARI. Tucumcari once was a crossroads of commerce and one of the busiest towns on Route 66. It was founded in 1901 when the Chicago, Rock Island and Pacific Railroad built a construction camp there called Ragtown. It later was called Six Gun Siding because of the frequent gunfights. Still later it was called Douglas. Finally in 1908 it was renamed Tucumcari after nearby Tucumcari Mountain. Legend has it that the mountain got its name from two lovers: Tucom and Kari, who died tragic deaths during a dispute between their parents over leadership of a band of Apaches.

Tucumcari is at the eastern end of the *Route 66 New Mexico Motor Tour,* in which classic cars are driven over the old alignment of Route 66 from Tucumcari to Gallup each June. It is sponsored by the New Mexico Route 66 Association.

Tucumcari also hosts *Wheels on 66,* which is a car show held in conjunction with the Motor Tour.

Tucumcari has many motels with vintage neon signs. Some are lit up at night even though the motels have long been closed.

The 1941 Blue Swallow at 815 E Route 66 has a bright blue neon sign (added in 1960) that announces its *100% Refrigerated Air.* This is perhaps the most photographed motel sign on Route 66 (the Munger Moss in Lebanon, Missouri, is up there too). All of the rooms have been restored to the original motor court style, including working rotary telephones. The rooms are well appointed with new mattresses, high thread count sheets and plush towels. Be sure to make reservations.

Stay cool in the
Refrigerated Air

The Pow Wow Motor Hotel at 801 W Tucumcari Ave is worn, but it is a good place to stay, mainly because the Lizard Lounge (the best bar in town) is attached to the Motel. It dates from the 1930's. There are some photos showing what Tucumcari was like when it was booming.

Tee Pee Curios at the corner of Route 66 and Park St is shaped like a Tee Pee.

Don't miss the Route 66 Historical Museum at 416 Adams St.

The Route 66 Monument at 1500 Route 66 is a sculpture by Tom Coffin dedicated in 1997 and is the newest Route 66 attraction in Tucumcari. It is in front of the Tucumcari Convention Center on the west end of town.

Bad Lands Customs at 328 Main St is the only motorcycle shop between Amarillo and Albuquerque. The owner has won awards for his custom bikes and hot rods.

Curious curios at the Tee Pee

The ride to Montoya will take you into the Frontage Rd and through a narrow tunnel under I-40. This tunnel gets muddy in wet weather, so if it's raining, stay on I-40.

West from Tucumcari to Santa Rosa

From **Tucumcari**, follow Bus 40 through town and get on I-40 • Get off at Exit 321 and go left • Take a right onto S Frontage Rd • Bear left at the next overpass and stay on S Frontage Rd • Go through a narrow tunnel, pass under I-40, get on N Frontage Rd and follow it through to **Montoya** • From Montoya, go left over I-40 at abandoned Richardson's Store, and follow it around a long curve onto S Frontage Rd • The Frontage Rd will cross over I-40 again • Follow it to **Newkirk** • From Newkirk, follow the Frontage Rd to **Cuervo** • From Cuervo, go straight through town and get on I-40 • Get off I-40 at Exit 277 and go onto Bus 40 through **Santa Rosa**

East to San Jon

Follow Bus 40 through **Tucumcari** until it dead ends • Go left on S Frontage Rd and follow it to San Jon

Montoya, Newkirk, Cuervo and Santa Rosa

Montoya. Montoya was founded in 1902 as a railhead serving local cattle ranchers. There is not much left except the abandoned 1925 Richardson's Store and Sinclair Station, which operated until the mid-1970's when the owner died.

Richardson's Store in Montoya

Newkirk. Newkirk was founded in 1901 when a railroad was built through there. In 1941 it had 115 residents, two gas stations and two lunch rooms.

Today, Newkirk has lots of relics, but also has a store where you can get gas, beer and food.

The ride to Cuervo follows the Frontage Rd, which is rough and bumpy much of the way. Be careful, especially for loose gravel.

Cuervo. There is no Cuervo in Cuervo. You can't even get a beer!

There are several small businesses, including Cuervo Gas, where you probably can't get gas.

Santa Rosa. Santa Rosa has vintage motels, some in good shape and some in decline.

Scuba in the desert at the Blue

The Club Café, which was opened in 1934 by Phil Craig and Floyd Shaw who had come from Texas to work on highway construction. Its Fat Man logo, which was a caricature of Phil Craig, appeared on on billboards all over Route 66 and later I-40. The Club Café went into decline, then later was bought and restored. Unfortunately, it finally closed in 1992. You can see the original Fat Man sign at Joseph's Bar & Grill at 1775 Route 66.

The Blue Hole at 1000 Blue Hole Rd is a pond of crystal clear water 60 feet in diameter and 81 feet deep that looks dark blue in the sunlight. The Blue Hole is popular for scuba diving, which must be a rare thing in the New Mexico Desert.

The Route 66 Auto Museum on the east end of town at 2866 Will Rogers Dr is an antique car museum with a hot rod elevated on the top of its sign. It costs a few dollars to visit, but folks who ride motorcycles are sure to enjoy viewing the vintage cars.

On the way out of town is a small portion of pre-1937 Route 66 following 4th St and Riverside Drive. This detour winds through a neighborhood that has seen better days, but when you get to the other end, you will be west of the Pecos!

At the west end of town is the Pecos Bar at 457 Route 66. It is a western style bar with several pool tables.

If you want to take a detour to see some Wild West history, Ft Sumner is about a 45 minute ride from Santa Rosa. Billy the Kid was killed there by Pat Garret, and the Kid is buried there. There also is a cheesy Billy the Kid Museum.

All that's left of the Fat Man's Café

When leaving Santa Rosa, I give you two options:

My main route is the pre-1937 route from Santa Rosa north through Santa Fe, then south through Albuquerque to Correro. There are at least three reasons to take this option. First, it is the older route. Second, you get to go to Santa Fe. Third, it's a beautiful ride. For directions and information about this route, continue reading below.

The alternate route follows I-40 to Moriarty then through Albuquerque to Rio Puerco. This route is quicker, but still has a lot to offer. It will take you through Tijeras Canyon and into Albuquerque on Central Ave, which is Albuquerque's main Route 66 drag. It also will take you through Old Town Albuquerque, which is a colorful historic area with lots of intact Route 66 buildings and businesses. For directions and information about this route, skip to page 167.

West from Santa Rosa to Santa Fe

From **Santa Rosa**, get on I-40 and follow it to Exit 256/Hwy 84 • Go right on Hwy 84 to **Dilia** • Stay on Hwy 84 through the I-25 intersection • Go to the Stop sign and get on the N Frontage Rd by the Phillips 66 Station • Follow N Frontage Rd to **Tecolote, Bernal** and on to Pecos River Station at **San Juan** • Cross I-25 and follow the S Frontage Rd to **Rowe** • Cross under I-25 at E T Padilla's abandoned store (I-25 Exit 307) and follow Hwy 63 N to **Pecos** • Get on Hwy 50 into **Glorieta** • Get on I-25 at Exit 299 and get off at Exit 294 (Canoncito) • Go left through Apache Canyon on the N Frontage Rd, which will be Old Las Vegas Hwy • Go past Bobcat Bite and Harry's Roadhouse • Go right on Old Pecos Trail/Hwy 466 • Go for about a mile to a light and go right staying on Old Pecos Trail (which will become Old Santa Fe Trail as you approach Downtown). • Cross Paseo de Peralta and De Vargas St • Go left on Alameda in the heart of **Santa Fe**

East From Santa Rosa to Tucumcari

Follow Bus 40 through **Santa Rosa** • Cross under I-40 then take an immediate left onto I-40 • Get off of I-40 at Exit 291 • Go left at the end of the off ramp • Go left under I-40 and then go right on N

Frontage Rd to **Cuervo** and **Newkirk** • Go straight at the Route 66 Gas Station • When approaching Montoya, stay straight following the Frontage Rd crossing I-40 onto the N Frontage Rd • Stay on the N Frontage Rd, cross over I-40 and follow S Frontage Rd • Cross I-40 again back onto N Frontage Rd to **Montoya** • Follow N Frontage Rd past the abandoned Richardson's Store • Follow the Frontage Rd through a narrow tunnel, cross under I-40, and get on S Frontage Rd • Go left toward the Dairy Queen where S Frontage Rd turns to gravel and get on I-40 • Get off I-40 at Exit 329 and follow Bus 40 through **Tucumcari**

Dilia, Tecolote, Bernal, San Juan, Rowe, Pecos, Glorieta and Santa Fe

DILIA. Dilia is the first of a series of small villages you will encounter on your way to and out of Santa Fe. Maestros Lounge is on the roadside. In back of Maestros is the Sacred Heart Catholic Church. You can go from Perdition to Redemption just a few feet away!

TECOLOTE. Tecolote is on an Indian Reservation that has a sign warning of the prosecution of trespassers. There is an adobe church that is painted white. Folks who have seen it say its impressive. I heeded the warning sign and didn't trespass.

Dilia's Sacred Heart Church

BERNAL. There is nothing in Bernal except abandoned buildings. But the ride is full of gentle turns and rolling hills with a great view of Glorieta Mesa and the valley below.

SAN JUAN. San Juan has the Pecos River Station, which is a general store and gas station.

The ride from San Juan to Rowe is on the opposite side of I-25 than you have been on, and it's not nearly as pretty. Still, it's not on the Interstate, and the riding is more fun than on the highway.

E D Padilla's Store and Victory Bar had whiskey, beer and wine

ROWE. Rowe has a Post Office and a few residences. ET Padilla's Store and Victory Bar that advertised *Whiskey-Wine-Beer* is long abandoned. Too bad. As the song says *These are a few of my favorite things.*

When you leave Rowe toward Pecos, you finally will get away from I-25 and go through some beautiful country on the way to Santa Fe.

PECOS. Pecos is on a mountain pass that has been used by travelers for centuries, including by nomadic Indian tribes.

There is a mix of thriving businesses, crumbling homes and abandoned store fronts. The Casa De Herrera Restaurant and Lounge at 387 Hwy 63 seems to be a good place to stop, eat and drink.

Adelo's Town & Country Store at 13 Pecos Hwy has it all. The sign says it has *Groceries, Meats, Hardware & Building Supplies, Clothing, Dry Goods and an ATM Machine.* It also sells liquor.

Pecos is near the Pecos National Historic Site. This settlement existed long before the Spanish came to New Mexico and long before it was called Pecos or was known as a pueblo. It was a center of trading with for the Plains Indians. At one time it had 2,000 residents. The site was abandoned by the Indians in the early 1800's. Today there is a self-guided walking tour through two Spanish missions and some ancient ruins.

The ride from Pecos to Glorieta is one of the nicest portions of this section of Route 66. Although the ride is not long, it is picturesque without much of the decaying and abandoned buildings present along much of New Mexico's Route 66.

Along the way, you will pass Griego's Market and Liquors/Nash's Night Club and Lounge, which are housed in the same building. I have been to the Market, which is a good place to stop for a snack and gas. I have not been to the Night Club, but hey, you can't go wrong with a bar.

GLORIETA. Glorieta has a small church by the entrance to I-25, but it is more known for the Baptist Conference Center, which has provided retreats in a Christian atmosphere for over 60 years.

The Battle of Glorieta Pass was fought on March 26-28, 1862 during the Civil War. It sometimes is referred to as the *Gettysburg of the West*. Confederate forces were unsuccessful in driving Union forces from the area. The Confederates had to withdraw to Arizona, and eventually back to Texas. It was the decisive battle of the New Mexican campaign.

SANTA FE. When you exit I-25 at Canoncito, before heading to Santa Fe, go right to see the Senora de la Luz Church. This still-used catholic mission built in the 1880's has a haunting look, especially because of the hillside cemetery with graves marked only by wooden crosses. Ansel Adams photographed this church and it is a favorite of local artists.

After viewing the Church, turn around and head through Apache Canyon for the 10 mile ride into Santa Fe. On the way you will pass Bobcat Bite at 418 Old Las Vegas Hwy and Harry's Roadhouse at 96 Old Las Vegas Hwy, both local biker destinations.

The Palace of the Governors on the Plaza is an adobe structure built in about 1610 to serve as Spain's seat of government in the southwest. It is the oldest continuously occupied public building in the United States. Lew Wallace wrote parts of *Ben Hur* there while he was territorial governor.

Loretto Chapel at 207 Old Santa Fe Trail with its Miraculous Staircase was built in 1878 by an unidentified carpenter who showed up with a tool box and a donkey. The Chapel had no staircase to access the choir loft. The carpenter figured out a way to build a circular staircase that solved the problem. Tradition has it that the unknown carpenter was St Joseph, the patron saint of carpenters.

The Chapel of San Miguel por Barrio de Analco at 401 Old Santa Fe Trail is the oldest continuously operated church in the United States.

The Mission of San Miguel of Santa Fe at 401 Old Santa Fe Trail has a bell from 1356.

The oldest house in the United States, dating from 1200, is at 201 E De Vargas St.

Evangelo's two blocks off the Plaza at 200 W San Francisco has cold beer, live music and good prices. The Shed at 113 E Palace Ave just off the Plaza is a fun spot

The cemetery at Senora de la Luz Church in Canoncito

that has been around forever. Its southwestern Mexican food is as good as you will get anywhere.

I usually stay at La Fonda at 100 E San Francisco. It is one of the oldest and best hotels in Santa Fe and has shops, a good bar and several restaurants.

When my friend Tracie and I stopped in Santa Fe on our way to Jackson Hole, we decided to stay at a more traditional Route 66 motel, and we found the El Rey Inn. Route 66 still passed through Santa Fe when it opened in 1936 with 12 rooms. It now has 86 rooms. The El Rey has been under the same management since 1973 and it must be a labor of love, because this is a wonderful place.

LA BAJADA HILL. The original alignment of Route 66 through Santa Fe followed the severely winding La Bajada Hill. It was so steep that cars driving up sometimes had to go in reverse so that gas could feed into their gravity fueled engines.

It currently is a dirt road that is passable only using four wheel drive vehicles, and even then it is

La Bajada Hill

dangerous. Also, it is on an Indian Reservation, so permission is needed for access whether you decide to ride or hike it.

To get to the bottom of the Hill, get off of I-25 at Exit 264, go right and follow Hwy 16 for 2.8 miles. Turn right on Tetilla Peak Rd and go one mile. Go right on Old Route 66. Go 1.5 miles and cross the 1928 Santa Fe River Bridge to the base of the Hill.

To get to the top of the Hill follow Cerrillos Rd out of Santa Fe. Go left on Airport Rd/Hwy 284. Go straight across onto Hwy 56 at the Junction with Veterans Memorial Hwy/Hwy 599. Go 3.3 miles and take a sharp right onto CR 56C. Go straight for about six miles on the dirt road to the top of the Hill.

West from Santa Fe to Albuquerque

From Alameda in **Santa Fe**, go left onto Paseo de Peralta and follow it across town to St Mary • Go left on St Mary and follow it to Carrillo. • Go right on Carrillo and follow it to I-25 and cross over bearing left with Hwy 14 • Go about a mile (going through a light), then go right on Hwy 599 • Go 100 yards to the first light and go left onto the Frontage Rd (there is no sign identifying the Frontage Rd) • Follow the Frontage Rd until it ends at a Stop sign, and get on I-25 • Get off I-25 at Exit 248 and take a right • Go left on Hwy 313 to **Algodones** and **Bernalillo** • Stay on Hwy 313 through town crossing Hwy 550 • Stay on Hwy 313 for several miles; when approaching the traffic circle for Hwy 556, get in the right lane and follow Hwy 566 west (the first turn off the traffic circle) and continue on to 4th St • Cross under I-40 into Downtown • Go left on Roma • Go right onto 3rd St • Go right onto Central Ave in **Albuquerque** • Take 4th St into Downtown

East from Santa Fe to Santa Rosa

From **Santa Fe,** follow Cerrillos onto Galisteo • Go right on Water St • At the corner of Old Santa Fe Trail, go straight (instead of going left following the Route 66 sign), go one block and go right on Old Santa Fe Trail • At a fork, go right on Old Pecos Trail • Go left at the Stop light at Old Santa Fe Trail/St Michaels • Go left at the Stop light at Old Las Vegas Hwy, which will become the Frontage Rd • Get on I-25 where the Frontage Rd dead ends at Canoncito (Exit 294) • Get off at Exit 299 into **Glorieta** • From Glorieta, go left at the end of the Exit ramp, cross I-25, and go right onto Hwy 50 to **Pecos** • From Hwy 50 in Pecos, go right on Hwy 63 • Go toward I-25 near Exit 307 • Go under I-25 and go left on S Frontage Rd • Follow the Frontage Rd to **Rowe** • From Rowe, stay on the S Frontage Rd to I-25 Exit 319.• Cross I-25 and follow N Frontage Rd to the Pecos River Station in **San Juan** • From San Juan, follow the N Frontage Rd to **Bernal**, **Tecolote** and on to the intersection with I-25 Exit 339 • Cross I-25 at the Phillips 66 Station and follow US 84 to **Dilia** • From Dilia, follow US 84 to I-40 • Get on I-40 East to Exit 256 • Take Exit 256 to Bus 40 through **Santa Rosa**

Algodones, Bernalillo and Albuquerque

ALGODONES. Algodones was founded as a military garrison to protect wagon trains traveling from Santa Fe to Chihuahua, Mexico. Later, it served as a military supply depot and in 1846 was occupied by General Kearney and the Army of the West.

The main attraction is the La Hacienda Vargas Bed and Breakfast at 1431 Hwy 313. The site once was used as a stagecoach stop and as a train station.

There also is a small market where you can gas up.

The ride to Bernalillo passes through neighborhoods of small desert homes and mobile home parks. The road follows some railroad tracks and is lined by sage brush and other desert plants. There is not all that much to see, but this will be the last rural ride before hitting traffic of the Albuquerque suburbs, so enjoy this quiet stretch of road.

BERNALILLO. Downtown features a *Welcome to Bernalillo* sign with a finned turquoise Cadillac. Across the street you will find The Flying Star Café at 200 N Camino del Pueblo. Down the street is the Range Café at 925 S Camino del Pueblo.

Welcome to Bernalillo

For bikers, there is Sylva's Saloon at 955 S Camino del Pueblo. It opened the day after prohibition ended. The last time I went by it had a *For Sale* sign on it, but it was open. Sylva's welcomes bikers but Club patches are not allowed.

ALBUQUERQUE. If you go into Albuquerque from Santa Fe on the pre-1937 route, you will come in on 4th St, which has several vintage motels and restaurants. The El Camino Motel at 6801 4th St NW and the El Camino Dining Room across the street stand out.

If you came into Albuquerque on Central Ave there is more to see. Central Ave is the main drag for Route 66 in Albuquerque. There are three distinct sections.

The first section is east Central Ave, which has has lots of vintage Route 66 hotels and other buildings, many of which are in good condition. As you get closer to town, the traffic will increase as you go through the University of New Mexico. There are lots of bars and restaurants with a college feel.

The second section is Downtown Central Ave, which is the heart of Albuquerque's Route 66. Be sure to see the KiMo Theatre at 423 Central Ave.

The Library at 312 Central Ave SW has long been a biker favorite. It has cold beer and the bartenders and waitresses are dressed in skimpy school girl outfits.

Knockouts Gentlemen's Club is across the street. It has lots of dancers, and the lap dances are only $5.00 (this is not a typo!).

Both the Library and Knockouts no longer allow patches. Apparently, there were a couple of brawls at a biker rally in the summer of 2011 and patches were banned in these clubs.

You can wear your patch at Maloney's at 325 Central Ave NW. It has better food and drinks than the Library or Knockouts, although the eye candy is not as good.

The 1927 KiMo Theater

Don't miss the 66 Diner and the Route 66 Association of New Mexico at 1405 Central Ave.

The 1939 La Posada Hotel at 125 2nd St NW is where Conrad Hilton and Zsa Zsa Gabor were married. It gets mixed reviews, mainly because of its expense and loud music played in the lobby at night. I've stayed there a few times and always liked it.

The Hotel Blue at 717 Central Ave NW is on the edge of the Downtown Central area. It has good prices and secure parking for bikes. The long-time family owned Villa de Casa Restaurant across the street serves home style Italian food at a good price.

One of the 12 Madonna of the Trail Statues put up by the Daughters of the American Revolution in the 1920's is in Downtown Albuquerque at 421 Gold Ave. There are two along Route 66. The other is in Upland, CA.

The third section of Central Ave is Old Town on the west side of Albuquerque's Route 66. It is not as busy as east Central or Downtown, but it has nicer motels and restaurants.

Home of the Wimpy Burger

You have a choice when you leave Albuquerque. You can take the pre-1937 route out of town on 4th St, which will take you through some old neighborhoods before getting to Correo and joining I-40 to Mesita, or you can take the post-1937 route out west Central Ave and the Frontage Rd to Rio Puerco, where you will join I-40 to Mesita. The pre-1937 route takes a little more time, but it is worth it. You will find the Red Ball Café at 1303 4th St SW (serving the Wimpy Burger since 1922), a 1950s Dairy Queen at 427 Iselta Blvd SW and Blue Castle Auto 2321 Iselta Blvd. There also is a giant statue of the Roadrunner at 2219 Iselta.

West from Albuquerque to Correro

From Central Ave in **Albuquerque,** go left onto 4th St · At Bridge Ave, go right, cross the Rio Grande, then go left at the light on Isleta Blvd · At Isleta Blvd/Goff Blvd light, go left to stay on Isleta · Stay on Isleta to **Armijo, Parajito** and **Los Padillas** · From Los Padillas, follow Isleta across I-25 · Go left on Hwy 147 · Cross the Rio Grande and go right on Hwy 47 to **Bosque Farms, Peralta** and **Valencia** · In Valencia, when Hwy 47 turns left, go straight onto Hwy 6 (Main St) following the signs to **Los Lunas** · From Los Lunas, stay on Main St · Cross Hwy 313 and I-25, and follow Hwy 6 for 32 miles to **Correro** · Go past the Wild Horse Mesa Bar to I-40, which ends the pre-1937 Santa Fe Route

East from Albuquerque to Santa Fe

From Central Ave in Downtown **Albuquerque**, go left on 3rd St · Go left on Marquette · Go right on 4th St and follow it out of town · Go several miles to the Junction with Hwy 556 and Hwy 313 · Follow the traffic circle to Hwy 313 to **Bernalillo** · Follow Hwy 313 to **Algodones** · From Hwy 313 in Algodones, go right at the Junction of

Hwy 313 and get on I-25 at Exit 248. • Get off at Exit 267 • At the end of the ramp, go right then take an immediate left onto the Frontage Rd • Follow the Frontage Rd to the Stop sign at Hwy 599 • Go right, then left onto Hwy 14 • Go under I-25 and stay on Hwy 14/Cerrillos Rd through to **Santa Fe** • Stay on Cerrillos Rd and merge onto Galisteo

Armijo, Parajito, Los Padillas, Bosque Farms, Peralta, Valencia, Los Lunas and Correro

ARMIJO, Armijo is so small no one who lives there ever heard of it. It is named for the family of Jose de Armijo, who came to the area in 1693. Apparently there is a ghost town, but I have not found it.

PARAJITO. Parajito, founded in about 1746, is on the original Camino Real as well as the pre-1937 Route 66. It is a largely Hispanic community that has a few restaurants, markets and stores. There are no Route 66 sites of note.

LOS PADILLAS. There is not much in Los Padillas. I came across a sign for Lone Wolf Motorcycles. I was there on a Sunday and it was closed, so I couldn't find out anything about it. The sign says they had their best year ever. Hopefully they are talking about this year.

Beep Beep!

BASQUE FARMS. Bosque Farms is a strip of small businesses. Not much hustle and bustle. I found the Longhorn Saloon at 395 Basque Farms Rd. I saw lots of bikes on the road. There must be something going on!

PERALTA. I didn't see much in Peralta, but right across the Town Line going into Valencia, there is the Two Minute Bar and Grill. Read on.

VALENCIA. The Two Minute Bar and Grill is at 3513 Hwy 47 (a Los Lunas address). It is a sports bar with a separate room with a stage where live music can be played.

On the way to Los Lunas, you will pass through the Iselta Pueblo. The mission church there was built in 1613, and is one of the oldest in New Mexico. Thomas Edison made the first motion picture there in 1898.

LOS LUNAS. The big spot in Los Lunas is the Luna Mansion at 110 Main St NE, which is an 1880's mansion that offers comparatively upscale dining. There also is an 1879 Santa Fe Railroad depot.

CORRERO. There is nothing in Correro except the Wild Horse Mesa Bar. It has not been opened when I have gone by. Too bad.

Across from the Wild Horse Mesa Bar is a Route 66 sign that leads down a dirt road to Mesita. I tried to ride my bike down this road, which is on private property, and it was too rough. I turned around in less than half a mile. As much fun as it is exploring the older parts of Route 66, you will be

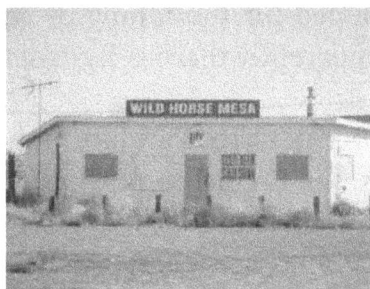

I hope this spot reopens!

better off passing up this portion of the Old Road if you are on two wheels.

West from Correro to Manuelito

From **Correro,** get on I-40 and get off at Exit 117 to **Mesita** · Go right at the end of the ramp then left onto the Frontage Rd · Go right onto Hwy 124 to **Laguna**, **New Laguna**, **Paraje**, **Budville**, **Cubero** and **San Fidel** · From San Fidel, stay on Hwy 124 to a dead end just past a Whiting Bros sign · Cross over I-40 and stay on Hwy 124 · Cross under I-40 through a narrow tunnel and get on Hwy 117 · Follow Hwy 117 onto Bus 40 in **Grants** · Follow Bus 40 through Grants and get on Hwy 122 to **Milan, Bluewater, Prewitt, Thoreau** and **Continental Divide** • Get on I-40 and get off at Exit 36 in Iyanbito • Get on Hwy 118 and follow it to Bus 40 in **Gallup** • Follow Bus 40/Hwy 118 through Gallup • Go left following Hwy 118 to **Defiance** (be careful not to miss the Hwy 118 sign; it is small and does not say Route 66 or direct you to Defiance) • Stay on Hwy 118 and go right at a Y • Cross under I-40 staying on Hwy 118 and follow it to **Manuelito**

East from Correro to Albuquerque

From **Correro**, take Hwy 6 for 32 miles then cross I-25 into **Los Lunas** • From Los Lunas, stay on Hwy 6 (Main St) to Hwy 47 • Take Hwy 47 N to **Valencia**, **Peralta** and **Bosque Farms** • From Bosque Farms, follow Hwy 47 N into the Iselta Indian Reservation • Go left on Hwy 147 • Follow Hwy 147 to Hwy 314 • Go right on Hwy 314, go under I-25 and get onto Iselta Blvd to **Los Padillas**, **Parajito** and **Armijo** • From Armijo, follow Iselta Blvd to the intersection with Goff Blvd/ Arenal Rd • Stay right with Iselta Blvd • Go right onto Bridge Blvd • Cross the Rio Grande, go past 8th St, and go left onto 4th St • Pass Gold St and then go right onto Central Ave

Mesita, Laguna, New Laguna, Paraje, Budville, Cubero, San Fidel, Grants, Milan, Bluewater, Prewitt, Thoreau, Continental Divide, Gallup, Defiance and Manuelito

MESITA. Mesita is a small Indian community that has strict rules about trespassing and taking photos, especially during religious activities.

The ride from Mesita to Laguna is a treat. It winds off of I-40 into the hills, and you will see spectacular red rock vistas as you traverse this windy and hilly road. Local sites on the way to Laguna include an outcropping called Owl Rock and a stretch of road known as Dead Man's Curve.

LAGUNA. Route 66 always has gone through the Laguna Pueblo, in both the pre-and post-1937 alignments.

Ancestors of the current residents of Laguna have been there since at least 1300 and people have inhabited this area since 3000 BC.

The Pueblo was founded in 1699, which remarkably, makes it the newest of the New Mexican pueblos. There are six villages: Laguna, Mesita, Paraje, Encinal, Seama and Paguate.

The 1699 St Joseph of the Lake Mission Church dominates the skyline. This mission has been redone but maintains the original adobe floor, beam ceiling and other vintage features.

Like the other villages in the Pueblo, Laguna has restrictions concerning taking photographs, but those restrictions appear to be limited to photos of religious activities. Taking photos of the Mission is permitted. Also, there are vendors and artists that sell their wares around the Mission.

NEW LAGUNA. New Laguna is part of the larger Laguna Pueblo. It does not have the character the Mission provides to Laguna. It mostly is ruins of old stone buildings and trailer-type homes.

There does not appear to be any commerce. Even so, the ride is peaceful and off of I-40. There is a short loop off of Hwy 124 (which is Route 66 along here) that you can follow to see the whole village.

Laguna's 1699 Lake Mission Church

PARAJE. Paraje is a ghost town that is the last of the Laguna Pueblo villages along Route 66. The name in Spanish means *place,* and often is combined with another word to designate a particular place, such as *Paraje de Belen.*

Although there is nothing in the way of a settlement, the ride through this part of the New Mexico has a unique beauty.

BUDVILLE. You've got to love a town called Budville, especially if you have been riding a motorcycle through the New Mexico dessert.

The Budville Trading Post was opened in 1928 by Bud and Flossie Rice. Bud was murdered when the store was robbed in 1967. Flossie ran it until 1979 when she closed it for good.

Get a Bud in Budville

Good news! When I've gone through there in the past, there were a couple of beer joints that were never open; however, the last few times through, the Midway Bar and Grill has been alive and kicking with cold beer. So, hopefully there will be Bud in Budville if you visit.

CUBERO. The Villa de Cubero Trading Post is one of the only reliably operating businesses between Puerco and Grants. In 1937, it had a trading post, a service station and ten cottages. It became a popular getaway spot for Hollywood types, and actors like Jean Tierney stayed there. Today, gas, food and beer are available.

Locals claim Hemingway wrote The Old Man and the Sea here

Some people claim that Ernest Hemingway wrote part of *The Old Man and the Sea* at a café (no longer there) across the street from the Tourist Court at the Villa de Cubero. As the story goes, the owner's mother, who worked at the café, didn't like Hemingway. Once when he came into the place, she said "Al viene el diablo puerco" ("Here comes the son of the devil"). Years later, actress Vivian Vance (aka Ethel Mertz of I Love Lucy fame), who owned a ranch near Cubero, brought the woman a copy of *The Old Man and the Sea* with the inscription "The Dirty Old Devil-EH".

I've heard similar stories about the writing of *The Old Man and the Sea* in several of places including Silvergate, Montana. Key West Florida sounds like a more likely spot. But what the hell, when choosing between fact and legend, it's a lot more fun to go with the legend.

SAN FIDEL. San Fidel is the last of the near ghost towns before getting to Grants. There is the Zodiac Bar and the San Fidel Trading Post, but neither one has been open when I have passed through. But I've always been through there in the day time. Maybe the Zodiac is a hot night spot.

San Fidel used to have several cafés and service stations. They are all gone, but there is a Catholic church and school in operation.

GRANTS. Grants is the only town with a significant population between Albuquerque and Gallup. The *Fire and Ice Motorcycle Rally* is held each July. I happened to be at the first of these rallies when I was riding from Houston, Texas to Vancouver, with a stop at the *Sturgis Rally* on the way home (8,400 miles round trip!). I have been back a couple of times. It always is well organized and well attended. There are bunches of Bandidos.

The Franciscan Lodge once was the most modern hotel in Grants

Grants was founded as a railroad camp in the 1880's during the construction of the Atlantic and Pacific Railroad. By the 1930's it was a logging town. Later, it's most notable industry was uranium mining until the mines were played out in the 1980's. Since then, Grants has survived from Route 66 tourism.

There are vintage motels, although they generally do not appear to be in good condition. One of the oldest is the Franciscan Lodge, which when opened

Old School biker bar

in 1950, was the most modern in town. The Franciscan has fallen into disrepair, but it is still there with its distinctive neon sign.

The best bar is Pat's Lounge at 305 W Santa Fe Dr. It has been family owned for a couple of generations. It's a big biker spot.

Outlaws Saloon at 1109 E Santa Fe Ave has dancing on the weekends. It's more of a kid's place than a biker place.

The Red Lion Hotel at 1501 E Santa Fe Ave appears to be the only hotel that has a bar and a restaurant.

MILAN. Milan was founded by Salvador Milan in 1939. Salvador was born in Mexico. His family was exiled in 1913 during the Mexican revolution. Salvador was mayor of Milan into the 1970's.

Today, the 1950's style Wow Diner at 1300 Motel Dr advertises that it will *Wow You* with its unique atmosphere and atypical diner fare.

BLUEWATER. Bluewater gets its name from nearby Bluewater Lake, which is spring fed and has a blue hue in the sunlight. There are a few homes and businesses, but it's pretty close to a ghost town. In the surrounding area you can visit Bluewater State Park for boating and fishing.

PREWETT. Prewitt hosts an annual *Labor Day Rodeo*. Prewitt also has the *Route 66 Swap Meet*, which has been closed every time I have passed through.

The Tomahawk Bar is up the road a bit. It once was a wild place. It was opened after WW II by *Pistol Pete* South, who started with an adobe bar that burned. He rebuilt and added a 20 x 40 foot steel Quonset hut and a concrete block facade. The only sign read *BAR*. Simple and to the point! *Tomahawk* was added later, maybe by a different owner. The bar business was closed in the last decade due to excessive fighting and repeated violations of liquor laws. Today it only sells package liquors and beer. Too bad. This must have been perfect for bikers.

THOREAU. Thoreau (pronounced Thuh-roo) is a bump in the road that was not named for Henry David (although some sources claim it was). It is located at the base of a beautiful red sandstone escarpment that continues north and west. You will be following these sublime formations nearly to the Arizona border.

This once was a rough place

Thoreau is a local trading center with craftsmen such as rug weavers, silversmiths, and turquoise jewelry artists. It has a strong Navajo influence and many residents speak that language.

Roxanne Trout Heath wrote a book about the history of Thoreau in 1982 called *Thoreau, Where the Trails Cross*. I tried to find this book on the Internet. While several book sites list it I could not find a copy for sale.

Thoreau has the Red Mountain Market & Deli. It isn't always open.

CONTINENTAL DIVIDE. Continental Divide has the Indian Village and Indian Market curio shops. There also is an old Whiting Bros Motel relic.

Signs claim this is the highest elevation on Route 66. It is not. The actual highest point is between Belmont and Parks, Arizona.

GALLUP. Be sure to tour Gallup at night, because it has one of the best collections of preserved neon signs along Route 66.

Gallup is known for its Native American jewelry shops. There are beautiful pieces and bargaining is expected.

The El Rancho Hotel in Gallup at 1000 E 66, with its bright neon sign that spells out the name of the Hotel in rope looking script, is my favorite hotel on Route 66. It boasts the *Charm of yesterday and the convenience of tomorrow*.

The El Rancho was built by D W Griffith's brother in the 1930's and was used by movie crews when filming in New Mexico. The unique lobby features an atrium that has ornate chandeliers with a western flare, along with hand crafted wooden furniture and a large fireplace. There is an old fashioned elevator that requires an operator for its use. There are autographed photos of John Wayne, Tom Mix, Ronald Regan, Humphrey Bogart, Allen Ladd, Mae West, Katherine Hepburn and a hundred more.

Each room is named after a movie star who stayed there. The biggest is the Ronald Reagan Room, but my favorite is the Kirk Douglas Room, which has a nice little portico.

Most importantly, the 49er Bar at the El Rancho was named one of *America's 50 best Dive Bars* by Esquire Magazine.

The American Bar at 221 W Coal Ave is a bit rough. On busy nights they have a policeman at the door to check for weapons and to act as a bouncer. There are several pool tables and lots of local photos and memorabilia.

Goodfella's at 1206 E Hwy 66 is a popular sports bar that always has a crowd.

Window Rock is close by in Window Rock, Arizona. It is a sacred Navajo place consisting of an immense face of red rock through which the wind has eroded a large hole or *window*. The seat of the Navajo government is there. If you are going to see just one Navajo site along your trip, this is the one to see. It is only a half an hour ride from Gallup.

The lobby of the El Rancho

Gallop is at the Western end of *The Route 66 New Mexico Motor Tour*, in which classic cars are driven over the old alignment of Route 66 from Tucumcari to Gallup each June. It is sponsored by the New Mexico Route 66 Association.

DEFIANCE. There must not be much to Defiance. There is no sign to let you know you are there. I have ever found it. The locals know where it is, but they have been unsuccessful in directing me to it.

The 1950 Kirk Douglas movie *Ace in the Hole* was filmed in this area.

MANUELITO. Manuelito is a Navajo village and is the last outpost in New Mexico before Arizona. It is named after Navajo Chief Manuelito, who signed a treaty with Kit Carson in Grants.

There are several trading posts offering Navajo jewelry. Those trading posts are on the site of the long-gone Atkinson's Trading Post, opened in 1942. Atkinson's was a rustic log cabin structure built of Navajo hogans.

The most spectacular features here are the views of the weather worn sandstone formations and arroyos that will lead you into Arizona.

West to Lupton, Arizona

From **Manuelito**, follow Hwy 118 across the Arizona line • Cross under I-40 at Indian Village and go right on S Frontage Rd through **Lupton**

East from Manuelito to Correro

From **Manuelito,** follow Hwy 118 under I-40 • Go left at Salt Water Marsh • Go right into **Defiance** • Follow Hwy 118/ Bus 40 to **Gallup** • Follow Hwy 118/Bus 40 out of Gallup to Iybanito and go straight onto I-40 • Get off I-40 at Exit 47 in **Continental Divide** • Follow the *Begin Route 66* sign to Hwy 122 and on to **Thoreau, Prewett, Bluewater, Milan** and **Grants** • From Bus 40, go left on Hwy 117 just before the I-40 overpass at the east end of Grants • Go left on Hwy 124 near a Shell Station • Follow Hwy 124 to **San Fidel, Cubero, Budville, Paraje, New Laguna** and **Laguna** • From Laguna, follow Hwy 124 across the San Jose River (often dry) • Go left at the *Laguna School Historic 66* sign • Follow Route 66 to the Stop sign at Mesita Rd in **Mesita** • Go right and get on I-40 East • Follow I-40 to Exit 126 • Go right onto Hwy 6 in **Correro**

POST 1937 ROUTE FROM SANTA ROSA THROUGH ALBUQUERQUE

Although there are a few places to stop on the way from Moriarty to Albuquerque, I have given you an express route. Along the way, you will pass the **Flying C Ranch** and **Kline's Corners.** Both of these places feature every tacky souvenir imaginable, but they both also have good road food, clean bathrooms and gas. If you have to pick one, I recommend Cline's Corners. It's bigger and it has its own restaurant rather than national franchises.

West From Santa Rosa to Mesita

From **Santa Rosa,** get on I-40 west and follow it to Exit 197 and Bus 40 in **Moriarty** · Just before the I-40 on ramp at the west end of town, go left on Hwy 333 and follow it to **Edgewood** · Follow Hwy 333 out of Edgewood · At the top of a hill leading into Tijeras Canyon, look for a right turn crossing I-40 onto Sedillo Hill Rd (if you reach the Sedillo Hill Travel Center you have gone too far) · At the intersection with Hwy 333, go right into **Zuzax** · Stay on Hwy 333 through **Tijeras, Carnuel** and into **Albuquerque** (333 becomes Central Ave) · Follow Central Ave out of town · Cross I-40 and get on N Frontage Rd to **Rio Puerco** (I-40 Exit 140) · Get on I-40 to Exit 117 in **Mesita** and rejoin the main route

Moriarty, Edgewood, Zuzax, Tijeras, Carnuel, Albuquerque, and Rio Puerco

MORIARTY. When you get off of I-40 in Moriarty, you will glide past the Southwest Soaring Museum, or soar past the Glider Museum. Both names are on the building.

Moriarty claims to have the last Whiting Bros Station still in operation on Route 66. It does not sell gas. It only repairs tires, changes oil and things like that. For some history about the Whiting Bros stations that once dominated Route 66, read the Holbrook, Arizonza information on page 174.

Last Whiting Bros Station on 66

The El Comedor de Anaya's Restaurant has the only neon rotosphere left on Route 66. It is a spiked neon globe with its hemispheres spinning in opposite directions. Very cool when lit up.

The Buford Steak House at 5 Carl Cannon Rd is the best restaurant and bar in town. There is live entertainment on the weekends and bikes are welcome.

Blackie's at 612 Route 66 is another local bar that gets some traffic.

EDGEWOOD. Edgewood has an RV park with an old Red Top diner (not open for business) similar to the one at the Route 66 Museum in Clinton, Oklahoma. Edgewood also has the Wild West Nature Park, which has mountain lions, coyotes and other interesting wildlife.

For bikers, stop by Knucklehead's Motorcycle Center on the west end of town.

The next town is Zuzax. You will be on Hwy 333 for part of the way, but then take a detour down Sedillo Hill Rd. If you are in a hurry, you can stay on Hwy 333 and skip the detour, but you will be missing a

Cool sign but the motel is closed

nice ride, and who knows whether you will get a chance to be here again.

ZUZAX. In the 1950s, Zuzax had a store and a chair lift out back. Today, there is not much except a small store (no gas) and an RV Park.

TIJERAS. Tijeras has Molly's bar. I've been by as early as 9:30 in the morning and have seen it open. Molly's doesn't have food, but there is a pizza place next door.

CARNUEL. Carnuel has the Mountain Lodge sign with its Mexican on a burro, but it doesn't have the Mountain Lodge itself. The old motel is now on private property.

ALBUQUERQUE. For a full description of Albuquerque go to page 154.

RIO PUERCO. Rio Puerco has the Route 66 Casino. It's a modern complex with Route 66 themed restaurants and gaming. It is nicer than most of the casinos you will find west of Albuquerque along New Mexico's Route 66.

Route 66 Casino in Rio Puerco

The 250 foot long Rio Puerco Bridge once was part of Route 66 into Albuquerque. The bridge is one of the longest single span steel truss bridges in New Mexico.

The next stop is Mesita to rejoin the main route. If you have taken this alternate route from Santa Rosa to Mesita, return to page 159.

Post 1937 Route East from Mesita to Santa Rosa

From **Mesita**, take I-40 to Exit 140 in **Rio Puerco** • At the end of the Exit, bear right through the traffic circle and cross I-40 to the N Frontage Rd • At the first Stop sign, cross I-40, then go left on S Frontage Rd • S Frontage Rd will become Central Ave • Follow Central Ave to Downtown **Albuquerque** (be sure not to accidentally go left on Lomas) • Stay on Central Ave through Downtown (it will become Hwy 333) • Follow Hwy 333 to **Carnuel, Tijeras** and **Zuzax**

• About one mile past Zuzax, go left and cross under I-40 onto Sedillo Hill Rd • After about 3½ miles, go right over I-40, then left onto Hwy 333 • Follow Hwy 333 to **Edgewood** • Follow Hwy 333 to a Stop sign with the Junction of I-40 • Go left and take an immediate right onto Bus 40 in **Moriarty** • Follow Bus 40 through Moriarty and get on I-40 • Get off of I-40 at Exit 273 into **Santa Rosa** • Go left at the Junction of US 54 onto Bus 40 through Santa Rosa

ARIZONA

In Arizona you'll spend a lot of time on I-40 but there is plenty of great riding.

The first few miles are bounded by huge rock formations that have caves carved from wind erosion. As you pass by these formations on your way to Holbrook, you can detour to see the Petrified Forest and the Painted Desert.

In Holbrook, you'll find one of the two remaining Wigwam Motels, which feature rooms made from concrete teepees. You'll also find the Winner's Circle Bar. It is one of the best biker bars in eastern Arizona.

On your way from Holbrook to Flagstaff, you'll pass the Meteor Crater, Twin Arrows and Two Guns. You also can stand on a corner in Winslow, Arizona without forgetting about Winona.

Flagstaff's altitude will keep you cool even in the summer. Scenes from *Easy Rider* were filmed in the Flagstaff area.

In nearby Belmont, you can see the Pine Breeze Inn where Peter Fonda and Dennis Hopper found there was NO VACANCY. You can even see the NO VACANCY sign at a local biker bar. You'll also pass over the highest altitude on Route 66.

Next is Williams, *The Gateway to the Grand Canyon*, which was the last Route 66 town bypassed by I-40. You can reach the Canyon on the Grand Canyon Railroad, which has been serving tourists since 1906. The World Famous Sultana Bar was a saloon and brothel before Arizona was a state and has Arizona's first liquor license.

Now get ready for some real fun. You are about to hit a 160 mile long uninterrupted stretch of Route 66.

You'll go through Seligman, which has the Snow Cap Drive-In, the Black Cat Bar and the Road Kill Café. The Hackberry Store is more of a museum than a store. Kingman, the home of Andy Devine, has vintage hotels and bars, and is the entrance way to the Oatman Hwy, which with all its twists and turns through the mountains is one of the best parts of Route 66 for motorcycle riding. In Oatman, you can see the room where Clark Gable and Carol Lombard spent their honey moon after they eloped.

From there, it's a short ride to the border.

West from Lupton to Holbrook

From **Lupton**, stay on S Frontage Rd and get on I-40 at Exit 354 • Get off at Exit 339 (St Johns Exit) and you will be in **Sanders** • From Sanders, follow the N Frontage Rd to the first Stop sign; you will be in **Chambers** • From Chambers, go left off the N Frontage Rd onto US 191 • Go about a quarter of a mile and get on I-40 • Get off I-40 at Exit 289 and go right on Navajo Blvd/Bus 40 into **Holbrook**

East to Manuelito

From **Lupton**, follow NM 118 to Bus 40 into **Manuelito**

Lupton, Sanders, Chambers and Holbrook

LUPTON. Lupton has the Largest Tee Pee in the Southwest; the Chief Yellow Horse Trading Post; and Indian Village. Some of these spots are seasonal, but others are open in the winter.

There is a Speedy's Truck Stop if you need gas.

When you cross under I-40 you will find the Indian Market, a long gone trading post in a geodesic dome.

On the Frontage Rd to Sanders, you will pass a Navajo hogan. They can have a variety

A traditional Navajo hogan

172

of styles. The one you will see is a traditional six sided wood dwelling with a doorway facing east and a smoke hole in the center. Navajos consider a hogan to be a gift from god that occupies a place in the sacred world. The hogan is symbolic of the sun and faces east so the sun is the first thing seen in the morning.

You also will pass several souvenir and jewelry places. I have not explored many of these. I sometimes stop at Ft Defiance for a bite to eat. It has a replica of an Old West fort. Some claim that scenes from the TV show *F Troop* were filmed there, but no one has been able to confirm that.

SANDERS. When you get off I-40 in Sanders you will be next to the local schools. A few hundred yards down the Frontage Rd is a boarded up Stop and Go, and next door, a Church of the Latter-Day Saints, which is in good shape.

Along the Frontage Rd to Chambers, you will pass some tired businesses hanging on. It's pretty grim.

CHAMBERS. Chambers has the Chambers Trading Co, which is spare, but you can get gas and food. It also is a pawn shop.

Next door is the Kiyaaaanii Gallery, which means Towering House (except for some accent marks that a normal computer cannot make, that's the correct spelling!).

The Apple Dumpling Restaurant was open last time I went by but it had a For Sale sign.

You can take a detour through the Petrified Forest, which has fossilized trees that lived 225 million ago. Humans first came to the area about 8,000 years ago, and pueblos were constructed beginning about 2,000 years ago. Due to changing climate conditions (no doubt caused by man-made carbons being emitted into the atmosphere), the last pueblos were abandoned about 1,400 years ago. There are over 600 archeological sites, including petrographs. It's illegal to pocket any artifacts but nearby stores sell them.

The Petrified Forest extends into the Painted Desert, which gets its name from the sweeping colors of the rock formations.

After Chambers, you will have a 45 mile ride on I-40 to Holbrook. It's a bummer being on the Interstate, but at least the speed limit is high.

HOLBROOK. Holbrook was founded in 1881 and named after the first chief engineer of the Atlantic and Pacific Railroad. At one time, it was a bawdy cow town.

Holbrook was the *de facto* home of the Whiting Bros chain of service stations that were all over Route 66. It was founded in 1926 by Eddie, Art, Ralph and Ernest Whiting in St Johns, Arizona. When they found that the newly designated Route 66 was going to go through Holbrook instead of St Johns, they moved to Holbrook. They expanded first to Winslow and Flagstaff and eventually had

Every night is bike night

over 100 outlets, with over 40 on Route 66. The remnants of these service stations can be seen all over Route 66. Today, Kaibab Industries, which was started by members of the Whiting Bros families in 1952, operates three modern stations in Arizona.

Downtown Holbrook has the Winner's Circle Bar at 466 Navajo Blvd. Every night is bike night, but the crowd can be sparse during the week. They have their own patch, although the patch holders are more a group that likes to ride together than a motorcycle club. There is pool, a great juke box and a cool collection of whiskey decanters depicting everybody from Robert E. Lee to Elvis.

Try the Empty Pockets Saloon at 2210 Navajo Blvd and the Mesa Grill Sports Bar, which is part of the Mesa Restaurant at 2318 Navajo Blvd.

Romo's at 121 W Hopi Dr Downtown has good Mexican food. Every order is individually made, so while it might take a few minutes to get served, the food is always fresh.

Spend a night in a tee pee

Across the street from Romo's is Joe and Aggies, which has been a Holbrook staple for years.

If you want a good steak, try Butterfield's Steak House at 609 W Hopi Dr.

Holbrook has one of the two remaining Wigwam Motels. It is at 811 W Hopi Dr. There originally were seven. The other remaining Wigwam is in Rialto, California. Each room is its own individual tee pee. The rooms are more spacious on the inside than they look from the outside. The surrounding motor court features antique cars. The office is only open a few hours a day, so you cannot check in until late afternoon.

There is a 1950's Dairy Queen at 1001 Navajo Blvd, but unfortunately, it is modern inside.

West from Holbrook to Flagstaff

Follow Bus 40/Navajo Blvd in **Holbrook**, go right on Hopi Dr, follow it out of town onto I-40 • Get off I-40 at Exit 277 • Follow Bus 40 into **Joseph City** • Follow Bus 40 out of town • At the *Dead End 2 Miles* sign, go left across I-40 • Go right onto S Frontage Rd and get on I-40 just past the **Jackrabbit Trading Post** • At Exit 257, cross I-40 and get on Hwy 87 S/Historic 66 into **Winslow** • Follow 3rd St out of town and get on I-40 • Get off I-40 at Exit 230 to **Two Guns** • Get back on I-40 and take Exit 219 to **Twin Arrows** • Get back on I-40 and take Exit 211 • Go right across the RR tracks and into **Winona** • Follow Townsend-Winona Rd to US 89 • Go left on US 89 and follow it into **Flagstaff**

East from Holbrook to Lupton

From **Holbrook**, follow Bus 40 through town and get on I-40 • Get off of I-40 at Exit 333 to **Chambers** (there is no *Chambers* sign) • From Exit 333 in Chambers, go left and in about half a mile, go right onto Apache CO 7060, which becomes N Frontage Rd, and follow it to **Sanders** (there is no sign for Sanders) • From Sanders, go right where the Frontage Rd ends and cross I-40 • Get on I-40 and get off at Exit 354 (Hawthorne Rd) • Go right, then immediately left onto the S Frontage Rd to **Lupton**

Joseph City, Winslow, Two Guns, Twin Arrows, Winona and Flagstaff

JOSEPH CITY. Joseph City was founded in 1876 by Mormons. It originally was called Allen's Camp, but the name was changed in 1878 to St Joseph after the Mormon profit Joseph Smith. In 1923, the name was changed to Joseph City so it would not be confused with St Joseph, Missouri. It is the oldest Mormon town in Arizona.

The entrance to Joseph City follows a line of aging pre-fab buildings and even older homes and businesses. There are a bunch of abandoned bars and road houses showing that Joseph City may have Rocked Out in its day, although that seems odd for a Mormon place.

A Route 66 stop off since 1949

There is a small building with a Route 66 sign with a local map featuring Betty Boop and a Harley-Davidson shield. It used to be a boutique, and although it is well maintained, it is now closed.

Next stop is the Jackrabbit Trading Post five miles west of Joseph City on the way to Winslow. It was opened in 1949 by James Taylor, who bought a snake farm and turned it into the Jackrabbit. He advertised with billboards with nothing but a silhouette of a giant rabbit. When you get there, you'll find one of those billboards with *Here it Is*

A corner in Winslow Arizona

printed beside it. There also is a giant rabbit with a saddle that children can mount for a good photo op.

The Jackrabbit has seen better days. Gas is no longer sold and on my last stop the restrooms were out of order. It doesn't matter: no Route 66 trip is complete without stopping here, at least for a few snap shots.

WINSLOW. Winslow has to be traveled east to west on 3rd St, and west to east on 2nd St. Second St is busier.

Stop and have your picture taken on the corner of 2nd and Kinsley next to the statue by sculptor Ron Adamson and the fire engine red Flatbed Ford parked nearby.

Winslow is proud of the 1928 La Posada Hotel located at 303 E 2nd St, which was the last Harvey House built. It was closed in 1957 and was used as offices for the Santa Fe Railroad until 1994. It once again is operating as a hotel.

The Lodge at 1914 W 3rd St on the west end of town looks better than most.

For bikers, try P T's Lounge at 1500 3rd St on the east end of town. It's an Old School biker place that has live bands and holds its own weekend long rally in the summer.

You can also try Bronco's Sports Bar at 2150 W Hwy 66 and Bojo's Grill and Sports Pub at 113 2nd St.

On your way to Flagstaff, you'll pass the Meteor Crater, which is about six miles off of I-40. The Crater is 570 feet deep and a mile across. It was formed 50,000 years ago when a 60,000 ton meteor slammed into the countryside. You should decide whether it is worth it in time or money. It is on private property and there is a pretty hefty fee to get in. Once in, there is an impressive museum you have you go through

These are the two guns in Two Guns

before you can actually see the Crater. They have some interesting literature about its origin and the unsuccessful search for the nickel of which the meteor was thought to be made. Once you get to the Crater, you can go on a walkway around part of the perimeter but you can't go down into it.

Two Guns. Two Guns was a tourist destination capitalizing on Canyon Diablo and the legend of Harry *Two Guns* Miller. The town had been named Canyon Lodge, but was renamed Two Guns after Miller, who was an Apache who had some tourist businesses in the Diablo Canyon area including a zoo that claimed to have *One of every beast in Arizona*. Miller killed a neighbor who was operating a competing business. He pled self defense and was acquitted even though it was determined that the victim had been unarmed. Miller later went to jail for defacing the grave marker of the man he killed because it said *Killed by Indian Miller*.

Two Guns was near the real ghost town of Canyon Diablo, which was founded in 1881 as railroad construction camp. The main drag was named Hell Street, which at one time had 14 saloons, 10 gambling houses, four whore houses and two dance halls. There were frequent gunfights and robberies. The first sheriff assumed office at 3:00 one afternoon and was killed at 8:00 the same night. There were five more sheriffs, and none lived more than a month. Canyon Diablo is now a ghost town but the ruins remain and are accessible.

Twin Arrows. Twin Arrows opened in about 1949 as the Canyon Padre Trading Post. The 20 foot tall Twin Arrows, which are made out of telephone poles, were constructed in 1954, and the Trading Post was renamed after its eyepopping new structures. There once was a curio shop, a gas station and a diner. It closed in 1998 and deteriorated quickly.

The Twin Arrows date from 1954

There has been some restoration. The Twin Arrows have been repainted and the outer structure of the Trading Post has had a facelift. However, it is not open for business. A $200,000,000 Navajo casino opened nearby in 2013. Maybe the casino traffic will encourage restoration efforts.

WINONA. When Bobby Troup was telling you how to get your kicks on Route 66, he warned "...don't forget Winona..." Well, it's hard to find these days. About all that's left is an old bridge that has been long abandoned.

Even so, the detour through Winona is worth it. You will be heading into Flagstaff through some beautiful pine woods with the mountains to your right and in front of you. The smell of the evergreens is one of the things tourists in cages will miss on this great stretch of road.

FLAGSTAFF. Flagstaff is a bit of a hippie town where you see folks wearing Eddie Bauer jackets and baggy shorts on cool summer evenings. There is snow on the peaks year round, and even in the middle of the summer, Flagstaff offers a welcome retreat from the heat of the Arizona desert. I once rode through a snowstorm there in late May.

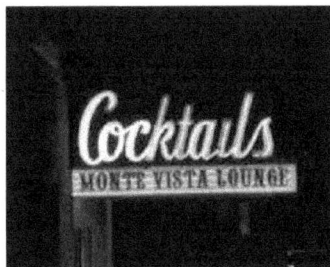

This bar gets an eclectic crowd

As you come into town, you'll pass the 1931 Museum Club at 3404 E Route 66, which has a guitar-shaped neon sign and live entertainment. It claims to be the biggest log cabin in the southwest. It may be, but there are bigger log cabins out there. The Old Faithful Inn in Yellowstone comes to mind.

There are period Route 66 motels along Bus 40, but I prefer to stay Downtown because I can park my bike and walk to good night spots.

The 1927 Monte Vista Hotel at 100 N San Francisco St Downtown is being remodeled. The rooms are named after famous people who stayed there, including John Wayne, Humphrey Bogart, Bob Hope, Zane Grey, Bing Crosby, Michael J Fox, Barbara Stanwyk, Bon Jovi, Spencer Tracey and Clark Gable. The Monte Vista Bar has an eclectic crowd. It's almost something out of the 1960's.

The Weatherford Hotel at 23 N Leroux St had Wyatt Earp as a frequent guest. The Weatherford is more upscale than the Monte Vista. It has a good restaurant and two ornate bars, one with a balcony.

Wyatt Earp stayed here

The 1917 Orpheum Theater at 15 W Aspen Ave was renovated and reopened on 2002. It has movies and live entertainment.

The Lowell Observatory, which was established in 1894, is where Pluto was discovered in 1930. The observatory operates four telescopes on two locations. The original observatory on Mars Rd houses the original 24 inch Clark Refracting telescope, which was built in 1926 for $20,000.

West from Flagstaff to Kingman

From **Flagstaff,** follow Hwy 89A/Bus 40 through Downtown until it merges onto I-40 • Get on I-40 and get off at Exit 185 at **Bellemont** • Go right and then go left onto the N Frontage Rd • Go straight onto the gravel road at the *Entering Private Land* sign • At the *To I-40* sign, go straight on CO Rd 146 staying on Route 66 • Go left following the sign to I-40/Deer Farm Rd in **Parks** • From Parks, follow CO Rd 146 • At the access road for I-40 Exit 171, go left and get on I-40 • Get off I-40 at Exit 165 and go left onto Bus 40 to **Williams** • From Williams, follow Bus 40 through town and get on I-40 • Get off at Exit 146 and follow Bus 40 through **Ash Fork** • Get back on I-40, get off at Exit 139 and go right on Crookton Rd • When the road comes to a T, go left into **Seligman** • From Seligman, follow Historic 66, which becomes AZ 66, through **Peach Springs**, **Truxton**, **Valentine**, **Hackberry** and into **Kingman**

East from Flagstaff to Holbrook

From **Flagstaff,** follow Hwy 89A/Bus 40, which becomes US Hwy 89 • Follow US 89 toward Page (ignoring the Route 66 signs that direct you to go right) to a Stop light at Townsend-Winona Rd • Go right on Townsend-Winona Rd and follow to **Winona** • From Winona, get on I-40 and get off at Exit 219 at **Twin Arrows** • Get back on I-40 and get off at Exit 230 at **Two Guns** • Get back on I-40 and take Exit 252 • Go right at the end of the off ramp, then go left following Bus 40/Route 66 through **Winslow** • Go past the I-40 signs and go straight onto Hwy 87 N • Cross the Little Colorado River • Go left at the Indian Trading Center and get on I-40 • Get off of I-40 at Exit 269 • At the end of the off ramp, go right and then take an immediate left onto S Frontage Rd • Go past the **Jackrabbit Trading Post** • Cross I-40 at the first opportunity and go right following Bus 40 through **Joseph City** • From Joseph City, get on I-40 and get off at Exit 285 to **Holbrook** • Follow Bus 40/Hopi Dr into town Holbrook • Go left on Navajo Blvd

Bellemont, Parks, Williams, Ash Fork, Seligman, Peach Springs, Truxton, Valentine, Hackberry and Kingman

BELLEMONT. Grand Canyon Harley-Davidson in Bellemont is a small shop compared to the huge dealerships that now seem to be the norm. I once stopped in to get a new rear tire and a fluid change. They were glad to help a road warrior on short notice.

The Pine Breeze Inn where Peter Fonda and Dennis Hopper found NO

No vacancy for bikers at the Pine Breeze Inn from *Easy Rider*

VACANCY is in Bellemont. To get there, go about a mile east on the Frontage Rd by Grand Canyon Harley-Davidson.

The Roadhouse Café next to Grand Canyon H-D has a full bar, serves food and has interesting museum pieces including the NO VACANCY sign from *Easy Rider*. You have to cook your food yourself. So, if you order a cheeseburger, they give you a burger patty, a roll and some cheese and send you to a large communal grill where other folks will be cooking their own meals. Beans and salad come with it and you serve yourself. It's odd, but it works.

When you leave Bellemont, you will get to ride through some pretty country on your way to Parks, then on to Williams. A couple of miles of this route is dirt road, but passable if it's dry. In wet weather, skip this route and instead stay on I-40 to Williams.

PARKS. The main reason to go through Parks is the beautiful wooded ride. There is a little village, along with the Parks in the Pines General Store, which was established in 1906.

WILLIAMS. Williams reminds me of how Jackson Hole, Wyoming was 25 years ago. The two towns don't look like each other, but they have the same feel. The air is fresh and crisp at night, and the stars are on top of you. Folks walk around in cowboy hats and boots that are not costumes. They listen to real country music. Stuff like George Jones, Ray Price, Don Williams and guys like that. Not the modern

The oldest bar in Arizona

Nashville stuff that Merle Haggard famously called "Nothing but bad rock and roll."

Williams was the last town to be bypassed by I-40, but unlike some of those towns, it continues to thrive because of Williams' proximity to the Grand Canyon and the cool mountain air during the summer. Railroad

Ave is one way going east to west and W Route 66 is one way going west to east. It's more lively on W Route 66.

The Grand Canyon Railroad at 233 N Grand Canyon Blvd gives rides to the Grand Canyon in vintage rail coaches pulled by a steam engine. There is a nice Bar Car. On at least some of the trips, they stage a train hold-up by masked horsemen who ride along side and then board the train. The bandits go from car to car robbing the passengers (of tips for the performance).

Lots of Williams' businesses claim to be *World Famous*, including the World Famous Sultana Bar at 301 W Route 66. It has been in continuous operation in the same building since 1906, which is six years before Arizona became a state. It has the oldest liquor license in Arizona. The atmosphere is Old West. There is an original tin ceiling that must be 15 feet high. There are trophies, including a moose, a mountain lion, a caribou and an elk.

The Canyon Club at 132 W Route 66 is another vintage bar on W Route 66. It is owned by the same folks who own the Sultana. They have cocktails and dancing.

I was in Seligman one night hitting the World Famous Black Cat Bar. It can get rowdy there sometimes, but this night it was Deadsville, so I rode over to Williams and hit the Canyon Club.

Dine, Dance and Drink

As I walked in, everyone was singing *Happy Birthday* to someone. It turned out to be a 72nd birthday party for a long-time Canyon Club regular.

It was a festive time and I enjoyed the lively atmosphere. After about 45 minutes, the birthday boy strolled over to me and said "How's it going Old Timer?" That really didn't make my day. I was 15 years younger than this guy! But, I took it with the grace and in the friendly spirit in which the remark was made, and bought us each a shot of Wild Turkey. Guys out west don't drink

The Red Garter
B&B

pussy shooters. I wound up passing out a bunch of Route66mc.com koozies and patches and had a wonderful time.

There is a biker looking place down the street from the Canyon Club called the Iron Horse Pub at 615 8th St with a motorcycle over the entrance way. It has not been opened when I have been by. Apparently, it opens seasonally or for special events.

Rod's Steak House at 301 E Route 66 also claims to be World Famous. It's an OK spot if you want a big meal. The small cocktail lounge downstairs is better than the restaurant.

The Red Garter Bed & Bakery at 137 W Railroad Ave is a B&B in a restored 1897 saloon and whore house. It is one of the best places to stay along Route 66. It operated as a brothel for decades after prostitution was outlawed in Arizona. The rooms are the ones where saloon girls plied their trade. They are well appointed with quality furnishings. Some have 12 foot ceilings with skylights. Lodging includes breakfast from its own bakery. There are stories of ghost sightings. The only thing that could improve this place would be the addition of a saloon (and the former pros!).

The Iron Horse

The Frey Marcus Hotel at 233 N Grand Canyon Ave was opened in 1908 inside the Williams Depot and became a Harvey House Hotel. The old hotel no longer is used for guests.

The Buffalo Points Inn at 437 W Route 66 is a pre-1930 house that has been turned into a B&B. It was voted as having the best porch in Williams. It's walking distance from everything.

Twisters Soda Fountain at 417 E Route 66 is a popular stop for sweet refreshments.

Don't forget Pete's Gas Station Museum at 101 E Route 66.

If you need help with your bike, stop in at Grand Canyon Motorsports.

ASH FORK. Ash Fork is known for selling flagstone. There are some vintage motels with cool signs, like the 1928 Copper State Motor Court at

101 Lewis Ave. It took four years to build, largely because it was constructed from cobblestones collected from the Ash Fork area. All of the motels in Ash Fork, including the Copper State, are either closed or in questionable repair.

Traveling east to west, you will come across the DeSoto Salon at 314 W Lewis Ave, with a DeSoto on the roof. Somehow, a DeSoto is cooler than say, a Pontiac.

Going west to east, you will find the Oasis Lounge at 356 W Park Ave, which is the only remaining bar in town. The Green Door Bar and the Arizona Café are long gone. The Oasis is small, and the crowd is totally local, but it's a pretty friendly place.

Ash Fork's DeSoto Salon

A sign at the west end of town will direct you to Route 66. This is a dead end road that leads to a Route 66 Museum at 901 W Old Route 66. It has not been open when I have passed by.

When you leave Ash Fork, you will be starting my favorite ride along Route 66. After a brief stint on I-40, you will head onto over 160 miles of original Route 66 that passes through a dozen little towns, some of which still have thriving motels, restaurants and shops. The road winds through rolling hills, beautiful grasslands and valleys, as well as evergreen forests. There are Burma Shave signs in and out of several towns. Almost all of the ride is out of sight of I-40, and by the end of this ride, you will be in California.

This is what motorcycles are all about. Enjoy!

SELIGMAN. Seligman was founded in 1895 after completion of the Peavine Railroad. I-40 bypassed Seligman's Route 66 in the late 1970's and the railroad discontinued service in 1985. Still, Seligman does pretty well.

The Snow Cap in the snow

Seligman is concentrated in two sections: one is on I-40 and the other is a Downtown area about half a mile off of I-40. Both locations have restaurants and motels, but the area away from I-40 is the more interesting.

The Snow Cap Drive-In at 301 W AZ 66 is one of the most sought out road side burger joints on Route 66. It's a snapshot from the past and a fun stop off. It has been known for decades as a place where the owners play practical jokes on their customers. The only problem is that sometimes the owners spend more time entertaining their customers than serving food. Service can be slooowwwwww. The good news is that you can have cold beer during your wait.

Down the street you will find the World Famous Black Cat Bar at 114 Chino St. It is opened from 9:00 am until 2:00 am. Things can get pretty lively on weekends. They have only bar food.

The the Rusty Bolt on Route 66 at Bolt Ave is three stores in one. The first two have Route 66 gifts and memorabilia. The third has biker accessories like leather jackets and boots.

Be sure to stop and see the Route 66 Motor Museum Downtown.

Near I-40, the Road Kill Café at 502 W AZ 66 is a popular stop off. The locals all say that

Open 9:00 am to 2:00 am

Lilo's across the street at 415 W Chino has the best food in town.

Seligman is at one end of the annual *Fun Run,* in which vintage car owners cruise Route 66 between Seligman and Topock, Arizona.

On the 35 mile ride from Seligman to Peach Springs, you will pass the Grand Canyon Caverns.

PEACH SPRINGS. Peach Springs is a village of only 600 and is the administrative headquarters of the Hualapai People (*People of the Tall Pine*).

In the 1880's, Peach Springs had a railroad water station, 10 saloons, no churches and no schools. It later had a roadhouse and a stage coach line.

In 1932, folks could gas up at Osterman's Shell Station and stay at the

Peach Springs Auto Court. A fire destroyed much of the Auto Court in 1946, but the owners rebuilt. In 1966, a flash flood took out the whole place, and the owners again rebuilt.

There is not much in Peach Springs today except the Hualapai Lodge, which features the River Runners Restaurant.

Truxton. There was no Truxton before Route 66. Truxton was founded in 1951 when Donald Dilts built a service station to accommodate Route 66 travelers. Almost everything is now gone except the Frontier Lounge and the Frontier Motel and Café across the street. The Frontier Motel sign recently has been restored. The Frontier Lounge has a sign saying it's open, but I'm not sure it is. It has not been when I've been by and I was unable to get a phone number.

Valentine. A small scene from *Easy Rider* in which Peter Fonda fixes a flat was filmed in Valentine. Other than that, there is not much in Valentine except an office of the Department of the Interior.

Valentine once offered Carrow's Cabins, which started as a stone restaurant featuring a spring fed swimming pool. Travelers could have a bite to eat and cool off in the pool. Later on, a garage and gas station were added, then later still, a motor court. Carrow's Cabins eventually closed after Valentine was bypassed.

The ride to Hackberry follows the train tracks so closely that you can feel the trains rumble as they chug by.

Hackberry. On the way to Hackberry, you'll pass Bert's Country Dancing. I can't tell whether it is still open, but it's a cool looking place.

The Hackberry Store was opened in 1934 as the Northside Grocery and Conoco Station. It closed in 1978 after I-40 bypassed the town. In 1992, Route 66 artist Bob Waldmire

The Hackberry Store

bought it and opened the Hackberry Store as a tourist center and souvenir shop. Waldmire sold it to the current owners in 1998.

Today, the Hackberry Store is more of a museum than a store, although souvenirs and refreshments are available. There is a 1950's Corvette out front, plus other vintage cars, trucks, signs, gas pumps and vending machines.

Inside are more museum pieces, including an entire diner and soda fountain (non-operational). There are autographed photos of luminaries who have stopped by, plus scores of other photos of TV and movie stars from the Route 66 era, including photos of Martin Milner and George Maharis. If you don't know who they are you should just go home!

The guys will love the photos in the Men's Room. I've never been in the Ladies Room, so I can't vouch for it.

A few miles out of town you'll pass the Kozy Corner Trailer Park. Check out the totem, which they call Giganticus Headicus.

On the 25 mile ride to Kingman, stop by the Outpost Saloon. It's a small, clean place with a cowboy motif. There are old guns, chaps and saddles, and a glass bar with western antiques on display. There also is a nice patio in the back. This is a biker spot despite the cowboy look.

KINGMAN. Kingman is the home of character actor Andy Devine. A lifelong friend of John Wayne, he's the corpulent guy with the froggy voice that played the stage driver in *Stagecoach* and the sheriff in *The Man Who Shot Liberty Vallance*. Kingman's Route 66 is called Andy Devine Blvd.

Andy Devine's father bought the Beale Hotel in 1906, and Andy grew up there. In 1923, the rates ranged from $1.50 to $4.00 per night. The Devine's sold the Beale in 1926 just as Route 66 was opening. It has been closed for years.

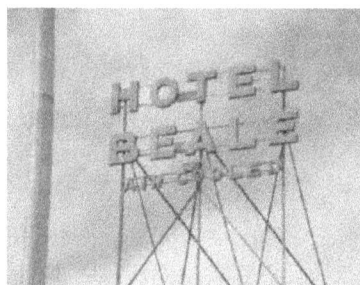

Actor Andy Devine grew up here

The Historic Route 66 Association of Arizona, with its Route 66 Museum, is in Kingman at 120 W Route 66. Locomotive Park, with a giant steam locomotive, is across the street at 310 W Beale St.

The Dambar Steak House at 1960 E Andy Devine welcomes bikers. There is a motorcycle in the entrance way to the bar. There is some nice eye candy too.

The Fireside Cocktail Lounge at 1716 Hoover St also is a good biker spot. It is more Old School than the Dambar.

Mr. D'z Diner at 105 E Andy Devine offers good food in a 1950's atmosphere.

If you are adventurous, try the Big Rig Doll House at 2770 S Hwy 66. It may be the roughest strip joint anywhere. The chicks are, well, edgy. It doesn't serve booze or beer, so everybody goes outside to drink. The doorman has a gun on his belt.

When you are leaving Kingman, you will get to ride the Oatman Hwy. Be careful. I wouldn't try it in bad weather.

West from Kingman to Topock

Follow Route 66/Andy Devine through **Kingman** • Go left at the Y by Locomotive Park following the sign to Oatman • Follow the signs to the Oatman Hwy, and follow it to **Cool Springs**, **Ed's Camp**, **Goldroad**, **Oatman**, **Golden Shores** and **Topock**

East from Kingman to Flagstaff

From **Kingman**, follow Bus 60/Route 66 out of town to **Hackberry** • Continue on AZ 66 to **Valentine**, **Truxton**, **Peach Springs** and **Seligman** • From Seligman, follow Route 66 and go right onto Crookton Rd/Historic 66 • Keep going to I-40 • Get on I-40 and get off at Exit 144 to **Ash Fork** • From Ash Fork, follow Bus 40 through town • Get on I-40 at Exit 146 • Get off I-40 at Exit 161, go left at the end of the off ramp, and follow Bus 40 into **Williams** • From Williams, follow Bus 40 out of town and get on I-40 • Get off at Exit 171 • Go left at the end of the off ramp across I-40, then go right at the dead end; this will be CO Rd 146, but there is no sign. • Follow CO Rd 146 to **Parks** • From Parks, follow CO Rd 146, which becomes N Frontage Rd, to I-40 Exit 185 in **Bellemont** • Get on I-40 at Exit 185 and get off at Exit 191 • Go under I-40 and go right on Bus 40/Route 66 into **Flagstaff**

Cool Springs, Ed's Camp, Goldroad, Oatman, Golden Shores and Topock

COOL SPRINGS. Cool Springs is the first settlement on the Oatman Hwy. It's 15 miles straight across a valley and sits at the foot of Sitgreaves Pass.

It was built in the 1920's, and from the beginning was an important stopping point for gas and supplies for Route 66 motorists. By the 1930's, there were eight cabins and a restaurant specializing in sandwiches and chicken dinners. After Cool Springs was bypassed, it held on for a while, but was burned to the ground in the mid-1960's. Today, all that is left is a small store, gift shop and museum built on the stone remnants of the burned out original structure.

In 1991, it was used as a set (that got blown up) in the Dolph Lundgren-Jean Claude Van Dam movie *Universal Soldier.*

ED'S CAMP. Ed's Camp was founded in the 1920's by Ed Edgerton, who set up the Kactus Café, a gas station, some campgrounds and related facilities to serve local miners. It looks like it has been abandoned for years.

Ed claimed to own the only living Saguaro cactus on Route 66, which he brought in from somewhere else in Arizona. When a Saguaro is transplanted, it needs to be replanted facing in the direction in which it was originally growing. Apparently Ed did not do that, because his cactus is dead.

Wait until you see the mountains on your way to Goldroad. Breathtaking, especially at the top of Sitgreaves Pass.

The Cool Springs Store

GOLDROAD. Goldroad was founded in 1902 when a post office was established there. The post office closed in 1942. Over $7,000,000 of gold was mined between 1903 and 1931. At its peak, Goldroad had 400 residents. Today there is mining going on but you can't see much of the operations.

OATMAN. The first time I visited Oatman I was riding across the Mojave Desert with my friend Connie, who is a full blooded Mescalero Apache. We were trying to get to Kingman coming west from LA. It must have been 120 degrees. We would stop every chance we could to drink water, and we would buy a bag of ice to put in between us. We also bought bottles of water that Connie would pour on us as to keep us a bit cool as we fought our way down the highway.

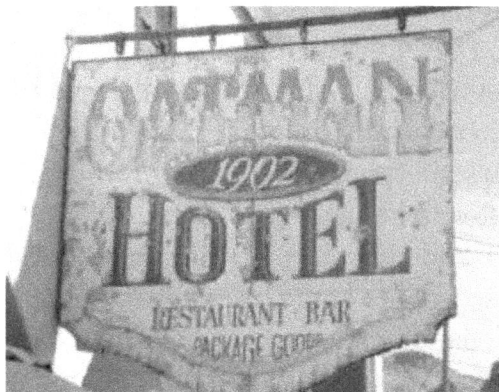

Clark Gable and Carol Lombard eloped to the Oatman Hotel

We decided to go through Oatman because we thought it would be cooler in the mountains and we could wait out the heat before moving on to Kingman. We wound up at the bar in the Oatman Hotel, which turned out to be the only air conditioned place for miles around. We were flat worn out and the Oatman Hotel was the oasis we needed.

As a poignant aside, while there we watched Payne Stewart win golf's US Open on TV. A couple of months later he was killed in a private jet on the way play in the Tour Championship at Champions Golf Club in Houston, where I was a member.

Anyway, keep Oatman in mind as a stop off if the Mojave is getting the better of you.

****

Oatman was a gold mining town named for Olive Oatman, a young girl who was kidnapped and enslaved by the Yavapai Indians. She was sold to the Mojave Indians, who adopted her and had her face tattooed in the Mojave tradition. She was released in 1855 near Oatman.

The Oatman Hotel is where Clark Gable and Carol Lombard went when they eloped. Gable reportedly loved the area and would go there to play poker with the miners. Depending on the state of repair of the Hotel, you can sometimes view the room where they stayed, but you can't check in. The Hotel no longer rents rooms.

Wild burros roam the streets and can be fed by hand. They are the descendants of the pack mules of the old time miners.

Oatman stages a cowboy shoot out in the middle of the street. The street is closed while it's going on. You might as well shut it down and have a beer at the Oatman Hotel Bar.

GOLDEN SHORES. Golden Shores was not developed as a Route 66 town. Instead, it has capitalized on its proximity to the Colorado River.

Uncle Bill's Bar advertises that bikers are welcome but it was closed last time I went by.

TOPOCK. There are some unusual pine trees on the way in to Topock.

Topock is known for boating. It also has the Old Arch Trails Bridge, which used to be the Old Route 66 Bridge. The Bridge was featured in the opening credits of *Easy Rider* and in *The Grapes of Wrath*. It crosses the Colorado River into California.

West to from Topock to Needles California

From **Topock**, get on I-40 and cross the Colorado River into California • Go past the first Exit (ignoring the Route 66 sign) • Go through the Inspection Station and get off I-40 at the Blythe Rd/ US 95 Exit • Go left toward US 95 • Go two miles to a Stop sign and bear right onto US 95 N (becomes Broadway) • Stay on Broadway through Downtown **Needles** • Follow Bus 40 and cross an overpass • Continue to a Stop sign and go left on Needles Hwy

East from Topock to Kingman

From **Topock,** cross I-40 to the Oatman Hwy • Follow the Oatman Hwy to **Golden Shores**, **Oatman**, **Goldroad, Ed's Camp** and **Cool Springs** • Stay on the Oatman Hwy to a Stop sign at I-40 • Go right and cross under I-40 • Go left on the Frontage Rd • Follow the Frontage Rd onto Andy Devine/Route 66 and through Downtown **Kingman**

CALIFORNIA

California here you come!

Route 66 through California has four sections.

The first section starts in Needles, which is a railroad town with lots of Route 66 motels, restaurants and relics. You will find the el Garces, which was a railroad depot and luxury hotel at the beginning of the 20th century. There also is an old covered wagon that the locals claim was used on the TV show *Death Valley Days*.

After leaving Needles, there is good news and bad news. The good news is that you will be traveling on one of the longest remaining stretches of the Old Road, which has such attractions as Roy's in Amboy, the Amboy Crater, the Bagdad Café and the Shoe Tree. The bad news is that this ride is through the Mojave Desert and summer temperatures can top 120 degrees. Take plenty of water and be sure to gas up, because it can be a long way between service stations.

The second section of California's Route 66 goes from Barstow to San Bernardino. You will have to spend time on Interstate highways, but the views over Cajon Pass are spectacular. There will be opportunities to get off of the Interstate and follow some Old Road through some very pretty country.

The third section is from San Bernardino to Pasadena. You will pass the Wigwam Motel in Rialto, and Bono's Deli in Fontana, which has been operated by Sonny's family since the 1930's. Much of this section is through modern towns that have lost their Route 66 *feel*. But it ends in Pasadena This modern city still holds much Route 66 charm, and you will find plenty of vintage motels, bars and restaurants.

The fourth section is from Pasadena to the terminus of Route 66 in Santa Monica. You will follow Santa Monica Blvd for only 10 miles, but those 10 miles can take hours. You will see the *Hollywood* sign, Rodeo Drive in Beverly Hills, the Troubadour, which is one of the legendary music venues in the world, and the Santa Monica Pier at the end of your journey.

Have fun in Sunny California, and congratulate yourself on having finished an honest motorcycle trip that riders worldwide dream of, but only the most adventurous finish.

West from Needles to Barstow

From **Needles**, follow Route 66/Needles Hwy out of town and keep bearing left until you reach a Stop sign • Turn left and get on I-40 • Get off at Exit 133 (Searchlight/Las Vegas) • Follow US 95 N/ Historic Route 66 for 6.4 miles • Before a RR crossing, go left on Goffs Rd • Follow Goffs Rd 14 miles to **Goffs** • From Goffs, follow Goffs Rd to **Fenner** • From Fenner, go under I-40 to the Stop sign at National Trails Hwy (about 4 miles). • Go right to **Essex** (about 2 miles) • From Essex, follow National Trails Hwy to **Chambless**, **Amboy** and **Luddlow** • In Ludlow, go right at the Stop sign onto Crucero Rd and cross over I-40. • Go left on N Frontage Rd/National Trails Hwy • Keep going to **Newberry Springs** • From Newberry Springs, stay on N Frontage Rd/National Trails Hwy for about 11.5 miles to a Stop sign at Dagett Rd • Go straight for about another 2.5 miles to a sharp curve left that will take you onto Nebo Rd • Get on I-40 • Get off at the next Exit, which will be Marine Corps Logistics base. • Go left under I-40 and continue to a Stop sign • Cross some lanes and go right onto the Frontage Rd • Go right at the light at Montara Rd, cross under I-40, and go left onto Bus 15/Main St in **Barstow**

East to Topock

From **Needles**, follow Broadway across I-40 and follow US 95 from town • Go four miles, and bear left onto Five Mile Rd • Get on I-40 and cross the Colorado River into Arizona • Take the Golden Shores/ Oatman Hwy Exit into **Topock**

Needles, Goffs, Fenner, Essex, Chambless, Amboy, Luddlow, Newberry Springs and Barstow

NEEDLES. Needles was known as a railroad hub. As you enter town you'll pass by a wagon that supposedly was used in the 1960's TV show *Death Valley Days*, which was hosted by the great Renaldus Magnus (aka Ronald Reagan). Who knows, maybe it was.

Needles has several vintage motels, the most interesting of which is Fender's River Road Resort at 3396 Needles Hwy. It has a red neon sign and offers river side rooms. It's a bit off of the main drag but there is not all that much on that drag.

The 1906 el Garces at 950 Front St was a hotel and Santa Fe Railroad Depot that has been long abandoned. Efforts have been underway to raise funds to restore this distinctive structure; however, today it is just a shell of a building without windows or doors, and it has been that way as long as I can remember. Still, it's easy to see how impressive it must have been.

The shell of the 1906 el Garces Hotel

Check out the Needles Regional Museum at 929 Front St.

The best biker bar is the Red Dog Saloon at 914 Broadway. This is a simple but clean place with a small bar room and a large room on the side where they sometimes have bands.

When you leave Needles, you will be off I-40 for over 100 miles. The road is sometimes rough, and with a few exceptions, there is not much out there. But the scenery is terrific, and after all, the reason for your trip is to see Old Route 66 in all its glory.

GOFFS. Goff's was a railroad town and a Route 66 stopping point until 1931 when a more direct route was built to connect Needles and Amboy.

The General Store building remains but has been abandoned. There is a restored 1914 school house that hosts a museum featuring the area's mining history.

There is not much else. *No phone. No lights. No motor cars. Not a single lux-u-ree!*

FENNER. Naja's Food and Drink Garden is offensively expensive and they make no apologies about it. On the other hand, it is the only gas or food between there and Ludlow, unless Roy's is open in Amboy, which is never a sure bet.

The first time I traveled this road, I thought I had plenty of gas when I went through Ludlow. I was on fumes by the time I got to Fenner. The thought of being stranded on this lonely stretch of road without water was not appealing. I was glad to pay any price for gas!

ESSEX. Legend has it that Essex was founded when someone had a flat tire and there were no garages for miles. So, he opened a service station that was known for providing free water to travelers. It did not get TV until 1977.

The town had only 89 residents in 2005, and the Elementary School had only four students.

CHAMBLESS. James Chambless and his family moved from Arkansas and established a series of homesteads in California in the early 1930's. Chambless Camp was founded in 1932 and ultimately had a café, a garage a grocery store and cabins available.

During WW II, General Patton trained soldiers near Chambless for desert fighting in the North Africa campaign. Chambless Camp would not serve beer but served lemonade for the soldiers and other customers.

Today, Chambless is owned by Gus Lizalde, who bought it a couple of decades ago out of his love for cars and Route 66.

A biker saloon called Bolo Station recently opened. It will be a good place to get refreshments while riding across the Mojave Desert. I hope it makes it.

Between Chambless and Amboy, look out for the Shoe Tree, where travelers have been tossing old shoes for years. It's located on an overpass on the left hand side of the road as you travel east to west.

Also look for the ruins of the Roadrunner Retreat Café and Station.

AMBOY. Amboy is home to Roy's Motel and Café. It's been in lots of movies and TV commercials.

Roy's was started as a garage in 1927 by Roy Crowls. Roy's daughter Betty married Buster Burris, and in 1940 Buster became Roy's partner. In 1945, Roy and Buster added a 24 hour café and in 1948 added a motel and expanded the café. At one time Roy's had 90 full-time employees.

Roy's once had 90 employees

Roy's did not fare well when I-40 bypassed Amboy and it has not offered full services for years. It currently has a small convenience store that sells soft drinks, pre-packaged food and gas, but there is no kitchen or motel. It is not always open, so don't count on being able to get gas there.

Despite having limited operations, the facility is in good repair. Rumors of restoration efforts are out there but there does not appear to be much progress.

The Amboy Crater is a few miles west toward Ludlow. This is a volcanic crater, not a meteor crater like the one in Arizona. It was formed about 6,000 years ago and last erupted about 500 years ago. It is 250 feet high and 1,500 feet across. Climbing is allowed, and there is a walking trail to the top that will let you peer into the crater.

LUDLOW. Ludlow prospered from the Tonopah and Tidewater Railroad, which shipped borax between Ludlow and Beatty, Nevada. The railroad shut down in 1940.

The Amboy Crater

The big site is the 1908 Ludlow Mercantile Company building. Ludlow Mercantile was opened by John Denair, who borrowed the money to build the store from Mother Preston, who owned a saloon and rooming house catering to railroad workers. Denair went broke, so Preston took over the store and operated it until 1918, when she sold it to one of her competitors, who moved his business into the Ludlow Mercantile building. He added a 24 hour garage and a motor court to take advantage of Route 66 traffic. The building has been abandoned and is falling down.

The Ludlow Café is open, and the Ludlow Motel gets pretty good reviews for a motel in the middle of nowhere.

Gas is available at a nearby Chevron Station. If you are heading east be sure to gas up. The next chance might be a long way away.

Route 66 between Ludlow and Newberry Springs is rough. It will rattle you (and your bike) to pieces. You might consider taking I-40 (which is pretty rough itself) for this stretch.

NEWBERRY SPRINGS. Newberry Springs has the Bagdad Café from the movie by that name. It is the original building used in the movie, but is not the original Bagdad Café, which was in in the now lost town of Bagdad near Amboy. The remnants of the motel used in the movie are nearby. There also is a well preserved fenced in Whiting Bros Station.

The Barn looks like a good bar.

BARSTOW. Downtown Barstow originally was situated along the railroad tracks. Today, it follows Bus 15 in a long straight shot through town. It's a perfect strip for cruising on a motorcycle or in a hot rod.

There are vintage motels with fun neon signs, including a miniature Roy's sign at the nowclosed Juan Pollo Mexican Restaurant. The El Rancho is built out of railroad ties.

Barstow's 1911 Casa del Desierto

There also are murals depicting Barstow's history.

On the way into town, you will see a sign for the Harvey House Hotel. This was the 1911 Casa del Desierto in the original Barstow Downtown area by the railroad tracks. It now serves as the Amtrak depot. The Barstow Route 66 Mother Road Museum and the Western America Railroad Museum are there. It is a bit hard to find. Although there is a big sign as you come into town, it actually is almost all the way across town, and the sign directing you there is small. Be on the look-out for a right hand turn near the Village Hotel sign.

West from Barstow to San Bernardino

From **Barstow**, follow Bus 15 out of town onto National Trails Hwy • Follow National Trails Hwy to **Lenwood,Hodge,Helendale** and **Oro Grande** • From Oro Grande, follow National Trails Hwy across an iron bridge over the Mojave River • Cross under I-15 to Bus 15/D St • Go right onto 7th St through **Victorville** • Get on I-15 toward San Bernardino • Follow I-15 for about 18 miles and get off at the Cleghorn Rd Exit • Go right at the end of the Exit onto Cajon Blvd • Go six miles to where the road dead ends and go left onto Kenwood Ave to I-15 • Get on I-15 S • Get in the left lanes and follow I-215 toward San Bernardino • Take the next Exit (Devore Rd) into **Devore** • Go left following the Historic Route 66 sign • From Devore, stay on Cajon Blvd for about 10 miles to Mt Vernon St • Go left on Mt Vernon into **San Bernardino**

East from Barstow to Needles

From **Barstow**, follow Main St/Bus 15 out of town • Go under I-40 and go left on E Main St/S Frontage Rd •At the next chance, get on I-40 • Get off at the next Exit (Nebo Rd), go left under I-40 on Nebo Rd, and follow National Trails Hwy going east • Go straight at the Stop sign at Daggett and keep going to **Newberry Springs** • From Newberry Springs, follow National Trails Hwy until the road comes to a T at Crucero Rd • Go right and cross I-40, then go left in front of the Ludlow Café onto National Trails Hwy into **Ludlow** • From Ludlow, follow National Trails Hwy to **Amboy**, **Chambless** and **Essex** • From Essex, follow National Trails Hwy for two miles • Watch for a *To I-40* sign • Go left on Goffs Rd (be alert; there is no sign) • Follow Goffs Rd under I-40 to **Fenner** and **Goffs** • From Goffs, follow Goffs Rd to US 95 • Go right onto US 95 to I-40 East • Take the River Rd Cutoff Exit, cross I-40, then go right on National Trails Hwy following the Route 66 signs • Merge into Needles Hwy, cross I-40, and follow Bus 40 into Needles • Bear right on Broadway following the Historic Route 66 signs through Downtown **Needles** (Route 66/Bus 40 will take a sharp right halfway through town; be careful not to miss the turn)

Lenwood, Hodge, Helendale, Oro Grande, Victorville, Devore and San Bernardino

LENWOOD. Barstow just fades away as you head out of Barstow toward Lenwood. Lenwood is sparse, but Gusto's Bar has a *Bikers Welcome* sign. It looks a bit rough.

HODGE. Hodge has the *Two 66s Co* sign. Locals tell me the Two 66s is a cattle ranch. I couldn't find any reference to it through a Google search. I have no clue whether the Two 66s relate to Route 66 or to something else. Anyway, it's a cool sign.

Yikes! Check out these gas prices

HELENDALE. Newton's Towing has an old Polly Gas Station sign featuring a large parrot and the prices for gas in a bygone era. I can't remember gas being 18.9 cents a gallon, but I can remember when it was less than a quarter.

Helendale has the Bottle Tree Ranch, which consists of hundreds of colorful bottles on metal stands arranged to look like trees. There also are lots of old Route 66 and other roadside style artifacts. Keep a sharp lookout or you will breeze right past it.

The Exotic World Burlesque Museum and Hall of Fame used to be on a goat farm just outside of Helendale. Unfortunately, it was moved to Las Vegas and has since closed.

Keep a lookout for a sign directing you to Roy Rodgers' Double R Bar Ranch.

ORO GRANDE. When riding into Oro Grande, you'll finally hit some soft curves and hills after being on the long straight road from Barstow.

The Bottle Tree Ranch

You'll pass by the Iron Hog Saloon. In the 1890's, it was a Wells Fargo switching station, and it has been a bar since the 1930's. Roy Rogers' ranch was nearby, and Roy and Dale Evans were frequent guests. They each carved the brand of the Ranch into the bar. It was in the movies *Easy Rider*, *Poker Run*, and *Erin Brockovitch*.

Today, the Iron Hog is an Old School biker joint with everything an Old School biker could want. There is cold beer, booze, an outside patio, Go Go Dancers, food, and a big property to have cook-outs.

I happened to stop in the night before their Grand Reopening. They

Roy Rogers frequented this bar

had been closed for nearly a year because a dispute with the local power company had left them without electricity. I drank Crown with the owner for a few hours and he told me about the history of the place and the plans he had for the reopening.

There were a bunch of chicks making home made hard candies that were going to be handed out at the Grand Opening. I grabbed one and popped it in my mouth. It tasted a bit odd, so I spit it out. I mentioned to one of the confectioners that the candy tasted funny. She told me "Of course it did, they are made with pot"! No more of that for me.

On your way to Victorville, you will find Emma Jean's Holland Burger. It's a small place where folks prefer to sit at the counter rather than the tables. Emma Jean's was opened in 1947 as the Holland Café by Bob and Katherine Holland. They sold it to Emma Jean in 1979 and she changed the name to Emma Jean's Holland Burger. Today it is run by Emma Jean's son Brian and his wife. This place has good food and a national following. Part of the movie *Kill Bill* was filmed there and it has been featured on *Dives, Drive-ins and Diners*.

VICTORVILLE. I've only stayed in Victorville once and it was *different*.

I had been planning to stay at the New Corral Motel because it has a distinctive restored Route 66 sign with a rearing neon palomino. I asked a local how it was, and he euphemistically told me that I could "meet some chicks" there. Not to be deterred, I stopped into a local bar and asked about the

The restored New Corral sign

New Corral, and the bartender told me that if I stayed there I "...definitely would get robbed."

So much for the New Corral. I wound up staying at the Green Tree Inn, which was pretty worn, but overall OK. It had its own bar and restaurant. I didn't meet any chicks, but at least I didn't get robbed.

I Googled local bars, and it appeared that a place called T-Zers was the place to go. I asked the clerk in the lobby of the Green Tree how to get there, and she told me it was closed because two people had been murdered there a couple of days previously. So much for T-Zers.

I looked for another bar and wound up at Johnnie Fingers Sports Bar at 15863 Lorene Dr. It turned out to be a pretty friendly place with cold beer and good drinks.

While I was there, someone came in and asked if we had any news about a shooting at the Dollar General. The bartender said she had heard about it an hour or so previously. The guys who had come in said that the police just got there.

Like I said, Victorville was *different*.

Be sure to visit the California Route 66 Museum at 16825 S D St just before following Route 66 along Bus 15 on Victorville's 7th Street, which is the main drag.

If you are hungry, just before getting on I-15 heading toward Devore and San Bernardino, try Richie's American Diner at 14326 Valley Center Dr. It has been around only about 20 years,but it has a 1950's feel, with its black and white checkered floor, turquoise upholstered booths and luncheonette counter. They smoke their own hams, chickens, steaks and other meats. There are some vintage Route 66 photos.

The next town is Devore, and you'll have to get on I-15 to get there, but it is a beautiful ride with views of mountain vistas. You'll also get off the interstate to follow the Old Road through a canyon following some railroad tracks with I-15 over 100 feet above you in some places. This short ride is one of the prettiest on California's Route 66, so don't be tempted to skip it by staying on I-15.

The Screaming Chicken: *Not for Posers, RUBS or Wannabes*

DEVORE. At the Devore Exit off of I-215, if you go right instead of left toward San Bernardino, you'll hit the Screaming Chicken Saloon at 18169 Cajon Blvd, which is an Old School biker bar. The signs outside say *Hot Babes* and *Not for Posers, RUBS or Wannabe's*. Sounds like a good joint.

The ride into San Bernardino follows railroad tracks and passes by industrial neighborhoods and several Route 66 relics, like the Palms Motel and the Lido Motel at the edge of town. The road can get a bit bumpy but it is tolerable.

SAN BERNARDINO. Depending on who you talk to, the Hells Angels were founded in San Berdoo (if the person you talk to is Sonny Barger, he might tell you it was Oakland).

San Bernardino along Route 66 follows Mt Vernon St down one long strip. There are lots of Route 66 relics and vintage motels along here but the motels look rough. There is a Holiday Inn that obviously is not part of the chain.

The 1937 Milta Café at 602 N Mt Vernon Ave serves pretty good Mexican food.

Will Rogers made his last appearance at the 1928 California Theater at 562 W 4th St.

West from San Bernardino to Santa Monica

Follow Mt Vernon through San Bernardino. • Go right on 5th St, which becomes Foothill Blvd, to **Rialto, Fontana, Rancho Cucamonga, Upland, Claremont, LaVerne, San Dimas, Glendora, Azusa,** and **Duart**e • From Duarte, follow Huntington Dr • Cross Mountain Ave • Go right on Shamrock Ave • Go left on Foothill Blvd in **Monrovia** • Go about 2½ miles then go left on Santa Anita Ave • Go right on Colorado Blvd into **Pasadena** • Follow Colorado Blvd across town• Cross Marenga and go left on Arroyo Pkwy/Hwy 110 • Take Exit 24B/ To Sunset Blvd • At the Stop sign, go left, cross the overpass and take an immediate right onto Figueroa St • Go right onto Sunset Blvd and follow it for about three miles through

Echo Park in **Los Angeles** ·After crossing Sanborne, go about 100 feet then go left on Manzania (this is a hard sign to see so keep alert) · Go 100 feet then go right on Santa Monica Blvd and follow it to **Santa Monica** · Cross 9th St and then go left on Lincoln Blvd to Olympic · **The corner of Lincoln and Olympic is the terminus of Route 66**

East from San Bernardino to Barstow

From **San Bernardino**, follow Mt Vernon out of town · Pass 19th St, get in the right hand lane and go straight onto Cajon Ave (if you reach 20th St you've gone too far) · Follow Cajon Ave to **Devore** · From Devore, follow Cajon Blvd to a Stop sign at Cajon Blvd/Devore Rd · Go right at the stop sign (the sign to Cajon/Devore Rd is small; if you miss the turn, you will wind up at a dead end a couple of hundred yards past the turn off) · Cross over I-215 and take an immediate right onto I-215 N · Follow I-215 past the I-15 S sign to I-15 N · Take the first Exit, which will be Kenwood Ave · Go left, cross under I-15, then go right onto Cajon Blvd · Go six miles, bear right from Cajon Blvd, go under I-15 and get on I-15 · Follow I-15 and get off at the Hwy 18/Palmdale Exit toward **Victorville.** · Follow Historic 66 to 7th St · Go right on 7th St and follow 7th St through town · Go left when 7th St dead ends at Bus 15/D St, which becomes National Trails Hwy · Keep going to **Oro Grande**, **Helendale**, **Hodge**, **Lenwood** and into **Barstow** on Bus 15

Rialto, Fontana, Rancho Cucamonga, Upland, Claremont, La Verne, San Dimas, Glendora, Azuza, Duarte, Monrovia, Pasadena, Los Angeles and Santa Monica

RIALTO. Rialto was settled by Indians before the year 1500. In 1769, the King of Spain awarded portions of current Rialto to certain well to do Spaniards.

Mormons came to the area in 1851. By 1854, families began migrating in and establishing vineyards, citrus groves and ranches. There is an adobe house from this period in Lilac Park.

The second of the Wigwam Motels is here at 2728 W Foothill Ave. It is in better shape than the one in Holbrook, Arizona. The rooms are bigger, and have modern

The Wigwam Motel in Rialto

furniture and flat screen TVs. If you like cigars, they often get smoked with management out by the pool. Be sure to make reservations in the warm weather months. Even if you can't stay, this photo op is a must.

Rialto's Pyro Spectaculars is one of the biggest fireworks companies in the United States.

FONTANA. This is another town (along with San Bernardino and Oakland) that claims to be where the Hells Angels were founded.

Bono's Deli has been in operation by the Bono family since 1936. Their Giant Orange Stand remains out front. There is a deli, a restaurant and a wine bar in the back. I stopped in and met Joe Bono, who gave me a tour. Joe is Sonny's cousin, and he showed me a picture of Sonny and his *other* wife with President Reagan.

Sonny's family's deli since 1936

The Bono family came to Fontana in the 1930's and owned a vineyard. There is a large wooden cask in the Deli's wine bar that the Bono's used to mash grapes during their vineyard days.

There once were over 50 bonded vineyards in the Fontana area. Now there are none. Joe tells me he can remember when Fontana was rural and Route 66 in front of the Deli was one lane in each direction.

Bono's was being remodeled when I was last there and hopefully it has reopened.

Near Bono's, you will find Downtown Cycle, which does a brisk custom and repair business.

In the 1950's and 60's, Fontana had Mickey Thompson's Fontana International Dragway, also called Fontana Drag City or the Fontana Drag Strip. It was on the NHRA circuit. The original drag strip is gone, but in 2006, the owners of NASCAR's Auto Club Speedway opened a new NHRA drag strip.

RANCHO CUCAMONGA. Rancho Cucamonga has two Route 66 icons. The first is the Sycamore Inn, which started as a stagecoach stop in 1848 and has been operating since then in ever nicer structures. The other is the Magic Lamp Inn, which has a cool magic lamp sign. They both are upscale places and are across the street from each other.

The Sycamore Inn since 1848

Hall of Fame pitcher Rollie Fingers is from Rancho Cucamonga. Also, the LA Dodgers Class A minor league Rancho Cucamonga Quakes are there.

UPLAND. Upland was founded in 1906 as an agricultural community focusing on citrus groves and grapes. There was a mule powered trolley to transport passengers from Upland to the Southern Pacific Railroad line in a neighboring town.

Today, Upland is a skateboarding Mecca because it is where vertical pool and pipe skateboarding originated. The Pipeline Skate Park opened in 1977 and featured a 20 foot pipe that was the predecessor of the Baldy Pipe and the Monster Bowl.

Madonna of the Trail

One of the 12 Madonna of the Trail statues put up across the country by the Daughters of the American Revolution is in Upland at the corner of Foothill and Euclid Ave. There are two on Route 66. The other is in Albuquerque.

CLAREMONT. Claremont calls itself *The City of Trees and PhD's* because of its tree lined streets and residents with doctoral degrees. The Claremont Colleges and the Claremont Institute are there. Money Magazine once named Claremont as the 5th best place to live in the United States. That was the highest rating of any California town.

Wolfe's Market has been operating in Claremont since 1917 and has been in its current Route 66 location since 1935. As its sign says, *It is not a supermarket, it's a Super Market.* It is small, but upscale, with first rate produce, meats and deli products. There also is a good wine selection. If you are hungry, you can get a quick sandwich and eat it outside on their deck.

Starting in Claremont, the ride west toward LA is more tree-lined and less congested. There still are lots of traffic lights, but you can make good time through here, and the ride is much less frustrating than the previous 20 miles or so.

LA VERNE. The University of La Verne is a nationally recognized private college founded in 1891.

Boxer Sugar Shane Mosley, football players Freddie Brown and Glenn Davis, and entertainers Jessica Albers and Jeffery Garcia all are from La Verne.

The La Paloma Café serves good Mexican food.

SAN DIMAS. San Dimas takes its name from San Dimas Canyon in the San Gabriel Mountains.

The street lights entering San Dimas have banners naming the local men and women who serve in the US military. Each banner names a different service person and the branch of the military service in which the they serve.

Good for you San Dimas!

San Dimas was where *Bill and Ted's Excellent Adventure* was filmed.

San Dimas is home to the Pinnacle Steak House at 269 W Foothill Blvd. It has a big steer and Conestoga Wagon sign.

GLENDORA. Glendora keeps up the San Dimas tribute to its service men and women by putting up banners honoring them by name and identifying their military branches.

Good for you Glendora!

Glendora has the Golden Spur Restaurant at 1223 E Route 66. It has a spurred boot neon sign.

The Our Place Lounge at 240 E Route 66 looks like a good stopping place for a cold beer.

AZUSA. Azuza is known as the Canyon City because it is near the entrance to San Gabriel Canyon.

Route 66 into Azusa follows a couple of hundred yards of double wide pre-fab homes that are shaded by some beautiful copper beach trees.

Azusa's 1960's drive in theater

The Foothills Drive-In Theatre has an angled marquis so it can be seen from both directions. It opened in 1961 with the movies *Babes in Arms* and *Misty*, and had its last showing in 2001 with *Harry Potter and the Sorcerer's Stone* and *Oceans's Eleven*. The theatre no longer is in operation but the marquis is to be preserved.

DUARTE. Duarte hosts an annual *Salute to Route 66 Parade* on the third weekend of September.

Duarte has a variation on the themes in San Dimas and Glendora, which have banners on their lamp posts honoring their military service men and women. Duarte has banners with the names of its recent high school graduates and the colleges they are attending. What a nice way to commemorate their achievements.

The Justice Brothers Racing Museum at 2734 E Huntington Dr sells car care products worldwide and has sponsored dozens of high profile drivers such as A J Foyt.

MONROVIA. On Shamrock Ave you will find Dale's Garage, which is a vintage gas station with well-preserved antique gas pumps.

The 1924 Aztec Hotel at 311 W Foothill Ave is said to be one of the best examples of Mayan revival architecture. So, you would think it would have been named the Mayan Hotel. In any event, it is being remodeled. It has an old time fan system where all the fans operate off of a single drive belt. The restaurant and bar have reopened. The rest of the hotel is scheduled to open in 2014.

Dale's Garage

Perhaps the best part of Monrovia is the stretch of buildings along Foothill Blvd. They look like they must have been 60 years ago when Route 66 was thriving. It looks so safe that grade school children can walk home unattended. It's a jump back in time to the days of Ward, June, Wally and the Beaver.

PASADENA. The little old lady from Pasadena is the terror of Colorado Blvd, which is Route 66 in Pasadena. Colorado Blvd is a wide street with two spacious lanes on each side lined with palm trees. There are vintage and modern motels and you won't have any problem finding a nice affordable place to stay. One of the best is the Saga at 1633 E Colorado Blvd.

As you come into town, look for R Place Cocktail Lounge at 3739 E Colorado Blvd on the right hand side of the street. It has wonderful turquoise upholstered booths. This Old School place has style and biker's are welcome.

A quarter mile or so past R Place, look for Villain Custom Cycles, which has Harley-Davidson parts and a service shop.

The Colorado Bar at 2460 E Colorado Blvd also is a good place with a bit of a younger crowd.

The Rite Spot Restaurant at 1500 W Colorado Blvd claims to have invented the cheeseburger in 1924. Louie's Lunch in New Haven, Connecticut may have an argument there. Louie's, a Yalie hangout for over a century, claims to have invented the hamburger in 1900.

Just a bit out of town to the east, you can find the 100-to-1 Cocktail Lounge at 100 W Huntington Dr near Santa Anita Park (the horse track). I found this bar when I was lost trying to find my way along Route 66. Some locals gave me directions that turned out to be perfect. This is a biker friendly place where you will have a terrific time.

The west end of town is the older section. There is a mix of modern construction that blends in well with the older buildings. It is a trendy area, but I got away with wearing my patch in Smitty's at 110 S Lake Ave, which is an upscale local favorite.

Great bar outside Pasadena

The Rose Bowl is nestled into a residential neighborhood on this side of town at 1001 Rose Bowl Dr.

LOS ANGELES. When you come into LA, you'll be near Dodger Stadium, and you soon will be in the Echo Park neighborhood. This is a colorful section of town with a bohemian atmosphere.

So far so good, but you are about to hit Santa Monica Blvd for the home stretch. Be prepared: the traffic is horrible almost all the time, and your 10 mile ride to Santa Monica and the terminus of Route 66 may take hours.

If you look to your right as you start down Santa Monica Blvd, you can catch a peek at the *Hollywood* sign. It's hard to see, but if you get a glimpse, you might want to take a brief detour down one of the side streets for a better view and a photo op.

You'll pass through West Hollywood near the corner of Hollywood and Vine. There are signs to the Avenue of the Stars. You'll also pass by Barney's Beanery, which is billed as the third oldest restaurant in LA.

Just before getting to Santa Monica, you'll go past the Troubadour at 9081 Santa Monica Blvd, which has been one of LA's best small venues for quality live music since 1957.

When you go through Beverly Hills, you'll see the palm tree lined streets to your right, and you'll go past Rodeo Drive on your left.

1950's diner on Route 66 in LA

SANTA MONICA. The terminus of Route 66 is a bit anti-climactic. It is not on the Pacific ocean. Rather, it is on the corner of Olympic and Lincoln a few blocks from the water. There is no sign indicating you are at the end of Route 66. Plus, it is a big intersection, and you can't tell which corner is the actual terminus. If you ask people who work in the surrounding buildings which corner is the end of Route 66 they won't have a clue what you are talking about.

The Will Rogers Hwy Marker at in Palisades Park at the Junction of Santa Monica Blvd and Ocean Ave is the better photo op for the end of your journey. Get your picture taken there, then head over to the Santa Monica Pier. It's fun, and there are some interesting Route 66 shops.

I usually stay at the Georgian Hotel at 1415 Ocean Ave across the street from the Will Rogers Hwy Marker. The prices are reasonable by Santa Monica standards. There are ocean views and nicely appointed rooms. There is safe bike parking in the

The Will Rogers Highway Marker near the terminus of Route 66

back. The only drawback is that although you can get a drink at a lobby bar, there is no real bar to hang out in. Not to worry; there are dozens of bars and restaurants nearby.

Congratulations, you have just completed one of the great road trip adventures in the world. Only one thing left to do. Turn around and ride back to Chicago!

East from Santa Monica to San Bernardino

From Olympic Blvd in **Santa Monica**, go to Lincoln Blvd then go right on Santa Monica Blvd • As you approach Downtown **Los Angeles**, pass Hoover and stay in the right lane of Santa Monica Blvd, which will merge into Sunset Blvd • From Sunset Blvd, go past the 110 Freeway to Figueroa • Go left on Figueroa, and get on Hwy 110 (Pasadena Freeway) toward Pasadena • When the freeway ends, keep going straight on Arroyo Pkwy to Colorado Blvd, go right and follow it through **Pasadena** • Pass Princeton St • Where Colorado Terrace and Colorado Blvd meet, go left at the light staying with Colorado Blvd (these are complicated turns and it's easy to miss Colorado Blvd at the east end of Pasadena; if you get to the Santa Anita Racetrack, you have missed the turn) • Go past a RR underpass and go left onto Santa Anita Ave in **Monrovia** • Cross under I-210 and go right onto Foothill Blvd • Go about 2.5 miles, cross California Ave and go right on Shamrock Ave • Go left on Huntington Dr, which will become Foothill Ave • Follow Foothill to **Duarte, Azusa, Glendora, San Dimas, La Verne, Claremont, Upland, Rancho Cucamonga, Fontana** and **Rialto** • From Rialto, follow Foothill Blvd into **San Bernardino** • Foothill Blvd will become 4th St and then curve left onto 5th St • Pass Roberts St and go left on Mt Vernon

MOTORCYCLE SHOPS

This chapter lists the motorcycle shops nearest to each town along my suggested pathway across Route 66. The dealerships for all the major motorcycle manufacturers are listed, along with all of the local custom and repair shops I could find. Shops in towns near but not on Route 66 have been included. The goal is for you to be able to find the nearest help in case of a break down. So, redundant listings are intentional.

The towns are listed in the order they arise on the suggested route from Chicago to Santa Monica. Towns in the alternate routes appear at the end of each State's listings.

ILLINOIS

CHICAGO

ACE Motorcycle and Scooter Co
1042 W Jackson Blvd
Chicago, IL 60607
(312) 432-0955

Capt'ns Chi City Cycles
4216 W Ogden Ave
Chicago, IL 60623
(773) 542-2004

Champion Cycle Center
3625 N Western Ave
Chicago, IL 60618
(773) 528-6500

Chewie's Motorbikes
2701 W Chicago Ave
Chicago, IL 60622
(773) 252-2439

Chicago Harley-Davidson
6868 N Western Ave
Chicago, IL 60645
(773) 338-6868

Chicago Harley-Davidson Downtown
66 E Ohio St
Chicago, IL 60611
(312) 274 9666

Motoworks Chicago
1901 S Western Ave
Chicago, IL 60608
(312) 738-4269

The Zone Honda Kawasaki
4520 W 63rd St
Chicago, IL 60629
(773) 767-7280

Village Cycle Center
1337 N Wells St
Chicago, IL 60610
(312) 751-2488

Windy City Harley-Davidson
O'Hare International
Airport Terminal 3
Chicago, IL 60666
(773) 686-4886

BERWYN

Illinois Harley-Davidson
1301 S Harlem Ave
Berwyn, IL 60402
(708) 788 1300

LYONS

Otto Brothers Honda
7837 Ogden Ave
Lyons, IL 60534
(708) 447-3040

COUNTRYSIDE

Highlands Yamaha
5320 East Ave
Countryside, IL 60525
(708) 246-4003

Joliet
Willy World Cycles
101 N Reed St
Joliet, IL 60435
(815) 725-4666

PONTIAC

Chuck's Harley-Davidson
2027 Ireland Grove Rd
Bloomington, IL 61704
(309) 662-1648

Garrels Honda
1101 E Howard St
Pontiac, IL 61764
(815) 842-3175

NORMAL

Team Automotive
1223 S Adelaide St
Normal, IL 61761
(309) 319-6829

BLOOMINGTON

Bombshell Handcrafted Customs
704 S McLean St
Bloomington, IL 61701
(309) 828-0700

Bombshell Handcrafted Customs
704 S McLean St
Bloomington, IL 61701
(309) 828-0700

Boss Hoss By Siron Automotive
2415 Bunn St
Bloomington, IL 61704
(309) 827-7611

Chuck's Harley-Davidson
2027 Ireland Grove Rd
Bloomington, IL 61704
(309) 662-1648

Sportland Motorsports
2045 Ireland Grove Rd
Bloomington, IL 61704
(309) 662-0508

Taurus Cycle
1 Lafayette Court
Bloomington, IL 61701
(309) 454-1565

LINCOLN

C & C Cycles
1314 5th St
Lincoln, IL 62656
(217) 735-1191

SPRINGFIELD

Capital City Motorsports
4863 Rodger St # A
Springfield, IL 62703
(217) 529-8850

Hall's Cycle
3801 N Dirksen Pkwy
Springfield, IL 62707
(217) 789-0107

Halls Harley-Davidson
2301 N Dirksen Pkwy
Springfield, IL 62702
(217) 528-8356

Kapitol City Kustoms
987 Estill Dr
Springfield, IL 62707
(217) 522-0875

Lost Highway Choppers & Hot Rods
2101 N Grand Ave E
Springfield, IL 62702
(217) 899-0630

Overturf Powersports
1633 N Dirksen Pkwy
Springfield, IL 62702
(217) 544-0126

RTD Motor Sports
2430 N Dirksen Pkwy
Springfield, IL 62702
(217) 528-5859

AUBURN

Lou's Cycle Services
115 N Iris Dr
Auburn, IL 62615
(217) 438-6043

CARLINVILLE

Right Way Motor Repair
210 Pershing St
Carlinville, IL 62626
(217) 854-8202

Ted's Harley-Davidson of Alton
4103 Humbert Rd
Alton, IL 62002
(618) 462-3030

STAUNTON

Crossbones Motorsports
717 N Edwardsville St
Staunton, IL 62088
(618) 635-8212

MITCHELL

J & J Speed Shop
2210 Nameoki Rd
Granite City, IL 62040
(618) 451-7974

LITCHFIELD

Action Cycle Vintage
1449 E Union Ave
Litchfield, IL 62056
(217) 324-6015

Niehaus Cycle Sales
718 N Sherman St
Litchfield, IL 62056
(217) 324-6565

Right Way Motor Repair
210 Pershing St
Carlinville, IL 62626
(217) 854-8202

Ted's Harley-Davidson of Alton
4103 Humbert Rd
Alton, IL 62002
(618) 462-3030

MISSOURI

ST LOUIS

Archway International Motorcycle
6300 Dr MLK Dr
St Louis, MO 63133
(314) 385-3334

Canyon Run
2222 S Jefferson Ave
St Louis, MO 63104
(314) 865-2665

Cycle House Performance
8732 Watson Rd
St Louis, MO 63119
(314) 270-3312

Donelson Cycles Inc
9851 Saint Charles Rock Rd
St Louis, MO 63074
(314) 427-1204

Gateway Harley-Davidson
3600 Lemay Ferry Rd
St Louis, MO 63125
(314) 845-9900

Motorcycle Mortuary
2400 S Jefferson Ave
St Louis, MO 63104
(314) 771-4105

Mungenast St Louis Honda
5939 S Lindbergh Blvd
St Louis, MO 63123
(314) 649-1330

Rich's Cycle Center
9500 Gravois Rd
St Louis, MO 63123
(314) 631-1300

Roadworthy Motorcycles Inc
7020 Page Ave
St Louis, MO 63133
(314) 725-9203

Royalty Racing
920 Dock St
St Louis, MO 63147
(314) 621-7777

Southside Custom Cycles
2327 Texas Ave
St Louis, MO 63104
(314) 773-3000

Widman Motorcycles
3628 S Broadway
St Louis, MO 63118
(314) 771-7100

WEBSTER GROVES

Cycle House Performance
8738 Watson Rd
Webster Groves, MO 63119
314 849 5577

Doc's Harley-Davidson
930 S Kirkwood Rd
Kirkwood, MO 63122
(314) 965-0166

ELLISVILLE

D & C Cycle Parts & Performance
123 N Central Ave
Eureka, MO 63025
(636) 938-4343

GRAY SUMMIT

BD & C Cycle Parts & Performance
123 N Central Ave
Eureka, MO 63025
(636) 938-4343

ST CLAIR

Bourbeuse Valley Harley-Davidson
1418 Hwy AT
Villa Ridge, MO 63089
(636) 742-2707

SULLIVAN

Moonlight Racing
State Hwy K
Sullivan, MO 63080
(636) 629-0223

CUBA

RJay's Speed Shop
7079 State Hwy ZZ
Cuba, MO 65453
(866) 439-7529

ST JAMES

Farris Customs
22331 Hwy KK
St James, MO 65559
(573) 205-8936

ROLLA

Hooligan Cycles
12975A S 63
Rolla, MO 65401
(573) 205-6311

Interstate Motorcycles
12570 Old Route 66
Rolla, MO 65401
(573) 265-6008

Stahlman Powersports
1387 S Bishop Ave
Rolla, MO 65401
(573) 364-6944

WAYNESVILLE

Skyline Honda Yamaha
25515 Hwy 17
Waynesville, MO 65583
(573) 774-2008

LEBANON

Lebanon Cycle Center
2410 Industrial Dr
Lebanon, MO 65536
(417) 532-9253

LSK Lebanon
801 N Jefferson Ave
Lebanon, MO 65536
(417) 588-3550

Ozark Harley-Davidson
2300 Evergreen Pkwy
Lebanon, MO 65536
(417) 532-2900

MARSHFIELD

Steel Thunder Custom Cycles
3410 Teague's Rd
Marshfield, MO 65706
(417) 468-2326

SPRINGFIELD

Chubby Customs
1666 E St Louis St
Springfield, MO 65802
(417) 655-0404

Cruisin' 66
1310 S Glenstone Ave
Springfield, MO 65804
(417) 891-9998

Denney's Harley-Davidson
3980 W Sunshine
Springfield, MO 65807
(417) 882-0100

JJ's Cycles
3670 S Glenstone Ave
Springfield, MO 65804
(417) 883-1065

Springfield Yamaha
5183 E Kearney St
Springfield, MO 65803
(417) 862-4343

Twin Motorcycle & Tattoo
2518 W College Rd
Springfield, MO 65802
(417) 832-1534

CARTHAGE

Carthage Auto Race Repair (C.A.R.R.)
2488 Old 66 Blvd
Carthage, MO 64836

Mike's Motorcycles
2007 Hazel St
Carthage, MO 64836
(417) 358-4943

Route 66 Ridley Motorcycles
2488 W Old 66 Blvd
Carthage, MO 64836
(417) 358-8441

JOPLIN

2 Bros Cycle
1402 Wisconsin Ave
Joplin, MO 64801
(417) 621-0557

Crazy Frank's Cycle
RR 3 Box 127
Joplin, MO 64801
(417) 781-6577

Cycle Connection Harley-Davidson
5014 Hearnes Blvd
Joplin, MO 64804
(417) 623-1054

Mid-America Motorcycle Rebuilders
8399 E 7th St
Joplin, MO 64801
(417) 781-9232

Mid-America Motorcycle Rebuilders
8399 E 7th St
Joplin, MO 64801
(417) 781-9232

Powersports of Joplin
4770 E 32nd St
Joplin, MO 64804
(417) 623-4661

KANSAS

GALENA

2 Bros Cycle
1402 Wisconsin Ave Suite B
Joplin, MO 64801
(417) 621-0557

Cycle Connection Harley-Davidson
5014 Hearnes Blvd
Joplin, MO 64804
(417) 623-1054

OKLAHOMA

COMMERCE

Bike-Go
108 Commerce St
Commerce, OK 74339
(918) 675-4090

PMI Performance Machine
701 N Main St
Commerce, OK 74339
(918) 442 8740

MIAMI

Route 66 Custom Cycles
214 S Main St
Miami, OK 74354
(918) 542-5090

Route 66 Vintage Iron Motorcycle Museum
128 S Main St
Miami, OK 74354
(918) 542-6170

TULSA

Action Power Sports
7465 E Admiral Place
Tulsa, OK 74115
(918) 838-8001

Brookside Motorcycle Company
4206 S Peoria Ave # A
Tulsa, OK 74105
(918) 743-2453

Honda of Tulsa
4926 E 21st St
Tulsa, OK 74114
(918) 744-5551

Jack's Motorcycle Service
5041 E Admiral Place
Tulsa, OK 74115
(918) 838-3100

K & N Motorcycles Inc
6105 New Sapulpa Rd
Tulsa, OK 74131
(918) 446-6657

Kinetic Playground Inc
4207 S Peoria Ave
Tulsa, OK 74105
(918) 743-6552

Metric Cycles
4941 E Admiral Place
Tulsa, OK 74115
(918) 835-7697

Myers-Duren Harley-Davidson
4848 S Peoria
Tulsa, OK 74105
(918) 743-4444

Ride Masters Motorcycle and ATV
1501 S Memorial Drive
Tulsa, OK 74112
(918) 828-0900

Roadhouse Motorsports
5700 S 107th E Ave
Tulsa, OK 74146
(918) 250-1400

Ron's Cycle Land
7120 E Pine St
Tulsa, OK 74115
(918) 835-8215

Route 66 Harley-Davidson
3637 S Memorial Dr
Tulsa, OK 74145
(918) 622-1340

Tulsa Cycle Supply
11121 E Pine St # A
Tulsa, OK 74116
(918) 834-0367

RED FORK

Gears and Beers
3908 SW Blvd
Red Fork, OK 918724
(918)724 8154

SAPULPA

Creek County Cycles
619 N Mission St
Sapulpa, OK 74066
(918) 227-9867

T & T Power Sports
301 S Main St
Sapulpa, OK 74066
(918) 227-2522

EDMOND

Harley-Davidson World Shop
3433 S Broadway
Edmond, OK 73013
(405) 478-4024

Mid America Cycle
640 Industrial Blvd
Edmond, OK 73034
(405) 282-0086

Road & Track
101 W 15th St
Edmond, OK 73013
(405) 348-5631

OKLAHOMA CITY

2 Brothers Custom Works
7780 N Rockwell Ave
Oklahoma City, OK 73132
(405) 720-1677

Ajax Kawasaki
8417 S I-35 Service Rd
Oklahoma City, OK 73149
(405) 634-8400

Baker Boys Yamaha
420 S Eagle Lane
Oklahoma City, OK 73128
(405) 789-3535

BS Unlimited
420 SW 59th St
Oklahoma City, OK 73109
(405) 708-6782

Colvin Motorcycle Co
3845 NW 10th St
Oklahoma City, OK 73107
(405) 946-6133

Fort Thunder Harley-Davidson
500 SW 11th St
Moore, OK 73160
(405) 793-8877

Harley-Davidson World
6904 W Reno Ave
Oklahoma City, OK 73127
(405) 631-8680

Heartland Cycles
7712 S Shields Blvd
Oklahoma City, OK 73149
(405) 634 1200

House of Kawasaki
7900 NW 10th Street St
Oklahoma City, OK 73127
(405) 787-7901

Matthews Performance Motorcycles
9005 NW 10th St
Oklahoma City, OK 73127
(405) 491-6000

Maxey's Cycle
4112 NW 39th St
Oklahoma City, OK 73112
405 946 0558 OKC

Thunder Cycles
800 W Memorial
Oklahoma City, OK
(405) 751 3706

Okie City Customs
2229 N Moore Ave
Moore , OK 73160
(405) 631-1133

R & B Cycles
2501 S Walker Ave
Oklahoma City, OK 73109
(405) 631-1218

Ray's Custom Cycles
2005 NW 39th St
Oklahoma City, OK 73118
(405) 528-0014

Thunder Roadhouse
900 W Memorial Rd
Oklahoma City, OK 73114
405 608 0416

Trinity Trikes & Customs
200 SE 19th St
Moore, OK
(405) 794 3935

Vee Twin Performance
400 SW 33rd St
Oklahoma City, OK 73109
(405) 631-1831

BETHANY

Performance Cycle
6200 Northwest 39th
Expressway
Bethany, OK 73008
(405) 787-4688

EL RENO

Phil's Cycle & ATV
2010 S Shepard Ave
El Reno, OK 73036
(405) 422-2887

Phil's Cycle & ATV
2010 S Shepard Ave
El Reno, OK 73036
(405) 422-2887

CLINTON

Xtreme Cycles ATV
1723 S 4th St
Clinton, OK 73601
(580) 323-7433

CANUTE

Elk City Honda
2111 S Main St
Elk City, OK 73644
(580) 225-3265

ProTeam Harley-Davidson
301 SE Interstate Dr
Lawton, OK 73501
(580) 353-5088

ELK CITY

Elk City Honda
2111 S Main St
Elk City, OK 73644
(580) 225-3265

McAlary ATV & Cycle Kawasaki
625 N Van Buren Ave
Elk City, OK 73644
(580) 225-6043

TEXAS

AMARILLO

A & M Cycles
6652 Canyon Dr # 8
Amarillo, TX 79109
(806) 353-7670

David Brown's Sport Center
4203 Canyon Dr
Amarillo, TX 79110
(806) 358-4572

Golden Spread Motorplex Inc.
4106 S Georgia St
Amarillo, TX 79110
(806) 352-6010

NEW MEXICO

Hog Heaven Motorcycles
4710 Canyon Dr
Amarillo, TX 79109
(806) 355-7300

Legends Custom Shop
10411 E Amarillo Blvd
Amarillo, TX 79108
(806) 418-2165

Mike Propes Repair Center
3814 Business Park Dr
Amarillo, TX 79110
(806) 463-1118

Sharp's Motorsports
4413 E Interstate 40
Amarillo, TX 79104
(806) 373-3051

Soncy Road Speed & Custom
8815 W Amarillo Blvd
Amarillo, TX 79106
(806) 331-4222

Tripp's Harley-Davidson
6040 I-40 West
Amarillo, TX 79106
(806) 352-2021

TUCUMCARI

Badlands Customs
3208 E Tucumcari Blvd
Tucumcari, NM 88401
(800) 746-9193

SANTA ROSA

High Velocity Cycles
6000 Zuni Road SE
Santa Rosa, NM 87108
(505) 237-2006

SANTA FE

Centaur Cycles & Scooters
3232 Cerrillos Rd
Santa Fe, NM 87507
(505) 471-5481

High Desert Custom V-Twins
97 Metro Blvd # C
Santa Fe, NM 87508
(505) 474-7800

Mika's Custom Motorcycles
1508 Cerrillos Rd
Santa Fe, NM 87505
(505) 984-0382

Santa Fe Harley-Davidson
4360 Rodeo Rd
Santa Fe, NM 87507
(505) 471-3808

Santa Fe Motor Sports
2594 Camino Entrada
Santa Fe, NM 87507
(505) 438-1888

SMR Motorsport
1116 Calle La Resolana
Santa Fe, NM 87507
(505) 473-3033

World Motorcycles
10 Bisbee Court
Santa Fe, NM 87508
(505) 428-0319

BERNALILLO

Demented Custom Cycles
845 S Hill Rd
Bernalillo, NM 87004
(505) 771-2205

Demented Custom Cycles
845 S Hill Rd
Bernalillo, NM 87004
(505) 771-2205

ALBUQUERQUE

Bobby J's Yamaha Inc
4724 Menaul Blvd NE
Albuquerque, NM 87110
(505) 884-3013

Eppie's Motorcycle Services
2701 4th St NW
Albuquerque, NM 87107
(505) 899-3800

High Velocity Cycles
6000 Zuni Rd SE
Albuquerque, NM 87108
(505) 237-2006

Honda Powersports Albuquerque
1220 S Renaissance Blvd NE
Albuquerque, NM 87107
(505) 999-2555

J&D Cycle
2524 Morningside Dr NE
Albuquerque, NM 87110
(505) 263-8227

New Mexico Motorcycle
4123 Broad SE
Albuquerque, NM 87105
(505) 877-4003

P J's Triumph Motorcycles LLC
12910 Central Ave SE
Albuquerque, NM 87123
(505) 323-6700

R & S Powersports Group
9601 Lomas Blvd NE
Albuquerque, NM 87112
(505) 292-6692

R & S Yamaha
3305 Juan Tabo Blvd NE
Albuquerque, NM 87111
(505) 292-8011

R&S Honda
1425 Wyoming Blvd NE
Albuquerque, NM 87112
(505) 293-1860

Rosedale Motorsports
8994 4th St NW
Albuquerque, NM 87114
(505) 897-1519

Thunderbird Harley-Davidson
5000 Alameda Blvd NE
Albuquerque, NM 87113
(505) 856-1600

LOS LUNAS

Dave's Motorcycle Parts and Repair
3161 NM 47
Los Lunas, NM 87031
(505) 865-4007

Los Lunas Motor Sports
2214 Sun Ranch Village Loop SW
Los Lunas, NM 87031
(505) 865-1700
(505) 856-1600

GRANTS

Bernie's Route 66 Motorcycle
1016 W Santa Fe Ave
Grants, NM 87020
(505) 287-5152

GALLUP

Desert Cycle
1315 Hamilton Rd # A
Gallup, NM 87301
(505) 722-3821

EDGEWOOD

Knucklehead's
1819 Old Hwy 66
Edgewood, NM 87015
(505) 281-2550

ARIZONA

FLAGSTAFF

Eagle Riders Motorcycles
800 W Route 66
Flagstaff, AZ 86001
928 637 6575

Eurogeek Motosport
555 S Blackbird Roost # 5
Flagstaff, AZ 86001
(928) 773-8913

Hi-Country Motorcycle & ATV Center
2800 N W St
Flagstaff, AZ 86004
(928) 214-8700

Mike's Bikes
3122 E Route 66
Flagstaff, AZ 86004
(928) 600-3508

Northland Motor Sports
1400 E Butler Ave # 9
Flagstaff, AZ 86001
(928) 526-7959

BELLEMONT

Grand Canyon Harley-Davidson
12000 Bellemont Rd
Bellemont, AZ 86015
(928) 774-3896

WILLIAMS

Grand Canyon Motorsports
516 N Grand Canyon Blvd
Williams, AZ 86046
(928) 635-3070

KINGMAN

Desert Thunder Victory
4180 Stockton Hill Rd
Kingman, AZ 86409
(928) 692-3232

Kelly's Performance Specialists
4906 N Olympic Dr
Kingman, AZ 86401
(928) 692-6601

Kingman Motorsports
2600 Northern Ave # 1
Kingman, AZ 86409
(928) 692-0008

Mother Road Harley-Davidson
2501 Beverly Ave
Kingman, AZ 86409
(928) 757-1166

River Rat Motorsports
2365 E Northern Ave
Kingman, AZ 86409
(928) 757-2480

Route 66 Motorsports
2501 E Beverly Ave
Kingman, AZ 86409
(928) 757-1166

CALIFORNIA

NEEDLES

J&J Classics
101 E Broadway St
Needles, CA 92363
(760) 326-6381

Route 66 Cycle Works
611 Front St
Needles, CA 92363
(760) 326-2925

BARSTOW

Barstow Motorcycle Center
2380 W Main St
Barstow, CA 92311
(760) 256-4090

Cycle Pros
820 E Williams St
Barstow, CA 92311
(760) 255-1816

VICTORVILLE

B & B Cycles
13815 Park Ave
Victorville, CA 92392
(760) 241-7387

Victor Valley Harley-Davidson
14522 Valley Center Dr
Victorville, CA 92395
(760) 951-1119

Victorville Motorcycle Center
14370 Valley Center Dr
Victorville, CA 92395
(760) 241-2386

SAN BERNARDINO

Chaparral Motorsports
555 S H St
San Bernardino, CA 92410
(800) 841-2960

Doug Douglas Motorcycles
24769 5th St
San Bernardino, CA 92410
(909) 884-4776

Norm's Cycle & ATV
273 S Pershing Ave # 3
San Bernardino, CA 92408
(909) 885-7667

Wisdom Motorsports
620 W Mill St # J
San Bernardino, CA 92410
(909) 888-3457

RIALTO

A & J Auto Repair
1260 N Fitzgerald Ave
Rialto, CA 92376
(909) 877-5698

Import Cycles Power Sports
1240 N Fitzgerald Ave
Rialto, CA 92376
(909) 875-3407

FONTANA

John Burr Cycles - Honda Yamaha Kawasaki
9008 Sierra Ave
Fontana, CA 92335
(909) 823-1338

Rancho Cucamonga C Motorsports
10002 6th St
Rancho Cucamonga, CA 91730
(909) 948-7975

Hellbound Steel
11031 Jersey Blvd
Rancho Cucamonga, CA 91730
(909) 944-7633

Lucky 7 Motorsports
8810 Archibald Ave
Rancho Cucamonga, CA 91730
(909) 948-2332

Yamaha of Cucamonga
9760 Foothill Blvd
Rancho Cucamonga, CA 91730
(909) 987-2411

UPLAND

BC Cycles
1777 Woodlawn St # G7
Upland, CA 91786
(909) 949-8100

LA VERNE

Forward Motion Motorcycles
1441 Palomares St
La Verne, CA 91750
(626) 457-6500

GLENDORA

M Racing
611 E Route 66
Glendora, CA 91741
(626) 963-3872

PASADENA

Holmes Power Sports
1200 E Colorado Blvd
Pasadena, CA 91106
(626) 376-4457

Lunatic Psycles
127 S Rosemead Blvd
Pasadena, CA 91107
(626) 577-9600

Pasadena Yamaha
2270 E Colorado Blvd
Pasadena, CA 91107
(626) 577-3000

Villain Custom Cycles
2762 E Colorado Blvd
Pasadena, CA 91107
(626) 568-8429

LOS ANGELES

Al's Cycle Shop
1645 Glendale Blvd
Los Angeles, CA 90026
(213) 353-0328

Cycle Depot
1644 Colorado Blvd
Los Angeles, CA 90041
(323) 254-6661

Cycle Parts
400 S Atlantic Blvd
Los Angeles, CA 90022
(323) 264-4107

Harley-Davidson of Glendale
3717 San Fernando Rd
Glendale, CA 91204
(818) 246-5618

Hollywood Harley Davidson
6810 Hollywood Blvd
Los Angeles, CA 90028
(818)2465-5618

Honda of Hollywood
6525 Santa Monica Blvd
Los Angeles, CA 90038
(323)466-7191

Los Angeles Harley-Davidson
13300 Paramount Blvd
S Gate, CA 90280
(562) 408-6088

Los Angeles Motorcycle Experts -Tecni Moto Cardoza
2609 Whittier Blvd
Los Angeles, CA 90023
(323) 207-7396

Motorcycle Performance Services Inc
1338 S La Brea Ave
Los Angeles, CA 90019
(323) 939-2370

Powerplant Custom Choppers
7368 1/2 Melrose Ave
Los Angeles, CA 90046
(323) 658-6711

Tony's Motorcycle Shop
1228 1/2 S Atlantic Blvd
Los Angeles, CA 90022
(323) 263-9282

SANTA MONICA

Moto Club di Santa Monica
2013 Lincoln Blvd
Santa Monica, CA 90405
(310) 882-5684

HOTELS AND CAMPGROUNDS; BARS, RESTAURANTS AND CASINOS; MUSEUMS

Hotels and Campgrounds

There are national chain hotels in or near almost every Route 66 town and finding lodging is easy. So, I generally limited the listings to historic Route 66 motels and to places I have visited. I especially avoided listings in larger cities (although I made exceptions in Chicago and Santa Monica because I thought a recommendation for the starting and ending points might be useful).

I included of all the campgrounds I could find in the towns along and near Route 66. There are not all that many of them, and in remote areas, finding a good campground might be more difficult than finding a motel. These campgrounds may be useful for the Old School riders who are camping along their journeys. I have not visited any of the listed campgrounds.

Bars, Restaurants and Casinos

I did not attempt to compile a definitive list of bars and restaurants along Route 66; rather I included only long-time Route 66 establishments and biker friendly bars and restaurants that I have visited or that were recommended by people I know. The limitation on the listings is designed to help you find fun places without your having to sort through a bunch of Squaresville spots. Visiting some of the places I have listed may involve a bit of a detour. But, trading stories with locals and bikers who are riding across the country is one of the fun things about motorcycles.

I listed casinos along Route 66 because some bikers like to gamble. However, I did not visit any of them, so you are on your own as far as casinos are concerned.

Museums

With a few exceptions, I have limited the listings of museums to those focusing on Route 66, motorcycles, hot rods and similar road trip fare. That's not to slight the other interesting museums along Route 66. I needed to cut off the scope of information I could include, and that cut off seemed appropriate.

ILLINOIS

CHICAGO

Hotels and Campgrounds

Congress Plaza Hotel
520 S Michigan Ave
Chicago, IL 60605
(312) 427-3800

Chicago Northwest KOA
8404 S Union Rd
Union, IL 60180
(815) 923-4206

Bars, and Restaurants

**Andy's Jazz Club &
Restaurant**
11 E Hubbard St
Chicago, IL 60611
(312) 642-6805

**Austin's Saloon &
Eatery**
481 Peterson Rd
Libertyville, IL 60048
847 549-1972

Billy Goat Tavern
430 N Michigan Ave
Chicago, IL
(312) 222-1525

Broken Oar
614 Rawson Bridge Rd
Chicago, IL 60013
(847) 639 6660

Buddy Guy's
700 S Wabash Ave
Chicago, IL 60605
(312) 427-1190

CC's Grove Inn
8258 Kean Ave
Chicago, IL 60480
(708) 839-1959

Delilah's
2771 N Lincoln Ave
Chicago, IL 60614
(773) 472-2771

Elephant & Castle
111 W Adams St
Chicago, IL 60603
(312) 236-6656

Goose Island Beer Co
1800 W Fulton St
Chicago, IL 60612
(312) 226-1119

**Haymarket Pub &
Brewery**
737 W Randolph St
Chicago, IL 60661
(312) 638-0700

Hogs & Honey's
1551 N Sheffield
Chicago, IL 60622
(312) 377-1773

J & J Lounge
1009 14th St
North Chicago, IL 60064
(847) 689-4280

Jesse Oaks
18490 W Old Gages Lake
Rd
Gages Lake, IL 60030
(847)223-2575

Kuma's Corner
2900 W Belmont Ave
Chicago, IL 60618
(773) 604-8769

Lou Mitchell's
565 W Jackson & Jefferson
Chicago, IL 60661
(312) 939-3111

Mack's Golden Pheasant
668 W North Ave
Elmhurst, IL 60126
(630) 279-8544

Miller's Pub
134 S Wabash Ave
Chicago, IL 60603
(312) 263-4988

Skylark Lounge
4007 W Ogden Ave
Chicago, IL 60623
(773) 522-9352

Snuggery
222 S Riverside Plaza
Chicago, IL 60606
(312) 441-9334

The Berghoff
17 W Adams St
Chicago, IL 60603
(312) 427-3170

Twisted Spoke
501 N Ogden Ave
Chicago, IL 60622
(312) 666 1500

CICERO

Hotels

Cindy Lyn Motel
5029 W Ogden Ave
Cicero, IL 60804
(708) 656-1730

Bars and Restaurants

Henry's Drive In
6031 W Ogden Ave
Cicero, IL 60804
(708) 656-9344

BERWYN

Bars and Restaurants

Fitzgerald's
6615 Roosevelt Rd
Berwyn, IL 60402
(708) 788-2118

Juniors Bar & Grill
7011 Ogden Ave
Berwyn, IL 60402
(708) 484-9465

Tiger O'Stylies
6300 W Ogden Ave
Berwyn, IL 60402
(708) 795-1298

LYONS

Bars and Restaurants

Ricky D's Place 7901
Ogden Ave # C
Lyons, IL 60534
(708) 442-8688

ROMEOVILLE

Bars and Restaurants

White Fence Farm
1376 Joliet Rd
Romeoville, IL 60446
(630) 739-1720

JOLIET

Museums

Route 66 Welcome Center
204 N Ottawa St
Joliet, IL 60432
(815) 723-5201

Hotels, Casinos and Campgrounds

Harrah's Casino Hotel
151 N Joliet St
Joliet, IL 60432
(815) 740-7800

Hollywood Casino
777 Hollywood Blvd
Joliet, IL 60436
(888) 436 7737

Kankakee South KOA
425 E 6000 S Rd
Chebanse, IL 60922
(815) 939-4603

Race View Farms
19100 Schweitzer Rd
Joliet, IL 60434
(815) 741-3010

Bars and Restaurants

Boz Hot Dogs
1601 S Chicago St
Joliet, IL 60436
(815) 722 9899

McBrody's Bar & Grill
73 W Jefferson St
Joliet, IL 60432
(815) 726-8960

Rich & Creamy
920 N Broadway St
Joliet, IL 60435
(815) 740-2899

Zelmo's Full Moon Saloon
1117 Plainfield Rd #1
Joliet, IL 60435
(815) 727-3840

ELWOOD

Bars and Restaurants

Best Food and Grub
South End
Across the Tracks
Elwood, IL 60609

Watson's Diner & Pub
115 W Mississippi St
Elwood, IL
(815) 423- 5125

WILMINGTON

Campgrounds

Fossil Rock Recreation Area
24615 Stripmine Rd
Wilmington, IL 60481
(815) 476-6784

Bars and Restaurants

Launching Pad Drive-In
810 E Baltimore St
Wilmington, IL 60481
(815) 476-6535

Rustic Inn
108 N Water St
Wilmington, IL 60481
(815) 476-7290

BRAIDWOOD

Hotels

Braidwood Motel
120 N Washington St
Braidwood, IL 60408
(815) 458-2321

Bars and Restaurants

Korner Keg & Kitchen
285 E Main St
Braidwood, IL 60408
(815) 458 2866

Polk-A-Dot Drive In
222 N Front St
Braidwood, IL 60408
(815) 458-3377

GARDNER

Bars and Restaurants

Vino's Bar & Grill
120 Depot St
Gardner, IL
(815) 237-8888

DWIGHT

Hotels

Whispering Pines
10940 S Dwight Rd
Dwight, IL 60420
(260) 433-4888

Bars and Restaurants

J T's Saloon
118 E Main St
Dwight, IL 60420
(815) 584-9510

Turtle's Tap
152 E Main St
Dwight, IL 60420
(815) 584-3663

ODELL

Bars and Restaurants

Pour Richard's Tap & Dining Room
419 Circle Dr
Odell, IL 60460
(815) 998-2556

Rentz's Tap & Dining
210 S Waupansie St
Odell, IL 60460
(815) 998 2383

Wishing Well Café
110 Tremont St
Odell, IL 60460
(815) 998-2100

PONTIAC

Museums

Route 66 Association of Illinois Hall of Fame & Museum
110 W Howard St
Pontiac, IL 61764
(815) 844-4566

Hotels

Lydia's Loft
1071/2 W Madison St
Pontiac, IL 61764
(309) 824-2490

Three Roses Bed and Breakfast
209 E Howard St
Pontiac, IL 61764
(815) 844-3404

Bars and Restaurants

Scotty's Place
1120 N Division St
Pontiac, IL 61764
(815) 844-2253

The Old Log Cabin
18700 Old Route 66
Pontiac, IL 61764
(815) 842-2908

LEXINGTON

Bars and Restaurants

Dat Bar at the End Row
402 W Main St
Lexington, IL 61753
(309) 365-3620

TOWANDA

Bars and Restaurants

Kicks on 66 Bar & Grill
19578 N 1960 E Rd
Towanda, IL 61776
(309) 728-2060

Normal

Bars and Restaurants

Avanti's Italian Restaurant
407 S Main St
Normal, IL 61761
(309) 452-4436

BLOOMINGTON

Hotels

Chateau Hotel and Conference Center
1601 Jumer Dr
Bloomington, IL 61704

Bars and Restaurants

Blue Line Nightclub
602 N Main St
Bloomington, IL 61701
(309) 585-2641

CJ's Restaurant
2901 E Empire St
Bloomington, IL 61704
(309) 663-4441

Daddios
527 N Main St
Bloomington, IL 61701
(309) 828-4434

Drifters Pub
612 N Main St
Bloomington, IL 61701
(309) 829-1920

Killarney's Irish Pub
523 N Main St
Bloomington, IL 61701
(309) 828-1186

Main Street Grill
517 N Main St
Bloomington, IL 61701
(309) 820-9241

Mulligans
531 N Main St
Bloomington, IL 61701
(309) 827-7796

Six Strings
525 N Main St
Bloomington, IL 61701
(309) 829-9977

Bars and Restaurants

Dixie Truckers Home
598 Main St
McLean, IL 61754
(309) 874-2323

Bars and Restaurants

Chubby's Bar & Grill
111 SE Vine St
Atlanta, IL 61723
(217) 648 -615

Palms Grill
110 SW Arch St
Atlanta, IL 61723
(217) 648-2233

Bars and Restaurants

Guzzardo's Italian Villa
509 Pulaski St
Lincoln, IL 62656
(217) 732-6370

Hallie's on the Square
111 S Kickapoo St
Lincoln, IL 62656
(217) 732-6923

SPRINGFIELD

Shea's Historic Route 66 Museum
2075 N Peoria Rd
Springfield, IL 62702
(217) 522-0475

Hotels and Campgrounds

Route 66 Hotel and Conference Center
625 E St Joseph St
Springfield, IL 62703
(217)529-6626

Mr. Lincoln's Campground RV Center
3045 Stanton St
Springfield, IL 62703
(217) 529-8206

Riverside Park Campground
4105 Sand Hill Rd
Springfield, IL 62702
(217) 753-06

Bars and Restaurants

Cove
1616 N Dirksen Pkwy
Springfield, IL 62702
(217) 753-1760

Cozy Dog Drive In
2935 S 6th St
Springfield, IL 62703
(217) 525-1992

Dude's Saloon
2001 N 11th St
Springfield, IL 62702
(217) 523-2346

Knuckleheads
2000 N Peoria Rd
Springfield, IL 62702
(217) 789-1488

Weebles Bar & Grill
4136 N Peoria Rd
Springfield, IL 62702
(217) 528-3337

CHATHAM

Campgrounds

Double J Campground & RV Park
9683 Palm Rd
Chatham, IL 62629
(217) 483-9998

Bars and Restaurants

AJs Tavern
101 E Mulberry St
Chatham, IL 62629
(217) 483-3213

Fat Willy's
109 E Mulberry St
Chatham, IL 62629
(217) 483-6969

GIRARD

Bars and Restaurants

Ron's Red Bird Café
112 W Center St
Girard, IL 62640
(217) 627-2045

CARLINVILLE

Hotels

Carlin Villa Motel
18891 IL 4
Carlinville, IL 62626
(217) 854-3201

Bars and Restaurants

Anchor Inn
33 Daley St
Carlinville, IL 62626
(217) 854 7516

Lucky Dog's Alehouse
230 E Side Square
Carlinville, IL 62626
(217)854-4448

St George Room
118 E Side Square
Carlinville, IL 62626
(217) 854-7018

GILLESPIE

Bars and Restaurants

Chiefs II
107 N Macoupin St
Gillespie, IL 62033
(217) 839-4299

STAUNTON

Bars and Restaurants

Decamp Junction
8767 State Route 4
Staunton, IL 62088
(618) 637-2951

Digger's Dugout
7708 State Route 4
Worden , IL 72097
(618) 633 1850

HAMEL

Bars and Restaurants

Weezy's
108 S Old Route 66
Hamel, IL 62046
(618) 633-2228

EDWARDSVILLE

Campgrounds

Red Barn Rendezvous RV Park
3955 County Rd 62
Edwardsville, IL 62025
(618) 692-9015

Stagger Inn
104 E Vandalia St
Edwardsville, IL 62025
(618) 656-4221

MITCHELL

Hotels

Apple Valley Motel
709 E Chain of Rocks Rd
Mitchell, IL 62040
(618) 931-6085

Greenway Motel
701 E Chain of Rocks Rd
Mitchell, IL 62040
(618) 219-2910

Bars and Restaurants

Luna Café
201 E Chain of Rocks Rd
Mitchell, IL 62040
(618) 931-3152

Towns in Alternate Route from Springfield to Staunton

DIVERNON

Bars and Restaurants

Corner Bar
200 S 1st St
Divernon, IL 62530
(217) 628 3605

FARMERSVILLE

Hotels
Bars and Restaurants

Art's Motel & Restaurant
101 Main St
Farmersville, IL 62533
(217) 227-3277

Silver Dollar
608 Elevator St
Farmersville, IL 62533
(217) 227-4580

LITCHFIELD

Hotels and Campgrounds

Kamper Kompanion
18388 E Frontage Rd
Litchfield, IL 62056
(217) 324-4747

Lazy Days Campground
22756 White Park La
Litchfield, IL 62056
(217) 324-3233

Bars and Restaurants

Ariston Café
413 N Old Route 66
Litchfield, IL 62056
(217) 324-2023

Route 66 Café
318 S Old Route 66
Litchfield, IL 62056
(217) 324-2771

Shaw's Club 66 Bar & Grill
901 S Old Route 66
Litchfield, IL 62056
(217) 324-9213

Stacey's Route 66 Café
318 Old Route 66
Litchfield, IL 62056
(217) 324-2771

MISSOURI

ST LOUIS

Hotels and Campgrounds

Holiday Inn
10709 Watson Rd
St Louis, MO
(800) 972-3145

St Louis RV Park
900 N Jefferson Ave
St Louis, MO 63106
(314) 241-3330

Granite City KOA
3157 W Chain of Rocks Rd
Granite City, MO 62040
(618) 931-5160

St Louis West / Historic Route 66 KOA
18475 Old Route 66
Eureka, MO 63025
(636) 257-3018

Bars and Restaurants

Bleeding Deacon Public House
4123 Chippewa St
St Louis, MO 63116
(314) 772-1813

Carl's Drive Inn
9033 Manchester Rd
St Louis, MO 63144
(314) 961-9652

Malone's Grill & Pub
8742 Watson Rd
St Louis, MO 63119
(314) 843-9904

Mile 277 Tap & Grill
10701 Watson Rd
St Louis, MO 63127
(314) 645-3277

Shot Heaven
5233 Gravois Ave
St Louis, MO 63116
(314) 351-9606

Ted Drewes Frozen Custard
6726 Chippewa St
St Louis, MO 63109
(314) 481-2652

Trainwreck Saloon
9243 Manchester Rd
St Louis, MO 63144
(314) 962-8148

POND

Bars and Restaurants

Big Chief Roadhouse
17352 Manchester Rd
Pond, MO 63038
(636) 458-3200

HOLLOW

Bars and Restaurants

Stovall's Grove Dance Hall and Saloon
18721 Stovall La
Wildwood , MO 63069
(636) 405-3024

GRAY SUMMIT

Motels

Sunset Motel
427 Hwy AT
Villa Ridge MO 63089
(314) 580-6417

Bars and Restaurants

Roadhouse Café
2763 MO 100
Gray Summit, MO 63039
(636) 451-2007

STANTON

Campgrounds

Stanton / Meramec KOA
74 Hwy W
Stanton, MO 63079
(573) 927-5215

SULLIVAN

Campgrounds

Meramec State Park
115 Meramec Park Dr
Sullivan, MO 63080
(573) 468-6072

BOURBON

Circle Inn Malt Shop
171 S Old Hwy 66
Bourbon, MO 65441
(573) 732-4470

Skippy's 66
247 Hwy H
Leesburg, MO 65535
(573) 245 6666

CUBA

Hotels and Campgrounds

Wagon Wheel Motel
901 E Washington Blvd
Cuba, MO 65453
(573) 885-3411

Ladybug RV Park & Campground
355 Hwy F
Cuba, MO 65453
(573) 885-3622

Meramec Valley RV Camp
1360 Hwy UU
Cuba, MO 65453
(573) 885-2541

Bars and Restaurants

East Office Bar and Grill
406 E Washington
Cuba, MO 65453
(573) 885 6804

Missouri Hick BBQ
913 E Washington St
Cuba, MO 65453
(573) 885-6791

The Rose
1109 E Washington St
Cuba, MO 65453
(573) 885-5646

Frisco's
121 S Smith St
Cuba, MO 65453
(573) 885 1522

St James
Bars and Restaurants
Johnnie's Bar
225 N Jefferson St
St James, MO 65559
(573) 265-8223

DOOLITTLE

Bars and Restaurants

Back Road Grill & Bar
195 Doolittle Outer Rd
Rolla, MO 65401
(573) 762-0125

DEVIL'S ELBOW

Hotels and Campgrounds

Route 66 Canoe Rental
1050 Trophy La
Devil's Elbow, MO 65457
(573) 336-2730

Piney Beach Cabins
12810 Tank La
Devil's Elbow, MO 65453
(573) 336-4321

Bars and Restaurants

Elbow Inn & Bar-B-Q Pit
21050 Teardrop Rd
Devil's Elbow, MO 65457
573 336-5375

Judy's Place

21754 Teardrop Rd
Devil's Elbow, MO 65457
573 336-4727

FORT LEONARD WOOD/ST ROBERT

Holiday Inn Express
605 Hwy Z
St Robert, MO 65584
(573) 336-2299

Bars and Restaurants

Area 151 Nightclub
819 State Hwy Z
St Robert, MO 65584
(573) 336-4244

Big Louie's Gentlemen's Club
14400 Hwy Z
St Robert, MO 65584
(573) 336-8783

Bottoms Up
1058 Old Route 66
St Robert, MO 65584
(573) 336-5505

WAYNESVILLE

**Hotels and
Campgrounds
Fort Wood Inn**
25755 Hwy 17
Waynesville, MO 65583
(573) 774-3600

Glen Oaks RV Park
26215 Hwy 17
Waynesville, MO 65583
(573) 774-2727

**Roubidoux Springs
Campground & RV Park**
601 Historic 66 W
Waynesville, MO 65583
(573) 74-6171 5

Hoppers Pub
318 Historic Route 66 E
Waynesville, MO 65583
(573) 774-0135

Steve's Place
202 Glenda Dr
Waynesville, MO 65583
(573) 774 6980

LEBANON

Museums

**Lebanon Route 66
Museum**
915 Jefferson
Lebanon, MO 65536
(417) 533 7667

Hotels and Campgrounds

**Forest Manor Motel &
RV Park**
1307 E Route 66
Lebanon, MO 65536
(417) 532-6114

Munger Moss Motel
1336 E Route 66
Lebanon, MO 65536
(417) 532-3111

**Menagerie
Campground**
1770 MO 64
Lebanon, MO 65536
(417) 532-3724

Niangua River Oasis
171 NRO Rd
Lebanon, MO 65536
(417) 532-6333

PHILLIPSBURG

Campgrounds

Happy Trails RV Park
18376 Campground Rd
Phillipsburg, MO 65722
(417) 532-3422

Conway

Museums

**Route 66 Welcome
Center**
726 W Jefferson Ave
Conway, MO 65632

STRAFFORD

Campgrounds

**Paradise in the Woods
RV Park**
2481 Grier Branch Rd
Strafford, MO 65757
(417) 859-2175

SPRINGFIELD

Hotels and Campgrounds

Best Western Rail Haven Motel
203 S Glenstone Ave
Springfield, MO 65802
(417) 866-1963

Rest Haven Court
2000 E Kearney St
Springfield, MO 65804
(417) 869-9114

Ozark Highlands Mobile Home Park
3731 S Glenstone Ave
Springfield, MO 65804
(417) 881-0066

Springfield/Route 66 KOA
5775 W Farm Rd 140
Springfield, MO 65802
(417) 831-3645

Bars and Restaurants

Andy's Frozen Custard
3147 E State Hwy D
Springfield, MO 65804
(417) 881-2820

Big Whiskey's American Bar & Grill
311 Park Central E
Springfield, MO 65806
(417) 862-2449

College St Café
1622 W College St
Springfield, MO 65806
(417) 864 0531

Mother's Brewing Company
215 S Grant Ave
Springfield, MO 65806
(417) 862-0423

Route 66 Café
2204 W College St
Springfield, MO 65806
417 987-4283

ALBATROSS

Bars and Restaurants

Route 66 Tavern
12221 Hwy 96
Albatross, MO 65707
(417) 452- 2266

AVILLA

Bars and Restaurants

Route 66 Café
Route 66
Avilla, MO

CARTHAGE, MO

Museums

Jasper County Courthouse Route 66 Museum
302 S Main St
Carthage, MO 64836

Hotels and Campgrounds Boots Motel
107 S Garrison St
Carthage, MO 64836
(417) 358 9453

Kel-Lake Motel
13071 MO 96
Carthage, MO 64836
(417) 358-9796

Big Red Barn RV Park
5089 County Lane 138
Carthage, MO 64836
(417) 358-2432

Coachlight Campground
5305 S Garrison Ave
Carthage, MO 64836
(417) 358-3666

Bars and Restaurants

Bamboo Garden
102 N Garrison Ave
Carthage, MO 64836
(417) 358-1611

Boomer Sooner BBQ & Catering
1220 Oak St
Carthage, MO 64836
(417) 358-8112

Jim's Bar
325 E 4th St
Carthage, MO 64836
(417) 358 8549

WEBB CITY

Bars and Restaurants

Fat Head's Hogs and Hot Rods
660 E Daugherty
Webb City, MO 64870
(417) 673-3399

Longhorn Bar & Grill
202 E Broadway
Webb City, MO 64870
(417) 673-5598

JOPLIN

Hotels and Campgrounds

Capri Motel
3401 N Main St
Joplin, MO 64801
(417) 206-0604

Joplin KOA Campground
4359 MO 43
Joplin, MO 64804
(417) 782-6711

Bars and Restaurants

Frank's Lounge
2112 Main St
Joplin, MO 64804
(417) 623-9651

Gallows
253 E US 160
Lamar, MO 64759
(417) 682-6869

Guitars Rock N Country Bar and Nightclub
1800 W 7th St
Joplin, MO 64801
(417) 782-6444

Hogs and Hotrods Saloon
7889 W Old Route 66
Joplin, MO 64804
(417) 206-2752

The Kitchen Pass
1212 S Main St
Joplin, MO 64801
(417) 624-9095

Turtleheads
4218 Main St
Joplin, MO 64804
(417) 782-4343

Undercliff Grill and Bar
6385 Old Hwy 71
Joplin, MO 64804
(417) 623-8382

Wilder's Steakhouse
1216 Main St
Joplin, MO 64801
(417) 623-7230

Towns in Alternate Route between Crestwood and Gray Summit

PACIFIC

Campgrounds

Yogi Bear's Jellystone Park
5300 Fox Creek Rd
Pacific, MO 63069
(636) 938-5925

Bars and Restaurants

Great Pacific Bar & Grill
220 S First St
Pacific, MO 63069
(636) 257-9911

Third Rail Bar & Grill
564 Old Route 66
Pacific, MO 63069
(636) 257-9909

KANSAS

GALENA

Bars and Restaurants

Cars On the Route
119 N Main St
Galena, KS 66739
(620) 783-1366

RIVERTON

Bars and Restaurants

Old Riverton Store
7109 Southeast Hwy 66
Riverton, KS 66770
(620) 848-3330

BAXTER SPRINGS

Museums

Baxter Springs Route 66 Visitors Center
Military Ave
Baxter Springs, KS 66713
(620) 856-2066

OKLAHOMA

QUAPAW

Bars, Restaurants and Casinos

Dallas' Dairyette
103 N Main St
Quapaw, OK 74363
(918) 674-9207

Hemi's Café
104 S Main St
Quapaw, OK 74363
(918) 674-2344

Downstream Casino
69300 Quapaw OK
58100 E 64 Rd
(918) 919-6000

COMMERCE, OK

Bars and Restaurants

Dairy King
100 N Main St
Commerce, OK 74339
(918) 675-4261

MIAMI

Museums

Route 66 Vintage Iron Motorcycle Museum
128 S Main St
Miami, OK 74354
(918) 542-6170

Bars, Restaurants and Casinos

Stone Hill Grill
1220 N Main St
Miami, OK 74354

Waylon's Ku-Ku
915 N Main St
Miami, OK 73454
(918) 542-1696

Buffalo Run Casino
1000 Buffalo Run Blvd
Miami, OK
(918) 542-7140

High Winds Casino
61475 E 100 Rd
Miami, OK 74354
(918) 541- 9463.

Stables Casino
530 H St
Miami, OK 74354
(918) 542-7884

VINITA

Hotels and Campgrounds

Park Hill Motel & RV Park
438415 E Hwy 60
Vinita, OK 74301
(918)256-5511

Vinita Inn Hotel
520 E Illinois Ave
Vinita, OK 74301
(918) 323-0899

Bars and Restaurants

Clanton's Café
319 E Illinois Ave
Vinita, OK 74301
(918) 256-9053

CHELSEA

Hotels

Chelsea Motor Inn
325 E Layton St
Chelsea, OK 74016
(918) 789-3437

Bars and Restaurants

Hilltop Bar
25062 E Hwy 66
Chelsea, OK 74106
(918) 789-9906

FOYIL

Bars and Restaurants

Tin Foyil Café
123 Main St
Foyil, OK 74031
(918) 550 9448

CLAREMORE

Museums

J M Davis Arms & Historical Museum
333 N Lynn Riggs Blvd
Claremore, OK 74017
(918) 341 5707

Will Rogers Memorial
1720 W Will Rogers Blvd
Claremore, OK 74017
(918) 341-0719

Hotels and Campgrounds

Claremore Motor Inn
1709 N Lynn Rogers Blvd
Claremore, OK 74017
(918) 342-4545

Will Rogers Magnuson Hotel
940 S Lynn Rogers Blvd
Claremore, OK 74017
(918) 341-4410

Blue Creek Cove
13400 E 390 Rd
Claremore, OK 74017
(918) 341-4244

Outpost Mobile Home Park and Campground
13505 S Hwy 88
Claremore, OK 74017
(918) 341-1014

Tulsa NE / Will Rogers Downs KOA
20900 S 4200 Rd
Claremore, OK 74019
(918) 283-8876

Bars and Restaurants

Billy Simms BBQ
2052 S Hwy 66
Claremore, OK 74109
(918) 923- 6771

Catoosa

Bars, Restaurants and Casinos

Aubrey's Hamburgers
19322 E Admiral Place
Catoosa, OK 74015
(918) 739-4044

Molly's Landing
3700 OK 66
Catoosa, OK 74015
(918) 266-7853

Toby Keith's I Love This Bar & Grill
777 W Cherokee St
Catoosa, OK 74015
(918) 739-4888

Cherokee Casino Inn Catoosa
19250 Timbercrest Circle
Catoosa, OK 74015
(918) 266-6700

Hard Rock Hotel & Casino
777 W Cherokee St
Catoosa, OK 74015
(918) 266-6700

TULSA

Hotels and Campgrounds

America's Value Inn
10117 E 11th St
Tulsa, OK 74128
918 836-2551

Brookshire Motel
11017 E 11th St
Tulsa, OK 74128
(918) 437-4746

Campbell Hotel
2636 E 11th St
Tulsa, OK 74104
(918) 744-5500

Desert Hills Motel
5320 E 11th St
Tulsa, OK 74112
(918) 834-3311

Mingo RV Park
801 N Mingo Rd
Tulsa, OK 74116
(918) 832-8824

Warrior Campground
5131 S Union Ave
Tulsa, OK 74107
(918) 446-3199

Bars and Restaurants

11th St Pub
6119 E 11th St
Tulsa, OK 74112
(918) 836-8873

Blue Dome Diner
313 2nd St
Tulsa, OK 74120
(918) 382-7866

Blues City Bar and Grill
3156 Mingo Rd
Tulsa, OK 71416
(918) 664-0356

Cain's Ballroom
423 N Main St
Tulsa, OK
(918) 584-2306

Corner Café
1103 S Peoria Ave
Tulsa, OK 74120
(918) 587-0081

Ed's Hurricane Lounge
3216 E 11th St
Tulsa, OK 74104
(918) 587-6426

El Rancho Grande
1629 E 11th St
Tulsa, OK 74120
(918) 584-0816

Knuckle Head
16001 E Pine
Tulsa, OK 74116
(918) 439-9995

Stryker's Route 66 Lounge
3748 SW Blvd
Tulsa, OK 74107
(918) 398-6326

Tally's Café
1102 S Yale Ave
Tulsa, OK 74112
(918) 835-8039

The Grey Snail
1334 E 15th St
Tulsa, OK 74120
(918) 587-7584

RED FORK

Bars and Restaurants

Gears and Beers
3908 SW Blvd
Red Fork, OK
(918) 724 8154

Ollie's Station Restaurant
4070 SW Blvd
Red Fork, OK 74107
(918) 446 0524

Stryker's Route 66 Lounge
3748 SW Blvd
Red Fork, OK
(918) 318 6326

SAPULPA

Campgrounds

Route 66 RV Park
9701 New Sapulpa Rd
Sapulpa, OK 74066
(918) 224-3750

Bars and Restaurants

Hickory House Barbeque
626 N Mission St
Sapulpa, OK 74066
(918) 224-7830

BRISTOW

Hotels and Campgrounds

Evergreen RV Park
37661 W Hwy 66 Bristow,
OK 74010

Bars, Restaurants and Casinos

Russ Ribs
223 S Main St
Bristow, OK 74010
(918) 367-5656

Creek Nation Casino
Bristow
121 W Lincoln
Bristow, OK 74010
(918) 367-2260

STROUD

Hotels and Campgrounds

Skyliner Motel
717 W Main St
Stroud, OK 74079
(918) 968-9556

Sac & Fox Mobile Home & RV Campground
RR 2
Stroud, OK 74079
(918) 968-3526

Bars, Restaurants and Casinos

Cue & Brew
417 W Main St
Stroud, OK 74079
(918) 968-9955

Rock Café
114 W Main St
Stroud, OK 74079
(918) 968-3990

Vallarta Mexican Restaurant
315 N 8th Ave
Stroud, OK 74079
(918) 987-1043

Sac & Fox Nation Stroud Casino
356120 E 926 Rd
Stroud, OK 74079
(918) 968-2540

DAVENPORT

Gar Wooly's
1025 Broadway
Davenport, OK 74026
(918) 377-2230

CHANDLER

Museums

Route 66 Interpretive Center
400 E 1st St
Chandler, OK 74834
(405) 258-1300

Jerry McClanahan's Art Gallery
306 Manvel Ave
Chandler, OK
(903) 467-6384

Hotels and Campgrounds

Lincoln Motel
740 E 1st St
Chandler, OK 74834
(405) 258-0200

Oak Glen RV Park
347203 E Hwy 66
Chandler, OK 74834
(405) 258-0904

WARWICK

Museums

Seaba Station Motorcycle Museum
336992 E Hwy 66
Warwick, OK 74834
(405) 258-9141

LUTHER

Bars and Restaurants

The Boundary on 66
16001 E Hwy 66
Luther, OK 73054
(405) 277-3532

County Line Bar
21940 E Hwy 66
Luther, OK
(405) 436 1007

ARCADIA

Campgrounds

Arcadia Lake
9000 E 2nd St
Arcadia, OK 73007
(405) 216 7470

Bars and Restaurants

POPS Restaurant
660 W Hwy 66
Arcadia , OK 73007
(405) 928-7677

EDMOND

Campgrounds

Scissotail Campground
9000 E 2nd St
Edmond, OK 73007
(405) 316-7470

Bars and Restaurants

Blue Moon Restaurant
1320 S Broadway
Edmond, OK 73034
(405) 340-3871

Dan McGuiness Pub
305 S Broadway
Edmond, OK 73103
(405) 359- 2222

Freddy's Frozen Custard
1925 E 2nd St
Edmond, OK 73034
(405) 844-1514

Henry Hudson's
2100 E 2nd St
Edmond, OK 73034
(405) 359-6707

OKLAHOMA CITY

Hotels and Campgrounds

Bricktown Hotel
2001 E Reno Ave
Oklahoma City, OK 73117
(405) 235-1647

Renaissance Oklahoma City Convention Center Hotel
10 N Broadway Ave
Oklahoma City, OK 73102
(405) 228-8000

Sheraton Oklahoma City
1 N Broadway
Oklahoma City, OK 73102
(405) 235-2780

The Skirvin Hilton Oklahoma City
1 Park Ave
Oklahoma City, OK 73102
(405) 272-3040

Twin Fountains RV Park
2727 Northeast 63rd St
Oklahoma City, OK 73111
(405) 475-5514

Bars, Restaurants and Casinos

Cattlemen's Steakhouse
1309 S Agnew Ave
Oklahoma City, OK 73108
(405) 236-0416

Mickey Mantle's Steakhouse
7 S Mickey Mantle Dr
Oklahoma City, OK 73114
(405) 752-6073

Hogwash Café/Bar and Grill
11 Council Rd
Oklahoma City, OK
(405) 793-6013

Hooters
111 E California St
Oklahoma City, OK 73104
(405) 231-1100

Thirsty Hog Saloon
720 Oklahoma City, OK 73128
(405) 604-4647

Thunder Roadhouse Café
900 W Memorial Rd
Oklahoma City , OK 73104
(405) 272 0777

Vick & Tim's
1001 N Western Ave
Oklahoma City, OK 73106
(405) 641-8712

Remington Park Racing Casino
1 Remington Place
Oklahoma City, OK 73111
(405) 424-1000

WARR ACRES

Hotels

Carlyle Motel
3600 NW 39th St
Warr Acres, OK 73112
(405) 946-3355

Nu Homa Motel
3528 NW 39th St
Warr Acres, OK 73112
(405) 943-0966

Bars and Restaurants

Ann's Chicken Fry House
4146 NW 39th St
Oklahoma City, OK 73112
(405) 943-8915

Hideaway
228 W Harmon Dr
Warr Acres, OK 73110
(405) 733-4500

Jack's Bar B Q
4418 NW 39th St
Warr Acres, OK 73112
(405) 605 -7990

Route 66 Roadhouse
4328 NW 39th St
Warr Acres, OK 73112
(405) 605-4500

BETHANY

Hotels

Western Motel
7600 NW 39th Expressway
Bethany, OK 73008
(405) 789-3809

YUKON

Bars and Restaurants

Grady's 66 Pub
444 W Main St
Yukon, OK 73099
(405) 354-8789

Hot Rod Café
400 E Main St
Youkon, OK 73099
(405) 577-6322

The Horseshoe Bar
445 W Main St
Youkon, OK 73099
(405) 350-1051

EL RENO

Campgrounds

El Reno West KOA
301 S Walbaun Rd
El Reno, OK 73014
(405) 884-2595

Bars and Restaurants

Charlie B's
1701 E Hwy 66
El Reno, OK 73036
(405) 295-6479

Gilmore's Pub & Barefoot Bar
112 S Choctaw
El Reno, OK
(405) 295-1996

Johnnie's Grill
301 S Rock Island Ave
El Reno, OK 73036
(405) 262-4721

S&S Bike Ranch Saloon
600 Sabra Pass
El Reno, OK
(405) 262-0866

CALUMET

Bars and Restaurants

Rumors Bar
103 N Calumet Rd
Calumet, OK 73014
(405) 893-2252

WEATHERFORD

Museums

Thomas P Stafford Air and Space Museum
3000 Logan Rd
Weatherford, OK 73096
(580) 772-5871

Bars and Restaurants

Benchwarmer Brown's Sports Bar and Grill
1108 E Main St
Weatherford, OK 73096
(580) 772-7682

Jerry's
1000 E Main St
Weatherford, OK 73096
(580) 772-3707

Lucille's Road House
1301 N Airport Rd
Weatherford, OK 73096
(580) 772-8808

CLINTON

Museums

Oklahoma Route 66 Museum
2229 W Gary Blvd
Clinton, OK 73601
(580)323 7866

Hotels and Campgrounds

Glancy Motor Hotel
217 E Gary Blvd
Clinton, OK 73601
(580) 323-0112

Trade Winds Inn
2128 W Gary Blvd
Clinton, OK 73601
(580) 323-2610

Bars, Restaurants and Casinos

Dairy Best
301 S 19th St
Clinton, OK 73601
(580)323-9843

Lucky Star Casino
10347 N 2274 Rd
Clinton, OK 73601
(580)323-6599

CANUTE

Campgrounds

Elk City/Clinton KOA
I-40, Exit 50 Clinton Lake
Canute, OK 73626
(580) 592-4409

Bars and Restaurants

Wild J's Gentlemen's Club
9th St
Canute, OK 73626
(580) 472-3932

ELK CITY

Museums

National Route 66 Museum
2717 3rd St
Elk City, OK 73648
(580) 225-6266

Hotels and Campgrounds

Elk City / Clinton KOA
I-40, Exit 50 Clinton Lake
Canute, OK 73626
(580) 592-4409

Elk Creek Mobile Park Inc
317 E 20th Street
Elk City, OK 73644
(580) 225-7865

Elk Run RV Park
Hwy 34 & I-40
Elk City, OK 73644
(580) 225-4888

Bars and Restaurants

Knucklehead Red's Saloon
2417 W Broadway Ave
Elk City, OK 73644
(580) 225-3141

Longhorn Bar
514 N Van Buren
Elk City, OK 73644
(580) 225-3113

TEXAS

SHAMROCK

Hotels and Campgrounds

Blarney Inn
402 E 12th St
Shamrock, TX 79079
(806) 256-2101

West Forty Camp Area
Interstate 40
Shamrock, TX 79079
(806) 256-3719

Bars and Restaurants

Big Vern's Steakhouse
200 E 12 St
Shamrock, TX 79079
(806) 256-2088

Silver Creek Sports Bar
1800 N Main St
Shamrock, TX 79079
(806) 256-1313

MCLEAN

Museums

Texas Route 66 Museum
100 Kingsley St
McLean, TX 79057
(806) 779-2225

Devil's Rope Museum
100 Kingsley St
McLean, TX 79057
(806)779-2225

Hotels

Cactus Inn
101 Pine St
McLean, TX 79057
(806)779-2346

Hotels

Alanreed Motel
13100 I-40 (Exit 135)
Alanreed, TX 79002
(806) 779-2202

Restaurants

Blessed Mary Restaurant
701 Front St
Groom, TX 79309
(806) 248-0170

Hotels and Campgrounds

Marriott Courtyard Downtown
724 S Polk St
Amarillo, TX 79101
(806) 553-4500

The Big Texan Motel
7701 W I-40
Amarillo, TX 79121
(806) 372-6000

Amarillo KOA
1100 Folsom Rd
Amarillo, TX 79108
(806) 335-1792

Amarillo Ranch RV Park
1414 Sunrise Dr
Amarillo, TX 79104
(806) 373-4962

AOK Camper Park
901 Spur 228
Amarillo, TX 79111
(806) 335-2677

Fort Amarillo RV Resort
10101 Business I-40
Amarillo, TX 79124
(806) 331-1700

Oasis RV Resort
2715 Arnot Rd
Amarillo, TX 79124
806 356-8408

Overnite RV Park
900 S Lakeside Dr
Amarillo, TX 79118
(806) 373-1431

Bars and Restaurants

Acapulco Restaurant
727 S Polk St
Amarillo, TX 79101
(806) 373-8889

Big Texan Steak Ranch
7701 E I-40
Amarillo, TX 79118
(806) 372-7000

Broken Spoke Lounge
3101 SW 6th Ave
Amarillo, TX 79106
(806) 373-9149

Scooters
4100 Bushland Blvd
Amarillo, TX 79106
(806) 355-6600

Smokey Joe's Texas Café
2903 Southwest 6th Ave
Amarillo, TX 79106
(806) 331-6698

VEGA

Hotels

Best Western Country Inn
1800 W Vega Blvd
Vega, TX 79092
(806) 267-2131

Bars and Restaurants

Boot Hill Saloon & Grill
909 Vega Blvd
Vega, TX 79092
(806) 267-2904

ADRIAN

Bars and Restaurants

Midpoint Café
Route 66
Adrian, TX 79001
(806) 538-6379

GLENRIO

Restaurants

Russell's Travel Center
1583 Frontage Rd
Glenrio, TX
(575) 576-8700

NEW MEXICO

SAN JON

Hotels

San Jon Motel
715 E Main Ave
San Jon, NM 88434
(575) 576-2911

TUCUMCARI

Hotels and Campgrounds

Motel Safari
722 E Route 66 Blvd
Tucumcari, NM 88401
(575) 461-1048

Pow Wow Inn
801 W Tucumcari Blvd
Tucumcari, NM 88401
(575) 461-0500

The Blue Swallow Motel
815 E Route 66 Blvd
Tucumcari, NM 88401
(575) 461-9849

Cactus RV Park
1316 E Tucumcari Blvd
Tucumcari, NM 88401
(575) 461-2501

Empty Saddle RV Park
2500 E Route 66 Blvd
Tucumcari, NM 88401
(575) 461-8623

Kiva RV Park
1416 E Route 66 Blvd
Tucumcari, NM 88401
(575) 461-156

Tucumcari KOA
6299A Quay Rd
Tucumcari, NM 88401
(575) 461-1841

Bars and Restaurants

Del's Restaurant
1202 E Route 66 Blvd
Tucumcari, NM 88401
(575) 461-1740

Lizard Lounge
801 W Tucumcari Blvd
Tucumcari, NM 88401
(505) 461-0500

SANTA ROSA

Hotels and Campgrounds
La Mesa Motel
2415 Historic Route 66
Santa Rosa, NM 88435
(575) 472-3021

Sun 'n Sand Motel
1120 Historic Route 66
Santa Rosa, NM 88435
(575) 472-5268

Sunset Motel
929 Will Rogers Dr
Santa Rosa, NM 88435
(575) 472-3762

La Loma Lodge & RV Park
1709 Historic Route 66
Santa Rosa, NM 88435
(575) 472-4379

Santa Rosa campground & RV Park
2136 Historic Route 66
Santa Rosa, NM 88435
(575) 472-3126

Bars and Restaurants

Comet II Drive In & Restaurant
217 Parker Ave
Santa Rosa, NM 88435
(575) 472-3663

Joseph's Bar & Grill
1775 Route 66
Santa Rosa, NM 88435
(575)472-3361

Pecos Bar
457 Historic Route 66
Santa Rosa, NM 88435
(575) 472-3344

Sun & Sand Restaurant
1124 Historic Route 66
Santa Rosa, NM 88435
(575) 472-3092

PECOS

Bars and Restaurants

Casa De Herrera Lounge
387 NM 63
Pecos, NM 87552
(505) 757-8559

SANTA FE

Hotels

Cottonwood Court
1742 Cerrillos Rd
Santa Fe, NM 87505
(505) 982-5571

El Rey Inn
1862 Cerrillos Rd
Santa Fe, NM 87505
(505) 982-1931

Inn of the Governors
101 W Alameda St
Santa Fe, NM 87501
(505) 982-4333

La Fonda
100 E San Francisco
Santa Fe, NM 87501
(505) 988-2952

Silver Saddle Motel
2810 Cerrillos Rd
Santa Fe, NM 87507
(505) 471-7663

Western Scene Motel
1608 Cerrillos Rd
Santa Fe, NM 87505
(505) 983-7484

Los Campos De Santa Fe RV Resort
3574 Cerrillos Rd
Santa Fe, NM 87507
(505) 473-9220

Rancheros De Santa Fe Campground
736 Old Las Vegas Hwy
Santa Fe, NM 87505
(505) 466-3482

Santa Fe KOA
934 Old Las Vegas Hwy
Santa Fe, NM 87505
(505) 466-1419

Santa Fe Skies RV Park
14 County Rd 48C
Santa Fe, NM 87508
(505) 473-5946

Trailer Ranch
3471 Cerrillos Rd # 27
Santa Fe, NM 87507
(505) 471-9970

Bars, Restaurants and Casinos

Blue Corn Café
133 W Water St
Santa Fe, NM 87501
(505) 984-1800

Bobcat Bite
418 Old Las Vegas Hwy
Santa Fe, NM 87505
(505) 983-5319

Coyote Café
132 W Water St
Santa Fe, NM 87501
(505) 983-1615

El Paseo Bar & Grill
208 Galisteo St
Santa Fe, NM 87501
(505) 992-2848

Evengelos Cocktail Lounge
200 W San Francisco St
Santa Fe, NM 87501
(505) 982-9014

Harry's Roadhouse
96 Old Las Vegas Hwy
Santa Fe, NM 87508
(505) 989-4629

Low 'n Slow Lowrider Bar
125 Washington Ave
Santa Fe, NM 87501
(505) 988-4900

ALGODONES

Hotels

Hacienda Vargas Bed and Breakfast
1431 Hwy 313
Algodones, NM 87001
(505) 867-9115

BERNALILLO

Campgrounds

Albuquerque/Bernalillo KOA
555 S Hill Rd
Bernalillo, NM 87004
(505) 867-5227

Coronado Campground
106 Monument Rd
Bernalillo, NM 87004
(505)980-8256

Bars and Restaurants

Flying Star Café
200 N Camino Del Pueblo
Bernalillo, NM 87004
(505) 404-2100

Silva's Saloon
955 S Camino Del Pueblo
Bernalillo, NM 87004
(505) 867-9976

The Range Café
925 S Camino Del Pueblo
Bernalillo, NM 87004
(505) 867-1700

ALBUQUERQUE

Hotels and Campgrounds

El Camino Motor Hotel
6801 4th St NW
Albuquerque, NM 87107
(505) 344-1606

La Posada Hotel
125 2nd St NW
Albuquerque, NM 87102
(505) 242-9090

The Hotel Blue
717 Central Ave NW
Albuquerque, NM 87102
(505) 924-2400

Albuquerque Central KOA
12400 Skyline Rd NE
Albuquerque, NM 87123
(505) 296-2729

American RV Park
13500 Central Ave SW
Albuquerque, NM 87121
(505) 831-3545

El Rancho Mobile Home Park
201 Wyoming Blvd SE # 90
Albuquerque, NM 87123
(505) 266-1455

Trails RV Park & Trading Post
14305 Central Ave NW
Albuquerque, NM 87121
(800) 326-6317

High Desert RV Park
13000 Frontage Rd SW
Albuquerque, NM 87121
(505) 839-9035

Palisades RV Park
9201 Central Ave NW
Albuquerque, NM 87121
(505) 831-5000

Bars and Restaurants

66 Diner
1405 Central Ave NE
Albuquerque, NM 87106
(505) 247-1421

El Camino Dining Room
6800 4th St NW
Los Ranchos, NM
(505) 344-0448

Kelly's Brew Pub
3222 Central Ave SE
Albuquerque, NM 87106
(505) 262-2739

Knockouts
311 Central Ave NW
Albuquerque, NM 87102
(505) 243-2446

Library Bar & Grill
312 Central Ave SW
Albuquerque, NM 87102
(505) 242-2992

Maloney's Tavern
325 Central Ave NW
Albuquerque, NM 87102
(505) 242-7422

Original Garcia's Kitchen
1113 4th St NW
Albuquerque, NM 87102
(505) 247-9149

Red Ball Café
1303 4th St SW
Albuquerque, NM 87102
(505) 247-9438

LOS LUNAS, NM

Hotels

Luna Mansion
110 Main St NE
Los Lunas, NM 87031
(505) 865-7333

BUDVILLE

Bars and Restaurants

Midway Bar and Grill
784 Old Hwy 66
Budville, NM 87014

GRANTS

Hotels and Campgrounds

Red Lion Motel
1501 E Santa Fe Ave
Grants, NM 87020
(505) 287-2843

Grants/Cibola Sands KOA
26 Cibola Sands Loop, S Hwy 53
Grants, NM 87020
(505) 287-4376

Lavaland RV Park
1901 E Santa Fe Ave
Grants, NM 87020
(505) 287-8665

Bars and Restaurants

Outlaws Saloon & Dance
1109 E Santa Fe Ave
Grants, NM 87020
(505) 287-5507

Pat's Lounge
304 W Santa Fe Ave
Grants, NM 87020
(505) 287-4722

Red Lion Motel Bar

1501 East Santa Fe Ave

Grants, NM 87020

(505) 287-2843

MILAN

Bars and Restaurants

Wow Diner

1300 Motel Dr

Milan, NM 87021

(505) 287-3801

GALLUP

Hotels and Campgrounds

Arrowhead Lodge

1115 E Historic Hwy 66

Gallup, NM 87301

(505) 863-5111

Blue Spruce Lodge

1119 E Historic Hwy 66

Gallup, NM 87301

(505) 863-5211

Desert Skies Motel

1703 W Historic Hwy 66

Gallup, NM 87301

(505) 863-4485

El Rancho Hotel

1000 E 66

Gallup, NM 87301

(505) 863-9311

USA RV Park

3009 W Historic Hwy 66

Gallup, NM 87301

(505) 863-5021

Bars, Restaurants and Casinos

American Bar

221 W Coal Ave

Gallup, NM 87301

Goodfellas Sports Lounge

1206 E Hwy 66

Gallup, NM 87301

(505) 863-0385

The 49er Lounge

1000 E 66

Gallup, NM 87301

(505) 863-9311

Virgie's Restaurant

2720 W Historic Hwy 66

Gallup, NM 87301

(505) 863-5152

Fire Rock Casino

249 Historic 66

Church Rock, NM 87311

(505) 905-7100

Towns in Alternate Route between Santa Rosa and Rio Puerco

MORIARTY

Bars and Restaurants

Blackie's

612 Route 66

Moriarty, NM 87035

(505) 832-0011

Buford Steakhouse

5 Carl Canon Rd

Moriarty, NM 87035

(505) 832 6525

El Comedor de Anayas

1009 Route 66

Moriarty, NM 87035

(505) 832-4442

TIJERAS

Campgrounds

Hidden Valley Camping Resort
844 NM 333 # B
Tijeras, NM 87059
(505) 281-3363

Bars and Restaurants

Molly's Bar
546 NM 333
Tijeras, NM 87059
(505) 281-9911

RIO PUERCO

Casinos
Route 66 Casino
14500 Central Ave
Rio Puerco, NM 87120
(505) 352-1500

ARIZONA

HOLBROOK

Hotels and Campgrounds

Wigwam Motel
811 W Hopi Dr
Holbrook, AZ 86025
(928)524-3048

Holbrook / Petrified Forest KOA
102 Hermosa Dr
Holbrook, AZ 86025
(928) 524-6689

OK RV Park
1576 Roadrunner Rd
Holbrook, AZ 86025
(928) 524-3226

Bars and Restaurants

Butterfield Steak House
609 W Hopi Dr
Holbrook, AZ 86025
(928) 524-3447

Empty Pockets Saloon
2210 Navajo Blvd
Holbrook, AZ 86025
(928) 524-6059

Joe & Aggie's Café
120 W Hopi Dr
Holbrook, AZ 86025
(928) 524-6540

Mesa Grill & Sports Bar
2318 Navajo Blvd
Holbrook, AZ 86025
(928) 524-6697

Mesa Italian Restaurant
2318 Navajo Blvd
Holbrook, AZ 86025
(928) 524-6696

Romo's Restaurant
121 W Hopi Dr
Holbrook, AZ 86025
(928) 524-2153

Winner's Circle
466 Navajo Blvd
Holbrook, AZ 86025
(928) 524-9600

WINSLOW

Hotels and Campgrounds

La Posada
303 E Second St
Winslow, AZ 86047
(928) 289-4366

The Lodge
1914 W 3rd St
Winslow, AZ 86047
(928) 289-4611

Meteor Crater
Meteor Crater Rd
Winslow, AZ 86047
(928) 289-4002

Bars and Restaurants

Bojo's Grill and Sports Pub
113 2nd St
Winslow, AZ 86047
(928)289-0616

Broncos Sports Bar
2150 W Hwy 66
Winslow, AZ 86047
(928) 289-3856

Falcon Restaurant & Lounge
1113 E 2nd St
Winslow, AZ 86047
(928) 289-2628

PT's
1500 E 3rd St
Winslow, AZ 86047
(928) 289-0787

FLAGSTAFF

Hotels and Campgrounds

Best Western Pony Soldier
3030 E Route 66
Flagstaff, AZ 86004
(928) 526-2388

The Hotel Monte Vista
100 N San Francisco St
Flagstaff, AZ 86001
(928) 779-6971

Weatherford Hotel
23 N Leroux St
Flagstaff, AZ 86001
(928) 779-1919

Western Hills Motel
1580 E Route 66
Flagstaff, AZ 86001
(928) 774-6633

Black Bart's RV Park
2760 E Butler Ave
Flagstaff, AZ 86004
(928) 774-1912

Flagstaff KOA
5803 N US Hwy 89
Flagstaff, AZ 86004
(928) 526-9926

Kit Carson RV Park
2101 W Route 66
Flagstaff, AZ 86001
(928) 774-6993

Woody Mountain Campground & RV Park
2727 W Route 66
Flagstaff, AZ 86001
(800) 732-7986

Bars and Restaurants

Monte Vista Cocktail Lounge
100 N San Francisco St
Flagstaff, AZ 86001
(928) 779 6971

Museum Club
3404 E Route 66
Flagstaff, AZ 86004
(928) 526-9434

WILLIAMS

Hotels and Campgrounds

Buffalo Points Inn B&B
437 W Route 66
Williams, AZ 86046
(928) 635-2349

Frey Marcus Hotel
233 N Grand Canyon Blvd
Williams, AZ 86406
(800) 843 8724

Grand Canyon Hotel
145 W Route 66
Williams, AZ 86046
(928) 635-1419

The Red Garter Bed & Bakery
137 W Railroad Ave
Williams, AZ 86046
(800)328-1484

Canyon Gateway RV
1060 N Grand Canyon Blvd
Williams, AZ 86046
(928) 635-2718

Grand Canyon/ Williams KOA
5333 Hwy 64
Williams, AZ 86046
(928) 635-2307

Grand Canyon Railway RV Park
233 N Grand Canyon Blvd
Williams, AZ 86046
(303) 843-8724

Railside RV Ranch
877 E Rodeo Rd
Williams, AZ 86046
(928) 635-4077

The Canyon Motel & RV Park
1900 E Rodeo Road Route 66
Williams, AZ 86046
(800) 482-3955

Williams Circle Pines KOA
1000 Circle Pines Rd
Williams, AZ 86046
(928) 635-2626

Bars and Restaurants

Canyon Club
132 W Route 66
Williams, AZ 86046
(928) 635-2582

Cruisers Café 66
233 W Route 66
Williams, AZ 86046
(928) 635-2445

Doc Holliday's Steakhouse
950 N Grand Canyon Blvd
Williams, AZ 86046
(928) 635-4797

Iron Horse Pub
615 8th St
Williams, AZ 76301
(940) 767-9488

Pancho McGillicuddy's Mexican Cantina
141 W Railroad Ave
Williams, AZ 86046
(928) 635-4150

Rod's Steakhouse
301 E Route 66
Williams, AZ 86046
(928) 635-2671

Sultana Bar
301 W Route 66
Williams, AZ 86406
(928) 635-2021

Twisters 50's Soda Fountain
417 E Route 66
Williams, AZ 86046
(928) 635-0266

ASH FORK

Bars and Restaurants

Oasis Lounge
346 W Park Ave
Ash Fork, AZ 86320
(928) 637-2650

SELIGMAN

Hotels and Campgrounds

Canyon Lodge
114 Chino St
Seligman, AZ 86337
(928) 422-3255

Deluxe Inn
22295 Old Hwy 66
Seligman, AZ 86337
(928) 422-3244

Historic Route 66 Motel
22750 W Hwy 66
Seligman, AZ 86337
(928) 422-3204

Romney Motel
22430 W Hwy Route 66
Seligman, AZ 86337
(310) 722-2943

Supai Motel
22450 Hwy 66
Seligman, AZ 86337
(928) 422-4153

Seligman / Route 66 KOA
801 E Hwy 66
Seligman, AZ 86337
(928) 422-3358

Bars and Restaurants

Snow Cap Drive In
301 AZ 66
Seligman, AZ 86337
(928)422-3291

Black Cat Bar
114 Chino St
Seligman, AZ 86337
(928) 422-3451

The Roadkill Café
502 W Hwy 66
Seligman, AZ 86337
(928) 422-3554

Westside Lilo's Café
415 W Chino
Seligman, AZ 86337
(928) 422-5456

PEACH SPRINGS

Hotels and Campgrounds

Grand Canyon Caverns Inn
Route 66, Mile Post Marker 115
Peach Springs, AZ 86434
(928) 422-3224

Hualapai Lodge
889 Hwy St
Peach Springs, AZ 86434
(928) 769-2230

Bars and Restaurants

Diamond Creek Restaurant
900 Route 66
Peach Springs, AZ 86434
(928) 769-2800

Frontier Motel & Café
16118 E Hwy 66
Peach Springs, AZ 86434
(928) 769-2238

HACKBERRY

Campgrounds

Kozy Corner Trailer Park
Hackberry, AZ
(928) 753 9732

Bars and Restaurants

Outpost Saloon
9321 E Hwy 66
Hackberry, AZ 86401
(928) 692 2166

KINGMAN

Hotels and Campgrounds

Arcadia Lodge
909 E Andy Devine Ave
Kingman, AZ 86401
(928) 753-6200

High Desert Inn
2803 E Andy Devine Ave
Kingman, AZ 86401
(928) 753-2935

Hill Top Motel
1901 E Andy Devine Ave
Kingman, AZ 86401
(928) 753-2198

Hillcrest Motel
2018 E Andy Devine Ave
Kingman, AZ 86401
(928) 718-1190

Ramblin Rose Motel
1001 E Andy Devine Ave
Kingman, AZ 86401
(928) 753-5541

Silver Queen Motel
3285 E Andy Devine Ave
Kingman, AZ 86401
(928) 757-4315

Blake Ranch RV Park
9315 E Blake Ranch Rd
Kingman, AZ 86401
(928) 757-3336

Fort Beale RV Park
300 Metcalfe Rd
Kingman, AZ 86401
(928) 753-3355

Kingman KOA

3820 N Roosevelt

Kingman, AZ 86409

(928)757-4397

Bars and Restaurants

Big Rig Doll House

2770 S Hwy 66

Kingman, AZ 86401

(928) 753-6558

Dambar Steakhouse

1960 E Andy Devine Ave

Kingman, AZ 86401

(928) 753-3523

Fireside Cocktail Lounge

1716 Hoover St

Kingman, AZ 86401

(928) 753-9110

Mr. D'z Route 66 Diner

105 E Andy Devine Ave

Kingman, AZ 86401

(928) 718-0066

Outpost Saloon

9321 E Hwy 66

Kingman, AZ 86401

(928) 692-2166

OATMAN

Bars and Restaurants

Judy's

260 Oatman

Oatman, AZ 86433

(928) 768-4463

Oatman Hotel Restaurant

181 Oatman, AZ 86433

(928)768-4408

Golden Shores

Bars and Restaurants

Uncle Bill's Roadhouse

5103 E Lake Powell Rd

Golden Shores, AZ

(928) 768-8303

CALIFORNIA

NEEDLES

Hotels and Campgrounds

Best Western Colorado River Inn

2371 W Broadway

Needles, CA 92363

(760) 326-4552

Fender's River Road Resort

3396 Needles Hwy

Needles, CA 92363

(760)326 3423

River Valley Motor Lodge

1707 Needles Hwy

Needles, CA 92363

(760) 326-3839

Calizona RV Park

1908 Five Mile Rd

Needles, CA 92363

(760) 326-5679

Desert View RV Resort
5300 Route 66
Needles, CA 92363
(760) 326-4000

Needles Koa Campground
5400 National Old Trails Rd
Needles, CA 92363
(760) 326-4207

River Road Resort & Motel
3396 Needles Hwy
Needles, CA 92363
(760) 326-3423

The Palms River Resort
4170 Needles Hwy
Needles, CA 92363
(760) 326-0333

Bars and Restaurants

66 Bar
1900 Needles Hwy
Needles, CA 92363
(760) 326-2277

B K's Pepper Lounge
533 Front St
Needles, CA 92363
(760) 326-8889

Juicy's River Café
2411 W Broadway
Needles, CA 92363
(760) 326-2233

Red Dog Saloon
914 Broadway
Needles, CA 92363
(760) 326-9919

FENNER

Bars and Restaurants

Naja's Food and Drink Garden
31251 Goffs Rd
Fenner, CA 92332

ESSEX

Bars and Restaurants

Hi Sahara Oasis
31251 Goffs Rd
Essex, CA 92332
(866) 721-7384

LUDLOW

Hotels

Ludlow Motel
National Trail Hwy
Ludlow, CA 92338
(760) 733-4463

Bars and Restaurants

Ludlow Café
68315 National Trails Hwy
Ludlow, CA 92338
(760) 733-4501

NEWBERRY SPRINGS

Campgrounds

Newberry Mt RV Park & Motel
47800 National Trails Hwy
Newberry Springs, CA 92365
(760) 257-0066

Bars and Restaurants

Bagdad Café
46548 National Trails Hwy
Newberry Springs, CA
92365
(760) 257-3101

The Barn
44560 National Trails Hwy
Newberry Springs, CA 92365
(760) 257-4110

BARSTOW

Hotels and Campgrounds

El Rancho Motel
112 E Main St
Barstow, CA 92311
(760) 256-2401

Route 66 Motel
195 W Main St
Barstow, CA 92311
(760) 256-7866

**The Best Western
Desert Villa Inn**
1984 E Main St
Barstow, CA 92311
(760) 256-1781

Barstow / Calico KOA
35250 Outer Hwy 15 N
Yermo, CA 92398
(760) 254-2311

Bars and Restaurants

DiNapoli's Firehouse
1358 E Main St
Barstow, CA 92311
(760) 256-1094

Gusto's Bar
25597 Main St
Barstow, CA 92311
(760) 253-3878

ORO GRANDE

Bars and Restaurants

Iron Hog Saloon
20848 National Trails Hwy
Oro Grande, CA 92368
(760) 843-0609

VICTORVILLE

Hotels and Campgrounds

New Corral Motel
14643 7th St
Victorville, CA 92395
(760) 245-9378

**Quality Inn & Suites
Green Tree**
14173 Green Tree Blvd # Q
Victorville, CA 92395
(760) 245-3461

**Shady Oasis
Kampground**
16530 Stoddard Wells Rd.
Victorville, CA 92395
(760) 245-6867

Bars and Restaurants

Gator's Sports Bar & Grill
12249 Hesperia Rd
Victorville, CA 92395
(760) 955-7860

Holland Burger
17143 N D St
Victorville, CA 92394
(760) 243-9938

Johnny Fingers Sports Bar
15863 Lorene Dr
Victorville, CA 92395
(760) 241-0804

Richie's Real American Diner
14326 Valley Center Dr
Victorville, CA 92395
(960) 955-1113

Steel Horse Saloon
14513 7th St
Victorville, CA 92395
(760) 245-6584

DEVORE

Bars and Restaurants

Screaming Chicken Saloon
18169 Cajon Blvd
San Bernardino, CA 92407
(909) 880-0056

SAN BERNARDINO

Bars and Restaurants

Milta Café
602 N Mt Vernon Ave
San Bernardino, CA 92411
(909) 888-0460

RIALTO

Hotels

Wigwam Motel
2728 W Foothill Blvd
Rialto, CA 92140
(909) 421 0844

FONTANA

Bars and Restaurants

Bono's Restaurant & Deli
15395 Foothill Blvd
Fontana, CA 92335
(909) 822-4036

RANCHO CUCAMONGA

Bars and Restaurants

Magic Lamp Inn
8189 Foothill Blvd
Rancho Cucamonga, CA 91730
(909) 981-8659

Sycamore Inn
8318 Foothill Blvd
Rancho Cucamonga, CA 91730
(909) 982-1104

The Deli
9671 Foothill Blvd
Rancho Cucamonga, CA 91730
(909) 989-8122

UPLAND

Bars and Restaurants

Joey's Bar-B-Q
1964 W Foothill Blvd
Upland, CA 91786
(909) 982-2128

The Buffalo Inn
1814 W Foothill Blvd
Upland, CA 91786
(909) 981-5515

CLAREMONT

Bars and Restaurants

Wolfe's Market
160 W Foothill Blvd
Claremont, CA 91771
(909) 626-8508

LA VERNE

Bars and Restaurants

La Paloma Restaurant
2975 Foothill Blvd
La Verne, CA 91750
(909) 593-7209

SAN DIMAS

Bars and Restaurants

**Pinnacle Peak
Steakhouse**
269 W Foothill Blvd
San Dimas, CA 91773
(909)599-5312

GLENDORA

Bars and Restaurants

Britestar Tavern
731 W Route 66
Glendora, CA 91740
(626) 335-1909

Golden Spur
1223 E Route 66
Glendora, CA 91740
(626) 963-9302

MONROVIA

Hotels

Aztec Hotel
311 W Foothill Blvd
Monrovia, CA 91016
(626) 358-3231

PASADENA

Hotels

Astro Motel
2818 E Colorado Blvd
Pasadena, CA 91107
(626) 449-3370

Pasadena Motor Inn
2097 E Colorado Blvd
Pasadena, CA 91107
(626) 796-3122

Saga Motor Hotel
1633 E Colorado Blvd
Pasadena, CA 91106
(626) 795-0431
Bars and Restaurants

**100 to 1 Cocktail
Lounge**
100 W Huntington Dr
Arcadia, CA 91007
(626) 445-3520

Colorado Bar
2640 E Colorado Blvd
Pasadena, CA 91107
(626) 449-3485

R Place
3739 E Colorado Blvd
Pasadena, CA 91107
(626) 792-7330

Smitty's Grill
110 S Lake Ave
Pasadena, CA 91101
(626) 792-9999

LOS ANGELES

Hotels and Campgrounds

Acton / Los Angeles KOA
7601 Soledad Canyon Rd
Acton, CA 93510
(661) 268-1214

Los Angeles / Pomona / Fairplex KOA
2200 N White Ave
Pomona, CA 91768
(909) 593-8915

Bars and Restaurants

Barney's Beanery
8447 Santa Monica Blvd
Los Angeles, CA 90069
(323) 654-2287

Troubadour
9081 Santa Monica Blvd
W Hollywood, CA 90069
(310) 276-6168

SANTA MONICA

Hotels

Best Western Plus Gateway Hotel
1920 Santa Monica Blvd
Santa Monica, CA 90404
(310) 829-9100

Ocean View Hotel
1447 Ocean Ave
Santa Monica, CA 90401
(310) 458-4888

The Georgian Hotel
1415 Ocean Ave
Santa Monica, CA 90401
(310)395-9945

Bars and Restaurants

O'Brien's Irish Pub & Restaurant
2226 Wilshire Blvd
Santa Monica, CA 90403
(310) 829-5303

Ocean Ave Seafood
1401 Ocean Ave
Santa Monica, CA 90401
(310) 394-5669

ROUTE 66 SOCIETIES

National Route 66 Federation
PO Box 1848
Lake Arrowhead, CA 92352
(909) 336-6131

Route 66 Association of Illinois
Route 66 Hall of Fame Museum
110 W Howard St
Pontiac, IL 61764
(815) 844-4566
www.il66assoc.org

Missouri Route 66 Association
102 East Dale St
Springfield, MO 65083
(417) 865-1318
www.missouri66.org

Oklahoma Route 66 Association
PO Box 446
Chandler, OK 74834
(405) 258 0008
www.oklahomaroute66.com

Old Route 66 Association of Texas
PO Box 66
McLean, TX 79057
(806) 373 7566 or 806 779-2225
www.mockturtlepress.com/texas

New Mexico Route 66 Association
14305 Central Ave NW
Albuquerque, NM 87121
(505) 831-6317
www.rt66nm.org

Historic Route 66 Association of Arizona
PO Box 66
Kingman, AZ
(928) 753-5001
www.azrt66.com

California Historic Route 66 Association
PO Box 66
Amboy, CA 92304
(909) 885-6324
www.route66ca.org

California Route 66 Preservation Foundation
PO Box 290066
Phelan ,CA 02329
(760) 868-3320
www.cart66pf.org

BIBLIOGRAPHY

Route 66 Dining and Lodging Guide, **Lake Arrowhead, CA, National Route 66 Association 15th Edition (2011).**
The National Route 66 Association has a group of volunteers called *Adopt-a-Hundred Members*. Each of those volunteers is assigned a stretch of Route 66 over which they collect the names, addresses and other valuable information about the hotels and restaurants along their assigned portions of Route 66. The information is updated every other year. No establishment can pay or otherwise advertise to be mentioned in the book. There are lots of black and white pictures.

FREETH, Nick, *Traveling Route 66,* **Norman, Oklahoma, University of Oklahoma Press (2001).**
This small book has hundreds of color pictures. It does not have the turn by turn directions or the detailed history of some other Route 66 books but it has interesting factoids not found elsewhere. It is a fun book to thumb through.

HINKLEY, Jim, *Ghost Towns of Route 66*, **Minneapolis, MN, Voyageur Press (2011).**
This book has wonderful photographs of Route 66 ghost towns along with a narrative providing interesting historical references and details of these long-abandoned places. This is much more than a coffee table book.

JENSEN, Jamie, *Road Trip USA Route 66*, **Berkeley, CA, Persius Book Group (2009).**
This is a book of manageable size that includes small color photos and nice descriptions of Route 66 history and attractions. The phone numbers of many attractions are provided. It does not have turn by turn directions.

KNOWLES, Drew, *Route 66 Adventure Handbook*, **Solana Beach, CA, Santa Monica Press LLC, Fourth Edition (2011).**

This is one of the more entertaining Route 66 guides. It has general, but not turn by turn directions. This is a great book for those who want to see the essentials of Route 66. The narratives are informative without giving excessive detail. There are black and white photos and plenty of helpful maps. One of the cool things about this book is that the author makes references to a 1957 Rand McNally Road Atlas he owns that still included Route 66 before the national highway system started bypassing towns.

McCLANAHAN, Jerry, *EZ 66 Guide for Travelers*, **Lake Arrowhead, CA, 2nd Edition, National Historic Route 66 Association (2008).**

This is perhaps the most complete guide to Route 66 available. It includes turn by turn directions going east and west for all alignments of Route 66 and a detailed history of the Mother Road. It is a spiral bound book that helps for easy use. There are no photos, but plenty of maps and drawings.

RITTENHOUSE, Jack D., *A Guidebook to Highway 66; a Facsimile of the 1946 First Edition,* **Albuquerque, NM, University of New Mexico Press (1989).**

This is the original guide to Route 66. It includes a new preface written in 1988 by Jack Rittenhouse in which he gives an interesting history of how he wrote and sold the book. The book itself is interesting both for the information it includes and for the for the information that is not included. The book makes clear that Route 66 in the early days was sparse. There are warnings about poor road surfaces and to watch out for open range livestock. Although motels that have become Route 66 icons, like the Rail Haven, the Wagon Wheel, the Blue Swallow and the El Rancho are mentioned, others like the Munger Moss are not included because they were not yet built. This slim volume wonderfully describes Route 66 as it was just after World War II and before the growth of the country during the 1950's.

SCOTT, Quinta, *Along Route 66,* **Norman, OK, University of Oklahoma Press (2000).**
This book focuses on architecture along Route 66 and has hundreds of vintage black and white photos along with interesting commentary. Many of the featured buildings still exist, so it's fun to compare how they looked decades ago with how they look today.

SNYDER, Tom, *Route 66 Traveler's Guide and Roadside Companion,* **New York, NY, St Martin's Griffin (2000).**
This book is written by the founder of the US Route 66 Association. It has good, but not turn by turn directions. There are lots of maps and photos but no color photos. The Route 66 history and descriptions of attractions are excellent.

WOODWARD, Kirk, *Motorcycle Guide to Historic Route 66, The Mother Road,* **Grapevine, TX, HHJM, Inc. (1995).**
This is the only book of which I am aware (other than this one) about Route 66 for bikers. It includes details of state motorcycle laws, listings of motorcycle shops along Route 66, as well turn by turn directions. It also has a diary of the author's experiences in his travels along Route 66. The biggest problem with this book is that it has not been updated in any meaningful way since its publication in 1995.

ABOUT THE AUTHOR

There were hints that Sam Allen was a bit twisted when he was arrested as the first *Streaker* at Ole Miss.

Despite his early legal transgressions, Sam's criminal record ultimately was expunged and he graduated from law school. He has been a lawyer for over 30 years, first practicing at a major New York City law firm and later as a partner in the corporate finance section of a Houston, Texas firm. He has been in private practice since 2011.

Sam the lawyer

While practicing law in New York, he boxed in Madison Square Garden and published an article about the experience in *New York Magazine*. After that, he was featured in *People Magazine* and on *NBC Nightly News* as New York's boxing lawyer. He resurrected his boxing career five years ago when he attended the Gleason's Gym Boxing Camp in upstate New York, where he went three rounds with former light heavyweight champ Bobby Czyz (and lived to tell about it).

Sam had never been on a motorcycle until he bought his first Harley-Davidson Road King in 1996. Later that year he rode over 3,500 miles from Houston to the Sturgis Motorcycle Rally and back. Since then, he has been to Sturgis over 10 times and has ridden his bike to every major motorcycle rally in the country. He rides over 20,000 miles a year, and has ridden through all of the lower 48 states and over 2,000 miles through Canada. Sam is a member of the Iron Butt Association, which sponsors extreme motorcycle rides, including the *Bun Burner Gold*, which requires a rider to cover 1,500 miles in less than 24 hours. He completed two Bun Burner Gold rides in a single month,

In 2002, Sam founded the Deacons of Deadwood Motorcycle Club. The Deacons started with 13 businessmen, and now has over 100 members. The Club has donated over $1,200,000 to charities benefiting children in the Houston area.

It took Sam over three years to gather the information and take the pictures in this book. He operates route66mc.com. He is working on a Route 66 GPS directional guide and is developing a Route 66 reality show.

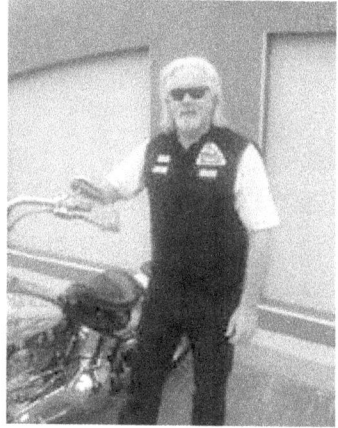

Sam the biker

www.ingramcontent.com/pod-product-compliance
Lightning Source LLC
Chambersburg PA
CBHW080455110426
42742CB00017B/2899